Writing Women's Worlds

BEDOUIN STORIES

LILA ABU-LUGHOD

University of California Press

Berkeley   Los Angeles   Oxford

Portions of the introduction were previously published in "Writing Against Culture," in *Recapturing Anthropology,* edited by Richard Fox (Santa Fe: School of American Research Press, 1991); and in "Can There Be a Feminist Ethnography?" *Women and Performance* 5 (1990): 7–27. A version of chapter 1 is appearing simultaneously as "Migdim: A Bedouin Matriarch," in *Struggle and Survival in the Modern Middle East,* edited by Edmund Burke III (Berkeley and Los Angeles: University of California Press, 1993). I reuse them with permission. All photographs, including the jacket illustration, by Lila Abu-Lughod/Anthro-Photo.

University of California Press
Berkeley and Los Angeles, California

University of California Press, Ltd.
Oxford, England

Library of Congress Cataloging-in-Publication Data

Abu-Lughod, Lila.
    Writing women's worlds : Bedouin stories / Lila Abu-Lughod.
       p.   cm.
    Includes bibliographical references.
    ISBN 0-520-07946-9 (alk. paper); ISBN 0-520-08304-0 (pbk.: alk. paper)
    1. Women, Muslim—Egypt—Social conditions.   2. Bedouins—Egypt.
3. Ethnology—Egypt—Biographical methods.   I. Title.
HQ1793.A68   1992
305.48'6971'0962—dc20
                                                            91-39685
                                                            CIP

Printed in the United States of America

9   8   7   6   5   4   3   2   1

The paper used in this publication meets the minimum requirements of American National Standard for Information Sciences—Permanence of Paper for Printed Library Materials, ANSI Z39.48-1984. ∞

For Fajriyya,
whose daughters may one day read this

CONTENTS

ILLUSTRATIONS

PREFACE

On a windy day in December 1989, just over eleven years since I had first taken the desert highway from Cairo to Alexandria, I sat with my aunt by the side of the road. My father had disappeared with the driver of our rented car, an agricultural engineer, and my husband to pick out the sheep we had just arranged to purchase. Meanwhile, my aunt and I bided our time.

Now, as in 1978, my father was accompanying me to visit a Bedouin family who lived not far off this desert road, people we had initially met together but with whom, in the intervening decade, I had lived on and off for more than two years. This was his first return visit to the community. Agreeing with me that it was only proper that he pay a call to express his appreciation for what they had done to help me, my father had routed himself through Egypt while on a trip to the Middle East. My father's sister had flown over from Jordan to see us and was curious to know the people with whom I had spent so much time. And my husband, although he had read most of what I had written about the families we were going to visit, including a draft of this book, had never met them. I wanted finally to introduce him to them.

When we set off again I was excited and proud. I was proud that we would pull up to the house in a Mercedes; it would confirm that I came from a good family and had, moreover, made a good marriage. (On my own, I had always straggled in from the bus and hot taxis that left me off on the road.) I was even prouder that we had a sheep of respectable size knocking about in the trunk of the car and that I sat wedged in the back seat with cartons full of unshelled peanuts, green tea, candy, and a jumble of combs, mirrors, kerchiefs, colognes, hairclips, pens, and cigarette lighters. My Bedouin friends would recognize that these were no ordinary gifts. This combination was the appropriate offering on the important occasion of a bride's first postmarital visit home, and I was pleased with myself for having arranged everything so well.

I was, I knew, a bit old for all this, and I wondered at my own reaction. Why should returning not just with members of my own family but as a daughter and new bride—a consummately patriarchal configuration—make me feel good? Had I not, years ago, established myself as a scholar and developed with the Bedouin family a relationship that was quite independent of these people who were accompanying me? Had I not distanced myself from that first encounter in which, shy, embarrassed, and feeling distinctly unlike an anthropologist, I had sat in the back of a van while my father discussed with the men of this family my need for hosts to help me learn about "the traditions and customs" of the Awlad ʿAli Bedouin? Had I not moved far enough beyond the dutiful daughter role I had once played to disagree with my host when he, assuming I shared his prejudices, criticized Europeans for their moral failings? On my last visit, when he complained about the lack of concern Europeans showed for their families, I had argued that the progressive breakdown of the extended family could be attributed to the need for mobile labor under modern capitalism; it could, I said, happen even to the Awlad ʿAli. As a feminist, I had also chided him for leaving his wives and daughters undernourished while he lavished attention on his guests. Had this community not registered its new view of me when some had asked me, as a respected outside authority, to present to their disdainful Egyptian compatriots— who consider them bandits or primitives—the truth about Bedouin social life and values?

Yet I was excited because I could anticipate their response to this visit. They consider family important, and part of what had made me acceptable to them in the first place was that they had met my family. My background as the daughter of an Arab and a Muslim had also been significant, compensating for my own apparent cultural incompetence. Arriving now from America with more family members would confirm me as, like them, not simply an individual, but part of a family, and one with which they had already established mutual ties. Over the years, I had often heard them discuss my father's concern for me and confidence in them; they would interpret his visit as an acknowledgment of their generosity and integrity.

I knew they would also be pleased to see me finally married. Most of the adolescent girls with whom I had first been associated were now married, each with one or two children. A bride whom I had helped welcome into the household was now the mother of five. The women of the family, and even some of the men, had often expressed concern that I had not married and begun a family of my own.

Furthermore, I was certain that they would appreciate our gesture of honoring them with these gifts. They knew that non-Bedouins do not offer sheep as gifts; they would realize that I had learned this sign of respect from them. And only the Awlad ʿAli celebrate the postmarital visit in this way. The symbolism would be clear. We would be affirming both a sort of belonging to this community and, more importantly, this particular family's status as "close kin" of mine. In 1988 I had scribbled on a sheet of paper a list of things a bride is traditionally expected to bring on her postmarital visit home. The woman doing the itemizing had teased me at the time about why I wanted this information: "Lila," she had joked, "we expect you to bring us these things when you get married!" She would not be expecting me to follow through, but she would remember our list.

This visit was of great personal importance because I hoped finally to bring together two parts of my life. The Bedouin families with whom I had lived had just as little knowledge of my social world in the United States as they had of my academic life, a life to which, in a peculiarly objectified form, they were so central. Introducing my husband to them was a way for me to begin to join the worlds. I was especially anxious that they accept him and condone my marriage to a foreigner, with its implications for my primary identity. Although my husband had done research in Egypt and speaks Arabic, he is English. And I knew they felt strongly that I, in their eyes an Arab Muslim woman, should marry within the community. I hoped that my father's very presence would indicate his approval of the match and validate my husband; but I could not be sure how they would react when confronted with the finality of my dual identity and divided loyalties.

I was relieved and touched by what happened. Predictably, the Haj, my Bedouin host, regaled us with his tales about the British troops in the Western Desert during the Second World War. He also politely inquired whether my husband knew his British friends: Wilfred Thesiger, the explorer, who had indeed once passed through, and Mark Allen, a British diplomat in Egypt in the early 1980s who had enjoyed falcon hunting with the Haj. The unexpected thing the Haj did, however, was to tell some stories I had never heard before: stories about the origins of the British, suggesting that the ancestors of many English people, including some of the royal family, had been Arabs. We did not quite realize what he was doing until, several hours later as we rose to leave after lunch, he looked closely at my husband and then turned to his brother for confirmation. "Just look at his face," he said. "You can see his Arab blood!"

In his own way, the Haj had sought to bring my two worlds together, enfolding the foreign world into his to draw me back in. The distance between these cultural and geographic worlds had been decreasing over the last decade anyway. The Haj's own daughter had recently married a young man whose older brother was studying medicine in England. Electricity had been tapped from the new power lines joining the coastal towns; the new cinder-block houses cropping up on what had been open land all had television sets in their front rooms. The Awlad ʿAli Bedouins, as former pastoralists moving herds of sheep, goats, and sometimes camels and involved in trade between Libya, the oases of the Western Desert, and the Nile Valley from Alexandria to Upper

Egypt, had never been isolated. Yet they were now more closely integrated into Egyptian state institutions and the national economy than even ten years earlier.

Many ethnographies open with the trope of arrival. My first book, *Veiled Sentiments,* began with a description of the road one took to the Bedouin hamlet that housed the families whose social world I would describe and analyze. Second books on the same community often begin with the image of return and the radical changes the author encounters after a long absence. I could not, however, follow this formula because less than a year had passed since my last visit and I had just spent five months in the community only two years earlier. Unlike my father, I had seen the desert highway go from two to four lanes and was not surprised to see the toll booths. I knew how the Haj detested this new road with its radar speed traps. I had seen the gradual extension of irrigation canals and the conversion of much of the barren land around the community into orchards. As the region became more crowded, fewer families pitched tents near their houses. I had also seen the sudden growth of the nearby market town where my host's brothers now owned a building that housed a café and several stores. They had come to find property investment more lucrative than the sheep herds that had earlier sustained them. Now only one brother still kept herds, and when one day he was kicked by one of his camels, even his old mother begged him to get rid of them. Their time had passed, she said.

I had written earlier about the Awlad ʿAli tribes of the Western Desert as culturally and linguistically distinct both from the Bedouin groups of Sinai and the Eastern Desert and from the Egyptians living in the villages and towns of the Nile Valley. The Awlad ʿAli trace their origins to Libya, and many would insistently point out their difference from the people who ran the country in which they found themselves uneasy citizens, resentful of increasing restrictions. Their children, however, who are in contact with non-Bedouins in government schools, seemed sometimes ambivalent about the features that set the Bedouins apart: the strength of the

bonds of kinship, the control of elder kin over younger, the independence that marks men's honor, and the voluntary veiling and
separation from men that indexes women's respectability.

The younger generation was becoming aware, as readers of this
book should be too, of how marginal their way of life is, whether
to the rest of Egypt or to the Arab world as a whole. If pastoralists
in the mid–twentieth century represented no more than 1 percent
of the population of the Middle East, their values and their ways
of organizing sociopolitical and economic life are now those of an
even smaller minority. This is clearest in the situation of women.
In most of Egypt working women in the 1980s were struggling
with the competing demands of employment and family: running
household farms while their men worked as migrant laborers in
Saudi Arabia, sewing clothes, peddling on the street, battling the
crowds in public transportation to get to their jobs in offices and
wealthy people's homes, or finding professional careers as politi-
cians, businesswomen, teachers, and medical doctors—some of
whom might also be feminist leaders or Islamic activists. For the
women in the families I know, however, these kinds of lives are
only distant possibilities. Given their differences from the majority
of Middle Eastern women, what purpose might be served by
recounting, as I do in *Writing Women's Worlds,* their stories?

This book is intended to present, in the form of a narrative
ethnography made up of these women's stories and conversations,
a general critique of ethnographic typification. I was searching, like
other anthropologists working today, for a new ethnographic style;
I was also intrigued by the insights on method and voice emerging
from feminist theorizing and sympathetic to concerns in Middle
East studies about the way Arab societies tend to be portrayed. I
decided to explore how the wonderfully complex stories of the
individuals I had come to know in this community in Egypt might
challenge the capacity of anthropological generalizations to render
lives, theirs or others', adequately. The resulting series of narratives
is organized around five anthropological themes associated with the
study of women in the Arab world: patrilineality, polygyny, re-

production, patrilateral parallel-cousin marriage, and honor and shame. Yet rather than the chapter titles explaining the stories, the stories are meant to undo the titles.

The narrative chapters are preceded by an introduction written in the more conventional form of an academic essay that locates the work in its appropriate theoretical and political contexts. My intention in this is to alert readers to the possibility of reading the book in a particular way. The narrative chapters are not meant to be just entertaining or illuminating stories about Bedouin life in the 1980s; they are also critical commentaries on anthropological modes of understanding human existence. As representations of Bedouin life, these narratives are organized deliberately in terms of a set of goals determined by the context in which they will be read, not the context in which they occurred. That is, I expect the audience—which I assume will be mostly Western or Western-educated, coming to the text informed by anthropology (and its current critics), feminism (and its internal dissenters, including Third World feminists), and Middle East studies (with its awareness of the problems of orientalism)—to approach the book critically, keeping in mind questions about the politics of ethnographic representation and sociological description, problems of feminist aspiration and method, and assumptions about the Muslim Middle East.

Although it opens with an introduction, the book has no formal conclusion. We plunge into the stories in chapter 1, and remain with them through the end of the book. A discursive conclusion would have given closure; it would have provided the reader with "the meaning" of all these stories about parents, children, husbands, wives, conflicts, joys, and hopes. Busy readers could then have skipped from the introduction to the conclusion, assuming that they had an adequate gloss for what was sandwiched between. Such a concluding commentary, pronouncing the lessons of all these rich and complex stories, would have restored the superiority of the interpretive/analytical mode being questioned by the very construction of narratives, would have reestablished the familiar authority of the expert's voice, and, most troubling, would inevitably have contained the stories. That I selected and organized them according to the themes designated by the chapter headings seemed limiting enough to their meanings. To have tried to sum up their significance would have reduced them further. It would, in the end, have diminished their power and their potential to overflow our analytical categories. In life, in their tellings in Egypt, these stories and conversations did not occur in themes, at least not these themes. And although I wanted the tales to be able to speak to a set of intellectual debates in various fields in the United States and Europe in the 1990s, I also wanted to let them be more.

ACKNOWLEDGMENTS

Perhaps more than most, this book has depended on the extraordinary talents and rich lives of those who are its subjects. To protect these generous families from strangers, I have chosen to use pseudonyms. Sadly, that prevents me from being able to thank them by name, although I owe them such a debt of gratitude. As a mediator between worlds, I have taken their words into another context and fixed them in a form they would find surprising. Yet I hope the women and men whose stories I retell here will someday understand why I did it. Until then, I hope they will give me the benefit of the doubt by having faith that, though it seems a strange way to do it, I have meant through this book to honor the kindness they have shown me over the years.

The list of other individuals and institutions who have supported this project is embarrassingly long. I have a debt to the reviewers at various foundations and institutions who recommended that my project, even in its inchoate stages, be supported; I hope this book will not disappoint them. An award from the National Endowment for the Humanities (College Teachers Award) in 1986 made possible an initial trip to Egypt to record material. More important, it gave me precious months for reading that helped me to formulate the project and lay its theoretical foundations. I am grateful to the Department of Anthropology and the Kevorkian Center for Near Eastern Studies at New York University for the use of their facilities and the stimulation of their company during that period. Bambi Schieffelin deserves special thanks for explaining to me how to begin transcribing my piles of cassette tapes. While in New York I was fortunate to find a group with whom to read the French feminists; my thanks to Carol Ockman for bringing us together.

The bulk of the fieldwork I undertook for this book was made possible by a Fulbright Award through the Islamic Civilization Program. The American Research Center in Egypt kindly gave me an affiliation and arranged for my permissions through the Egyptian Ministry of Higher Education. Amira Khattab was wonderfully helpful. Ann Radwan and the staff of the Fulbright Commission in Cairo saw to it that I could get on with my research; they offered assistance with transportation and occasional lodging, for which I was grateful during those long hot months of 1987. Friends in Cairo gave me good advice, good conversation, and comfortable places to stay; special thanks go to Soraya Altorki, Marilyn Booth, Ken Cuno, Nick Hopkins, Soheir Morsy, and Cynthia Nelson.

I transcribed and transcribed and transcribed (to use a favorite convention of Bedouin storytelling) and finally began writing while a member of the Institute for Advanced Study in Princeton. I am deeply grateful to Clifford Geertz and Joan Scott for affording me the privilege of that extraordinary year. The other regular participants in the "Gender Seminar," especially Judith Butler, Yasmine Ergas, Evelyn Fox Keller, Donna Haraway, Dorinne Kondo, Rayna Rapp, Carroll Smith-Rosenberg, and Louise Tilly, were helpful in forcing me to rethink much about feminist scholarship before it was too late. My gratitude to the National Endowment for the Humanities increased for their contribution, along with the Rockefeller Foundation, to my support at the Institute.

I managed to complete much of the rest of the writing while a Mellon Fellow at the University of Pennsylvania. I benefited enormously from colleagues and seminars there, but Arjun Appadurai, Carol Breckenridge, Margaret Mills, and the enlightening (if not always civilized) seminar on "Orientalism and Beyond" sponsored by the South Asia Program deserve particular mention. The anthropology department made me welcome, and Diana Long gave me an enjoyable home in Philadelphia.

Although the project seemed radical when I first conceived of it, the many talented anthropologists who have published narrative ethnographies since then have given it something of a school to swim with. The final form and intent of the book owe much to them and to the responses of many audiences and readers. If I can no longer remember what came from where, I am no less appreciative of all the comments and questions I have received. I will single out only a few individuals for thanks. The participants in the lively seminar "Representing Anthropology," organized by Richard Fox at the School of American Research in Santa Fe, helped me think through some of the issues raised in the introduction and showed me how much fun intellectual exchange could be. Susan Slyomovics and Ruth Behar were supportive critics. Wendy Brown gently but insistently asked me, in the final hour, what I had repressed. Catherine Lutz was a careful critic and good friend throughout. At the University of California Press I was glad to work again with Sheila Levine and Anne Canright and impressed, as before, with the attention my book received. The two anonymous reviewers suggested areas worth reworking; they delayed an already long overdue project but helped make it better. Without Mary and Ted Cross's generous offer of an exquisite place to work, I would not have enjoyed the process of doing these final revisions so much.

In the acknowledgments to my first book, I buried my thanks to Tim Mitchell in a long list of friends because he had come at its end. This book, which has shared our life together, owes much to him in details large and small (though none of its weaknesses can be blamed on him). He cheerfully read more of it and my other writings than anyone should have to; I am ever grateful for his optimism and the gift of his shared thoughts.

KEEPING THE NAMES STRAIGHT

FIRST GENERATION

Migdim: the old mother
Jawwad: Migdim's husband, deceased

SECOND GENERATION

Hamid: Migdim's eldest son
Sagr: (or *Haj Sagr*) Migdim's second son
Dhahab: Migdim's eldest daughter
Ngawa: Migdim's second daughter
Lawz: Migdim's youngest daughter
Gateefa: Sagr's senior wife and first cousin
Safiyya: Sagr's second wife
Azza: Sagr's third wife
Fayga: wife of one of Migdim's other sons

THIRD GENERATION

Sabra: eldest daughter of Gateefa and Sagr
Kamla: second daughter of Gateefa and Sagr
Selima: Hamid's daughter
Aisha: family friend and Kamla's future sister-in-law
Khwayyir: Migdim's grandson
Salih: Migdim's grandson

FOURTH GENERATION

Kafy: Migdim's great-grandson, grandson of Sagr and Safiyya

INTRODUCTION

Every book tells tales, some intended, some not. This is a book of
stories by and about some women in a small Bedouin community
in Egypt. It is made up of conversations, narratives, arguments,
songs, reminiscences, even an essay, that these women shared with
each other or with me. I recall them here in a certain order with a
very different audience in mind. In the way I have retold these tales
and the very fact that I have chosen to keep them as "just stories"
lies a tale meant for my professional colleagues—the anthropologists, feminist scholars, and students of the Muslim Middle East to
whom this introduction is largely addressed.

In one sense, of course, the unusual form of this ethnography
owes much to the remarkable women in the Awlad 'Ali Bedouin
community with whom I lived. During my first stay in this small
hamlet on the northwest coast of Egypt, a stay of nearly two years
in the late 1970s, I rarely felt comfortable tape-recording. After I
returned to the United States, I wrote a book based on eighteen
tattered notebooks in which I had scribbled notes. In it I tried to
present a general analysis of social life, morality, and poetry in this
community, with a special focus on gender relations (Abu-Lughod
1986).

I felt, however, that there was so much more richness in people's
conversations and complexity to their lives than I had managed to
convey in that book that I had to try again. I shared with many a
sense of the limitations of the standard anthropological monograph, however sophisticated, sensitive, or well written, and wondered if there could be a style of ethnographic writing that would

better capture the qualities of "life as lived" in this community.[1] A crucial aspect of this way of living was the way it was caught up in stories. The vividness and style with which women recounted stories of everyday life impressed me. The rhythms of their conversations, the voices dropping to a whisper then rising to dramatic pitches in enactments of reported speech, the expressions, the exaggerations, the detail—all lent intensity, even urgency, to the tellings. Those of us for whom newspapers and television define what is news and books and films constitute our imaginative spaces may find it hard to grasp what stories about life and people mean in such a social world—a world in which everyone is known (or is related to someone one knows) and the only events that matter are ones that happen to them.

I returned to Egypt several times between 1986 and 1989 with the hope that if I could manage to tape-record these expressive narratives, the qualities of life that I had sensed when with these women would not so easily elude me or those for whom I wanted to write.[2] I did not expect that just because I would work from recorded speech, some directed at me, some uttered with scarce awareness of my presence, that I would be able to represent more faithfully the realities of life in this community. We have learned to be suspicious of claims about the transparency of texts and the capacity of representations to mirror reality. No less than any other sort of ethnography, this book of stories involves analysis and is shaped by the questions asked and the point of view taken. It presents, as Clifford (1986a) argues all ethnographies do, a "partial

1. The phrase "life as lived" comes from Riesman (1977). For recent and interesting expressions of dissatisfaction with the gap between the written monograph and life as lived in the field, see, among others, Jackson 1989, on the body; R. Rosaldo 1989, on emotion; and Stoller 1989, on the senses.

2. By then, needless to say, I knew people well; more important, they knew me. I began to tape-record in the presence of those who did not mind, thus gathering most of the material out of which this book has been constructed.

truth." But I like to think that this book, with its fuller use of narrative and its greater reliance on recorded speech, conveys something that my first book could not.

Intersections

My vague longing for some way to write differently about the experience of living in that particular community in Egypt initially seemed to find legitimation in the debates about women's writing and feminist method. Sympathetic to feminist critiques of scholarship in various fields (including my own), I began to wonder if what I was seeking to do was write an ethnography "in a different voice" (to borrow Gilligan's [1982] phrase). In my early formulations of the project, I argued that this book would be written in the voice of Bedouin women (not men); more important, it would be in the voice of a woman ethnographer.[3] This framing of the problem seemed especially apt given the ferment in anthropological circles about ethnographic writing. In his introduction to *Writing Culture,* Clifford (1986a, 19) made the controversial claim that feminist anthropologists had not been involved in textual innovation, a statement that only later gave me pause.[4] At the time, I simply proposed that my project would fill this gap.

Over the years I became increasingly skeptical of my initial conceptions. First came a discomfort with the notion of a specifically female voice in writing. Any attempt to isolate what was specific to women writers eventually foundered on false essentialism and culture blindness.[5] Feminist anthropologists had done too

3. For a summary of this position, see Abu-Lughod 1988a.

4. My critique of this position can be found in Abu-Lughod 1990a. Other feminist anthropologists were working on compelling critiques at the same time; see Gordon 1988; Mascia-Lees, Sharpe, and Cohen 1989; and Visweswaran 1988.

5. See Echols 1984 for a good critique of cultural feminism. Haraway's (1985) cautions about a false organicist association with women are

much excellent work on the variety of women's experiences and the variability of gender systems for anyone to imagine that there might be some universal "woman's experience" or "woman's style," even if in many societies men and women did live in somewhat different worlds.[6] Feminist scholarship in the 1980s itself was shaken by self-critiques brought about by the realization of how many groups of women (lesbians, African-Americans, "women of color," Third World women, and others) had been excluded from consideration or participation in the development of theory. However attractive the prospect of associating certain positive qualities such as sensitivity, care, attention, embodiment, or egalitarianism with women and their projects, one finally had to confront the fact that these "feminine virtues" belonged strictly to a contemporary Euro-American subculture.[7]

If there was not "a different voice" for women, how should I define what I was aiming for? The next formulation for the book I wanted to write was as feminist ethnography. This raised a second set of problems, the most basic and tendentious of which was what it meant to be "feminist." A minimal definition might include a concern with women's conditions and with the political, economic, social, and cultural implications of systems of gender for them. But if feminism also implied some sort of emancipatory project applied to the subjects of the ethnography, it would not fit. Ong (1988, 90) was correct to insist that feminists should "recognize other forms of gender- and culture-based subjectivities, and accept that others

---

important, and Butler's (1990) critique of essentialism is especially lucid. The literature on women's writing is vast. I discuss some of it in Abu-Lughod 1990a.

6. Feminist anthropology or the anthropology of women, as it is variously known (with different implications), is now a major field. For recent guides to the field and the issues, see Collier and Yanagisako 1987; di Leonardo 1991; Moore 1988; Morgen 1989; and Sanday and Goodenough 1990.

7. Lutz's (1988, 1990) explorations of the associations between gender and emotion in Western ideology are especially interesting.

often choose to conduct their lives separate from our particular vision of the future."[8]

The ethnographic project could, however, be feminist vis-à-vis the world of scholarship in which it was embedded; it could direct itself meaningfully to assumptions of anthropology in general and the anthropology of the Arab world in particular using feminist insights. In an important article, Strathern (1987) characterized as awkward the relationship between anthropology and feminism. As I have argued elsewhere (Abu-Lughod 1991), she was right in her assessment but wrong in her analysis of the source of the tension. She located the tension in the differing relations of self and other of the feminist and the anthropologist, recognizing the power dynamic in the first relation but not in the second. By underplaying the inequality inherent in the anthropological self's position as (usually) a Westerner studying non-Western others, she disregarded the first lesson of feminist analyses from Simone de Beauvoir on: relations—or, more accurately, constructions—of self and other are rarely innocent of power.[9] To be feminist entails being sensitive to domination; for the ethnographer that means being aware of domination in the society being described and in the relationship between the writer (and readers) and the people being written about.

Also relevant to my project was the lively concern of feminist scholars in the social sciences, the history of science, and philosophy with questions of method. Building on the apprehension of how much knowledge had been generated with no attention to women and scant attention to gender, these writers had reexamined the implications of the claims to objectivity that accompanied this knowledge. Some sought to undermine these claims by showing the partiality of various kinds of knowledge; others exposed the

8. Further sophisticated discussions of the relationships among Western feminism, Third World or "Eastern" feminists, and other non-Western women can be found in Lazreg 1988; Mohanty 1984; and Spivak 1987.

9. The alternative and increasingly popular tradition of studying one's own society or European societies requires separate treatment.

gender-related associations in the West of the binary distinction between objective and subjective (Keller 1985) and analyzed the power effects of assertions of objectivity (MacKinnon 1982; D. Smith 1987). Many proposed alternative ways of knowing or seeking knowledge based on "women's experiences" (variously described as the experience of being subalterns, mothers, sexual beings or objects, daughters, and so forth), proposals sensibly criticized as unworkable (Harding 1987; Stacey 1988). These efforts have made one important contribution: they have sharpened our awareness of the charged nature of claims to objectivity and the situatedness of all knowledge (Haraway 1988). Positionality, feminist theorizing teaches, not only is not a handicap but must be made explicit and explored.

Feminist work thus encouraged a heightened consciousness of two issues—standpoint and the power dynamics of self and other—that dovetailed with anthropologists' increasingly sophisticated attention to reflexivity in fieldwork and writing. Critiques of anthropology were emerging from various quarters prodding us to question what we worked on, how we wrote, and for whom we wrote. Relations of self and other were central to the dilemma of cultural difference; the question of method and its connection to stance were critical to the politics of representation (in ethnographic texts), if not the politics of anthropology as a discipline. In this convergence between feminist and anthropological theorizing during what Marcus and Fischer (1986) called an "experimental moment," I began to see more clearly what issues I wanted to engage with in my second ethnography of this small community in Egypt's Western Desert.

Writing Against Culture

Why would an anthropologist trained in the professional analytic language of social science choose to compose an ethnography of narratives and conversations? There are, after all, only certain things such a book can do. Speaking of modes of writing about societies, Jackson (1989, 186) has noted that "the value and place of different discursive styles have to be decided by the situation we find ourselves in and the problems we address."[10] A book of stories cannot present in a systematic fashion or in the theoretical terms in which anthropologists usually work the logic of social life in the community I studied.[11] For that, the reader should turn to other discussions of the Awlad ʿAli (e.g., Abou-Zeid 1966; Abu-Lughod 1986; Mohsen 1975).

This book of tales can, however, speak to a set of theoretical concerns about the politics of representation. What became for me the most troubling aspect of ethnographic description was that it, like other social scientific discourses, trafficked in generalizations. Whether "seeking" laws of human sociality or simply characterizing and interpreting ways of life, our goal as anthropologists is usually to use details and the particulars of individual lives to produce typifications. The drawback, as I will argue, for those working with people living in other societies is that generalization can make these "others" seem simultaneously more coherent, self-contained, and different from ourselves than they might be. Generalization, however useful for other projects, helps make concepts like "culture" and "cultures" seem sensible. This in turn allows for the fixing of boundaries between self and other.

My concern about the generalizing mode of social scientific discourse is thus not that it abstracts and reifies, although I am responsive to critiques like D. Smith's (1987) that make this

10. Taussig (1987) has argued that the very horrors of colonial terror in Latin America forced him to write in a different style. Pandolfo (1991) has worked to mimic in her writing the concepts, Moroccan and other, she was trying to explore.

11. See Herzfeld 1987 for a very interesting discussion of what he calls the "theory-practice conundrum" in which he argues that the opposition between ethnography and theory is symbolic.

point.[12] Nor am I arguing for particularity versus generality as a way of privileging micro- over macro-processes. Analysts of everyday life who examine micro-interactions are just as fond of generalization as social scientists analyzing social movements or global interactions. In any event, attending to the particulars of individuals' lives need not imply disregard for forces and dynamics that are not locally based; the effects of extralocal or long-term processes are always manifested locally and specifically.

Anthropologists do, however, have two reasons to be especially wary of generalization. The first is that as part of a professional discourse of objectivity and expertise, it is inevitably a language of power. It is the language of those who seem to stand apart from and outside of what they are describing. Again, D. Smith's critique of sociological discourse is relevant. She has argued (1987, 62) that this seemingly detached mode of reflecting on social life is actually located: it represents the perspective of those involved in professional, managerial, and administrative structures, and its origins lie in the management of internal social groups like workers, women, blacks, the poor, or prisoners. It is thus part of what she calls "the ruling apparatus of this society." This critique might apply as easily to anthropology, with its inter- rather than intrasocietal perspective and its origins not in domestic political problems but in the exploration and colonization of the non-European world.[13] Furthermore, the very gap between the professional and authoritative discourses of generalization and the languages of everyday life (our own and those of others) establishes a fundamental separation

12. Speaking of sociological discourse, D. Smith (1987, 130) notes, for example, that "the complex organization of activities of actual individuals and their actual relations is entered into the discourse through concepts such as class, modernization, formal organization. A realm of theoretically constituted objects is created, freeing the discursive realm from its ground in the lives and work of actual individuals and liberating sociological inquiry to graze on a field of conceptual entities."

13. These ideas about the relationship between academic disciplines and social management are explored more fully in Foucault 1978, 1980.

between the anthropologist and his or her readers, on the one hand, and the people being written about, on the other, that in turn facilitates the construction of these others as simultaneously different and inferior.

For the anthropologist, the second and more serious problem with generalization is that by producing the effects of homogeneity, coherence, and timelessness, it contributes to the creation of "cultures." In the process of generalizing from experiences and conversations with a number of specific people in a community, the anthropologist may flatten out their differences and homogenize them. The effort to produce general ethnographic descriptions of people's beliefs or actions risks smoothing over contradictions, conflicts of interest, doubts, and arguments, not to mention changing motivations and historical circumstances. Besides being theoretically unsound, this erasure of time and conflict is misleading because it makes what is inside the external boundary set up by homogenization seem essential and fixed. The appearance of a lack of internal differentiation makes it easier to conceive of groups of people as discrete, bounded entities, like the "cultures" of "the Nuer," "the Balinese," or "the Awlad ʿAli Bedouin," populated by generic cultural beings who do this or that and believe such-and-such. Although we have come to take this notion of separate cultures for granted, there are good reasons to consider such entities dangerous fictions and to argue for what I have called writing *against* culture (Abu-Lughod 1991).

This stance might seem surprising. As the replacement for the scientific concept of race, popular in the nineteenth century but now discredited as a means of establishing essential differences between groups of people, culture was a positive concept. It seemed at first to solve the moral and analytical difficulties inherent in "race" by removing difference from the realm of the natural or innate. Whether conceived of as a set of behaviors, customs, traditions, rules, plans, recipes, instructions, or programs (to list the range of definitions Geertz [1973a, 44] furnishes), culture was something that was learned and therefore could change. More important, unlike race, and unlike even the earlier concept of "culture" as a synonym for civilization (contrasted to barbarism), the modern idea allowed for multiple rather than binary differences. The shift to "culture" ("lower case *c* with the possibility of a final *s*," as Clifford [1988a, 234] puts it) thus immediately checked an easy move to hierarchizing and, indeed, had a relativizing effect. The hallmark of twentieth-century anthropology, then, has been its promotion of cultural relativism over evaluation and judgment. In many cases, as Marcus and Fischer (1986) have argued, anthropology has even used its knowledge of others as a form of self-critique.[14]

Despite its anti-essentialist intent, however, the culture concept retains the tendency to make difference seem self-evident and people seem "other."[15] Many anthropologists have expressed concern

14. See Stocking 1989 for an interesting analysis of the meanings of "culture" in the 1920s.

15. Said (1978) has shown how the scholarly discourse of Orientalism, in mapping geography, race, and culture onto one another, fixes differences between people of "the West" and people of "the East" in ways so rigid that they might as well be considered innate. Some anticolonial movements and present-day struggles have worked by what could be labeled reverse Orientalism, where attempts to reverse the power relationship proceed by seeking to valorize for the self what in the former system had been devalued as other. A Gandhian appeal to the greater spirituality of a Hindu India, compared with the materialism and violence of the West, and an Islamist appeal to a greater faith in God, compared with the immorality and corruption of the West, both accept the essentialist terms of Orientalist constructions. While turning those constructs on their heads, the appeals preserve the rigid sense of difference based on culture.

A parallel can be drawn with feminism. It is a basic tenet of feminism that "women are not born, they are made." It has been important for most feminists to locate sex differences in culture, not biology or nature. While this approach has inspired some feminist theorists to attend to the social and personal effects of gender as a system of difference, for many others it has led to explorations of and strategies built on the notion of a women's culture. Cultural feminism (see Echols 1984) takes many forms, but it has many of the qualities of reverse Orientalism just discussed.

about how the notion of culture tends to make difference into something solid and timeless. Appadurai (1988b), in his radical argument that "natives" are a figment of the anthropological imagination, shows the complicity of the anthropological concept of culture in a continuing "incarceration" of non-Western peoples in time and place. He argues that by not looking to their histories, we have denied these people the same capacity for movement, travel, and geographical interaction that Westerners take for granted. The fluidity of group boundaries, languages, and practices, in other words, has been masked by the concept of culture. E. Wolf's (1982) work on "the people without history" has similarly uncovered massive movements of people and transformations in local life under the impact of Western expansion and the ensuing interactions with European economies—all this in communities that anthropologists often treat as representing untouched or enduring cultures. R. Rosaldo (1989) has argued not only that the "myth of the

---

For French feminists like Irigaray (1985a, 1985b), Cixous (1983), and Kristeva (1981), masculine and feminine, if not actually male and female, represent essentially different modes of being. Anglo-American feminists follow a different tack. Some attempt to "describe" the cultural differences between men and women—Gilligan (1982) and her followers (e.g., Belenky et al. 1986), who elaborate the notion of "a different voice," are popular examples. Others try to "explain" the differences, whether through a socially informed psychoanalytic theory (e.g., Chodorow 1978), a Marxist-derived theory of the effects of the division of labor and women's role in social reproduction (Hartsock 1985), an analysis of maternal practice (Ruddick 1989), or even a theory of sexual exploitation (MacKinnon 1982). Much feminist theorizing and practice seeks to build or reform social life along the lines of this "women's culture." There have been proposals for a woman-centered university (Rich 1979), a feminist science (H. Rose 1983, 1986), a feminist methodology in the sciences and social sciences (Meis 1983; Reinharz 1983; D. Smith 1987; Stanley and Wise 1983), even a feminist spirituality (e.g., Christ and Plaskow 1979) and ecology. These proposals nearly always build on values traditionally associated in the West with women: a sense of care and connectedness, maternal nurturing, immediacy of experience, involvement in the bodily (versus the abstract), and so forth.

Lone Ethnographer" and his product, the classic ethnography, produce the myth of separate and timeless cultures, but also that we would do better to focus on the border zones.[16]

Others have suggested as well that cultural theories tend to overemphasize coherence within these self-contained entities (Abu-Lughod 1990c). Clifford notes that "the discipline of fieldwork-based anthropology, in constituting its authority, constructs and reconstructs coherent cultural others and interpreting selves" (Clifford 1988b, 112). Ethnography, he says, is a form of culture collecting (like art collecting) in which "diverse experiences and facts are selected, gathered, detached from their original temporal occasions, and given enduring value in a new arrangement" (Clifford 1988a, 231). Organic metaphors of wholeness and the methodology of holism that characterizes anthropology both favor coherence, which in turn contributes to the perception of communities as bounded and discrete—at some fundamental level cut off from one another and different.

The problem with the concept of culture, therefore, is that despite its positive intent, it seems to work as an essential tool for making "other." As a professional discourse that elaborates on the meaning of culture in order to account for, explain, and understand cultural difference, anthropology ends up also constructing, producing, and maintaining difference. Anthropological discourse helps give cultural difference (and the separation between groups of people that it implies) the air of the self-evident.

Does difference always smuggle in hierarchy, as the feminist theorists have suggested? Anthropology seems to have high stakes in sustaining and perpetuating a belief in the existence of cultures that are identifiable as discrete, different, and separate from our own.[17] It has been argued that otherness and difference may have

16. For an earlier and more celebratory view of the way ethnographic writing exaggerates cultural differences, see Boon 1982, 26.

17. Arens (1979), for example, has asked the provocative question of why anthropologists cling so tenaciously to the belief that in some cultures

assumed for anthropologists "talismanic qualities."[18] Whether its goal is to engage in cultural self-critique or to assert enlightened tolerance through relativism, anthropology needs others that are different from the self. Yet a difference between self and other will always be hierarchical because the self is sensed as primary, self-formed, active, and complex, if not positive. At the very least, the self is always the interpreter and the other the interpreted.

Anyone interested in working against this hierarchizing must seek ways to undermine the essentialized notion of "cultures" different from ours and peoples separate from us. There are surely many ways to do this, but in this book I have sought to "write against culture" by working against generalization. Telling stories, it has seemed to me, could be a powerful tool for unsettling the culture concept and subverting the process of "othering" it entails.[19] Anthropologists commonly generalize about communities by saying that they are characterized by certain institutions, rules, or ways of doing things. For example, we can and often do say things like "The Bongo-Bongo are polygynous." What if one refused to typify in this way and instead asked how a particular set of individuals—three women and their husband in one community, for example—in fact live the "institution" that we call polygyny? Societies of the circum-Mediterranean have often been characterized as "honor and shame" societies. What if one asked how an Egyptian schoolgirl waiting for her marriage to be arranged by an important family in the 1980s lived this "cultural" complex?

By stressing the particularity of that girl's experiences or of that single marriage and by building a picture of polygyny or honor

---

cannibalism is an accepted ritual practice when the evidence (in the form of eyewitness accounts) is so meager (if not, as he argues, absent).

18. Said (1989, 213) used this term in his discussion of the current state of anthropology.

19. I have referred elsewhere (1991) to some of the powerful alternative strategies scholars have adopted for writing against culture, in particular the study of global interconnections, historical transformation, and theoretical explorations of notions like "practice" and "discourse."

from individuals' discussions, recollections, disagreements, and actions, one could make tangible several larger theoretical points. First, the refusal to generalize would highlight the constructed quality of that "typicality" so regularly produced in conventional social scientific accounts. Second, description of the actual circumstances and histories of individuals and their relationships would suggest that such particulars, which are always present (as we know from our own lives), are also always crucial to the constitution of experience. Third, reconstruction of people's arguments about, justifications for, and interpretations of what they and others are doing would allow clearer understanding of how social life proceeds. It would show that, within limited discourses (that may be contradictory and certainly are historically changing), people strategize, feel pain, contest interpretations of what is happening—in short, live their lives. In one sense this is not new. Bourdieu (1977), for example, theorizes about social practice in a similar way. The difference here is that one would represent through textual means how this happens rather than simply assert that it does so.

By focusing closely on particular individuals and their changing relationships, one could also subvert the most problematic connotations of "culture": homogeneity, coherence, and timelessness. In the face of the complexity of individual lives even in a single family, a term like "Bedouin culture" comes to seem meaningless, whether in the sense of rules that people follow or of a community that shares such rules. Individuals are confronted with choices; they struggle with others, make conflicting statements, argue about points of view on the same events, undergo ups and downs in various relationships and changes in their circumstances and desires, face new pressures, and fail to predict what will happen to them or those around them. Particular events always happen in time, becoming part of the history of the family, of the individuals involved, and of their relationships. In the events described in the women's stories I retell, one can even read the "larger forces" that made them possible.[20]

Storytelling

If one merit of the textual technique of storytelling is that it draws attention to, even as it refuses, the power of social scientific generalization to produce "cultures" (with their differentiation of selves and others), the other merit has to do with feminism's second lesson: the inevitability of positionality. A story is always situated; it has both a teller and an audience. Its perspective is partial (in both senses of the word), and its telling is motivated. The Bedouin women's tales presented here are no exception. While these stories may seem to reveal to us a great deal about the social and emotional dynamics in this Bedouin community in the 1980s, it must be remembered that in the original context each was told with a purpose. I have not tried to reproduce those contexts, nor have I undertaken an analysis of the role of these stories in the life of the community, although both would have been interesting projects.[21]

20. Even ritual, that communal practice for which time seems to have such a different (perhaps cyclical) meaning and which in anthropological discourse so perfectly marks the (exotic, primitive) cultural other as different, turns out to be particular and anything but timeless. A glance at Bedouin weddings (chapter 4), when one does not filter out the participants and sequences of events, reveals unpredictability to be a central feature.

21. The rich possibilities of the analysis of storytelling itself are apparent in the many excellent studies by folklorists (see Bauman 1986 for a discussion and Mills 1991 for an example) and in recent work by anthropologists such as Gilsenan's forthcoming *Lords of the Lebanese Marches,* which explores the complex role of telling tales in the construction of men of honor (and dishonor) in a Lebanese village; Narayan 1989, analyzing the role of stories in a Hindu swami's religious teachings; and

Instead, recognizing that with the inclusion of these stories in this book the tellers and audiences, as well as their purposes, have fundamentally shifted, I have tried to use these tales to construct what could be called a critical ethnography. I selected the stories and wove them into a pattern on the basis of a conjunction between Bedouin women's interest in and attention to certain issues and the salience of these issues for specific audiences in the West. Initially, I was guided in my selection by the subjects that excited, moved, and concerned the women I knew, the subjects most often discussed. In that sense, the stories represent women's voices in Awlad 'Ali society and their perspective on many matters that have generally entered the anthropological literature through men's voices.[22] But I have excluded neither men's stories nor stories about issues that concerned men and women equally (like land disputes, fights between families, or the past) because despite day-to-day sexual segregation, women define themselves in terms of their families, speak often with their husbands, brothers, fathers, uncles, nephews, and cousins, and are interested in all matters that concern those to whom they are close.

Most important, I do not pretend that these stories "lift" or get "behind" the veil, as reviewers of books on Middle Eastern women frequently say. As Bruner (1986) reminds us, ethnographies are themselves narratives. I have therefore sought, by crafting, reconfiguring, and juxtaposing these women's and men's stories, to make them speak particularly to my concerns and those of my audience. As the new teller of these tales, I wanted to draw out the ways they challenged simultaneously three sorts of constructions:

K. Stewart 1988 and 1991, which do wonders with the narratives of men and women in the Appalachian coal mining camps of West Virginia. Natalie Davis's *Fiction in the Archives* (1988) is a wonderful example of the use to which tales can be put for historical understanding of another time and place—in her case, sixteenth-century France.

22. I have discussed elsewhere the way the anthropological literature has treated tribalism primarily from a male perspective (Abu-Lughod 1989).

standard anthropological generalizations about social structure and culture; common feminist interpretations of gender relations in non-Western societies; and widely shared understandings of Muslim Arab society. That is the sense in which this ethnography is critical.

If this use of women's stories makes me something of a ventriloquist, as Appadurai (1988a, 16) has suggested all anthropologists are, it does not thereby undermine the worth of these retold tales. Only a false belief in the possibility of a nonsituated story (or "objectivity") could make one ask that stories reflect the way things, over there, "really" are.[23] Scholars like Kapferer (1988) and Mascia-Lees, Sharpe, and Cohen (1989), who worry about the hidden power to orchestrate "native" voices, merely articulate unsympathetically what many anthropologists have already become highly conscious of and troubled by: our role in shaping the words of people living in societies other than our own.[24] There is

23. I have discussed positionality at greater length in the context of the boundaries of self and other that feminists and "halfies" (people of mixed background or between two worlds) must deal with (Abu-Lughod 1991). R. Rosaldo (1989) presents an important argument regarding the relationship of personal experience to research. Haraway's (1988) consideration of the issues about situated knowledge is among the best. Other perceptive discussions of the implications of positionality in scholarship about the non-West and the whole problem of "location" can be found in Mani 1989 and John 1989.

24. A particularly heated debate has gone on in Middle East women's studies regarding Margot Badran's translated edition of the memoirs of the early Egyptian feminist Huda Sha'rawi (1986). Among the questions raised by reviewers (e.g., Ahmed 1987; Hatem 1988) were those about the hidden editorial hand used in selecting passages from the original manuscript, the choice to focus on the early years, and the decision to title the book in terms of Orientalist stereotypes. Lazreg (1988, 106) has criticized Mernissi (1988) for attempting "to speak for other women while rising above them." However appealing, books like Atiya's *Khul Khaal* are problematic because no information is provided on how the material was collected and what the relationship of the author was to the Egyptian women interviewed.

clearly no way to avoid doing this if we want to continue writing. What may alleviate some of the difficulties of the process of constructing a narrative is to make explicit, as I will try to do, how one has worked.

The arrangement of the stories into chapters follows an anthropological logic. Anthropologists often characterize societies in terms of social "institutions" like patrilineality (a mode of social organization based on kinship), patrilateral parallel-cousin marriage (a regular pattern of prescribed or preferred marriage), or polygyny. These constructs allow one to compare different groups and to grasp, in a nutshell, some basic facts about the way things work in a particular place. Although intended as analytical categories, these terms can, however, have the unfortunate effect of creating a mechanistic vision of society in which members play designated roles. No matter how much sophisticated theoretical discussion of strategies, dialectics, and articulations we engage in, thereby refining our understanding of the processes involved in producing such patterns, we are still left with little sense of individuals' experiences of such forms of organization and the individual acts that constitute them.

Whereas British social anthropology has focused on social organization, both French and American anthropological traditions have shown greater concern for "cultural" phenomena such as belief systems, modes of thought, or worldview. In this discourse, societies like those of the Middle East have come to be characterized as obsessed with honor and shame, marked by Islamic fatalism, or rife with agonistic jockeying between fragmenting tribal segments or calculating individuals.

I wanted the stories in this book to allow subtler thinking about such sociological and cultural characterizations by revealing how the various elements of such depictions, although often present, do not necessarily take the form one would expect or fall neatly into simple patterns. The stark contrast between the simple analytic frame—indicated by the abstract chapter titles—and the complex contents of the chapters, which consist of detailed and often highly personal arguments, experiences, and stories, is meant to be jarring.

In all cases, it seems to me, the moral of the stories is that things are and are not what they seem. The Awlad ʿAli are patrilineal, but reckoning descent, tribal affiliation, and inheritance through the male line does not foreclose women's opportunities or desires to shape their own lives or those of their sons and daughters, or to oppose the decisions of their fathers. Marriages are arranged by families in terms of a set of ideals, including a preference for marriage between first cousins, but the circumstances of each family and relations between families at any given moment make certain possibilities desirable, realizable, or not. Polygyny is an institution oppressive to women in that it causes them pain, but it is not necessarily the pleasure for husbands that Western fantasies about harems suggest. Given their expectations about marriage in general, the tensions that this sort of marriage generates for Awlad ʿAli women differ from those we might ourselves imagine; still, there *are* tensions, in relations both between husband and wife and between co-wives. Furthermore, although polygynous marriages may share some characteristics, no two are the same. As chapter 2, on Gateefa, Safiyya, Azza, and their husband, Sagr, makes clear, the experiences of those involved depend in part on their personalities and circumstances. They also change over time, since no relationship is ever static. Even at the level of social function, polygyny seems not always to increase reproduction and strengthen lineages or to forge political alliances: sometimes it backfires; sometimes such aims are simply beyond reach. Finally, although some turn to the Qurʾan to justify polygyny as Islamic, others use the same passage to condemn the practice as not favored by God.

Like polygyny, the other issues to which these stories speak are ones that carry multiple charges across the Western discourses of anthropology, feminism, Middle East studies, and popular orientalism. Patrilineality and reproduction, the "topics" of chapters 1 and 3, respectively, are loaded terms for Western audiences. In

Middle East anthropology, patrilineality and tribalism blend imperceptibly. Feminists, however, easily conflate patrilineality with "patriarchy," and focus on it in debates about male domination, gender hierarchy, and sexual difference. Feminist anthropologists thus interpret patrilineality as either a form of male domination or a system within which women develop numerous strategies and cause endless problems. In discussions of Arab society, the form of social organization and system of inheritance based on patrilineality is sometimes justified as Islamic; other times Islam is portrayed as trying to move beyond patrilineality by legislating inheritance for women and promoting wider associations based on religion rather than kinship. In chapter 1, the stories of the old matriarch Migdim reveal some of the implications over time of patrilineality. Covering subjects ranging from resistance to a father's authority to the meaning of giving birth to sons versus daughters, the struggles with grown sons over decisions affecting future generations, and the conflicts of loyalty between family and the women's community, Migdim's stories make vivid the conflicts and emotional ambivalence generated in her circumstances.[25]

Reproduction occupies an even more complex field than polygyny or patrilineality. In social scientific jargon it refers to the process of keeping society going; in Marxist scholarship, to the form women's work takes in the political economy. Feminist debates grant reproduction a different but still key role, analyzing it variously as the root of women's vulnerability to male oppression, the reason for the sexual division of labor, the symbolic basis for their social inferiority, the source of their alternative modes of thought and social interaction, the basis for a different experience of sexuality, the determinant of the firmness of their ego boundaries, and the genesis of their special relationship to language.[26] In

25. For a discussion of stories of resistance and an argument for using resistance as a diagnostic of power, see Abu-Lughod 1990b.

26. References to the feminist literature on reproduction would take up pages. A sampling of key texts, however, would have to include the following: de Beauvoir [1953] 1974; Chodorow 1978; Hartsock 1985;

the popular discourses about the Third World, and especially about Egypt, reproduction plays into other debates as well—about family planning and so-called overpopulation, on the one hand, and about high rates of child mortality and whether Egyptians value life as we do, on the other. Chapter 3, built around stories about giving birth, wanting children, having too many children, loving children, resenting children, raising children, scolding children, and telling them tales, tries to open up the field defined by these other discourses. Motherhood, these stories suggest, means many things.

The final two chapters, both about the younger generation, deal with two important dimensions of marriage, although the overlap in issues is so strong that the titles—"Patrilateral Parallel-Cousin Marriage" and "Honor and Shame"—are virtually interchangeable. What the anthropologist dispassionately calls arranged marriage is considered in many feminist circles (Middle Eastern as well as Western) a form of male control over women's sexuality and lives. In popular thinking about the Middle East, the practice is self-righteously made emblematic of Arab backwardness and lack of freedom. For sympathetic interpreters of Middle Eastern societies, however, much as for the participants, such marriages are seen as positive evidence of the high value people place on family ties. Nevertheless, a system in which it is accepted that marriages are arranged for young women by their families makes for complex experiences.

The preferential union known as patrilateral parallel-cousin marriage (marrying one's father's brother's daughter or son) has been a staple of Middle East anthropology.[27] Evoking in the popular mind the horrors of inbreeding, it is the perfect instance of an

Kristeva 1980; J. Mitchell 1974; O'Brien 1981; Ortner 1974; Rich 1986; M. Rosaldo 1974; and Ruddick 1989. These do not include other feminist and antifeminist debates such as those in sociobiology or in American popular culture, especially in the controversy over abortion. For a comprehensive review, see Ginsburg and Rapp 1991.

27. The best guide to the literature on this subject, among many others of Middle East anthropology, is Eickelman 1989.

"institution" that should neither be seen as mechanical nor treated out of context. Praised in the songs of women and girls at weddings between cousins, this form of marriage so warmly spoken about can also be resisted when relations between families are tense. As chapter 4 on the still-unmarried Sabra shows, circumstances of age and personality can always come into play, and with just a word life will take a different path. Although in all marriages, the bride's virginity at her wedding is linked to family pride in surprisingly positive ways, when groom and bride are cousins the taking of the girl's virginity becomes the business of all the women of the family. The blunt way older women speak of their participation in the wedding-day defloration of their nieces by their nephews suggests how profoundly marriage and even sexuality are public family matters.

The last chapter speaks to a "cultural" complex rather than a social "institution." Honor and shame, the values widely thought to regulate interactions in circum-Mediterranean societies, have been seen as a mechanism for the sexual control of women. Associating honor with men and shame with women, discussions of this complex have generally treated women's role as negative or, at best, passive. Yet Kamla, the young woman who has been to school, proudly asserts the honor (through modesty) of girls like herself and struggles to maintain this modesty as part of her cultural identity. Moreover, although she talks in terms of these seemingly timeless values, she rejects some of their entailments using arguments derived paradoxically from both her religious education and the romantic mass-media soap operas that enthrall her. Honor and shame in Egypt in the 1980s for a young Bedouin woman with some education, influenced by the ideas of urban Egyptians and sensitive to the moral pressures of increasingly persuasive Islamic groups, take on specific meanings. Indeed, the very possibility of an abstract moral code like "honor and shame" or a principle of preferential marriage involving arranged marriage backed by parental authority is thrown into question by the relentless specificity of Kamla's case.

One final issue frames all of the women's stories in this book, whether about children, parents, siblings, sex, marriage, death, drinking, schooling, or the Second World War, and that is religious identity. Given the place of Islam in the Western imagination—at times menacing, sometimes merely "other"—and its attributed power to determine the lives and thoughts of all Muslims, the stories in a critical ethnography must speak to this image. Yet the frame of faith in God or Muslim identity, represented here by the quotations from the Qur'an or the sayings (*aḥadīth*) of the Prophet Muhammad at the head of each chapter, functions in a more complex way than do the short chapter titles.[28] Not only is a contrast being drawn between foreign general concepts and local terms and complexity, but also an "internal" contrast is being set up between simple religious prescription and complex practices and circumstances.

Intriguingly, the religious framework is significant, in somewhat different ways, to both the Western reader and the women in the Awlad 'Ali Bedouin community whose stories I relate. In popular and much scholarly thinking in the West, Islam is perceived as all-determining. This view corresponds to that of many Muslims who believe that they should indeed be guided by the ideals of Islamic faith and practice. As someone who stands in between, however, I want to show both groups, through this critical ethnography, that not all events or utterances can be explained by reference to Islam.

Women often affirm their acceptance of what happens with the phrase "What God brings," which suggests to the Western reader Islam's notorious fatalism. Yet from the stories one can see that asserting this sentiment does not make women submissive.

28. Only one of the two *ḥadīth*s I quote did I hear anyone in the Awlad 'Ali community repeat. My source for the *ḥadīth* that opens chapter 1 is Schleifer 1986, 8. I have reworked her translation. After comparing the major translations into English of the Qur'an, I decided to follow that found in *The Holy Qur'ān* printed by the King Fahd Holy Qur'ān Printing Complex in Saudi Arabia. The translator is not listed.

Women are not prevented from struggling with and resisting decisions they do not like; trying every healing technique they know to cure pain, relieve suffering, or conceive and raise healthy children; or calling out oaths and curses when their disobedient children exasperate them.

Piety and religious observance have positive meanings for all the women in this Bedouin community, whereas to many secular people they suggest a certain sobriety, if not humorlessness. For old Migdim, however, piety—expressed through such practices as organizing her daily schedule around prayer and praising God even as she moans about her arthritic hands—does not seem to preclude chuckling over a risqué folktale, enjoying a sexually explicit song, or energetically bad-mouthing a neighbor.[29]

In addition to these qualities, both believers and outside scholars grant Islam a sort of timeless and supralocal existence. Yet whether we take the view of those in the Bedouin community, who see truth in the Qur'an and the model of the Prophet and strive to follow them, or of the outsider, who reifies a set of complex practices and statements in a notion like "the religion of Islam," we fail to grasp the real dilemmas people face because of Islam's grounding in social and historic specifics. The Awlad 'Ali women whose stories fill this book have been shaken up in the last decade by their indirect contact with members of the new Islamic movements in Egypt and their association with Egyptian state institutions like schools and media where new moral claims about the "good Muslim" are made. Educated daughters argue with their mothers about traditional practices, backing their positions by referring to Egyptian orderliness and employing knowledge of religion. The older women now wonder whether they are wrong to visit the tombs of saints or to seek out holymen to write amulets, as some people in the towns tell them, people who go to the

---

29. For a discussion of the tension between the Islamic discourse and other discourses in this Bedouin community and a sense of how to analyze these tensions, see my "Islam and the Gendered Discourses of Death" (forthcoming).

mosque and can read the Qur'an—and have beards, the women sometimes joke irreverently, that resemble pubic hair.

I chose not to devote a separate chapter to stories that spoke specifically to the issue of "Islam," for faith in God and the importance of Muslim identity were constant elements in women's discourse, invoked in myriad contexts to justify, implore, reprimand, explain, and comfort. The stories in this book bring out numerous tensions that relate to this identity: between practices and their justifications, between ideals and behavior, between simple prescriptions and multiple interpretations, between a sense of the universal and the complexity of local and individual experience. It is hoped that these stories will help draw out the distinction between reference to and determination by Muslim traditions.

Tactical Humanism

My argument for writing this book of stories is that cultural difference, which is both the ground and product of anthropological discourse, is a problematic construction. The strategy I use to write against culture involves playing, as many anthropologists are doing, with writing. Does writing make a difference?

Geertz's (1973b, 1988) insight that anthropologists are writers has been the starting point of a good deal of serious thinking about textuality, the practice of ethnographic writing, and the fieldwork encounter. Suspicions that those with literary leanings have too readily collapsed the politics of ethnography into its poetics have also been voiced in response. Fox (1991) puts it best when he wonders if what he calls the postmodern critique does not reinforce among anthropologists a "false consciousness about their scholarly labor processes" by underwriting their self-image as artisans. Noting that anthropology is produced not only in "the field" but also in the factory conditions of university departments, professional meetings, granting agencies, and the politically and historically determined context of previously authorized texts, he questions how much control we have over the context for our work and how much liberty we have in altering it. Others have raised challenging questions about why, at this moment in history, and in the United States in particular, there should have developed among anthropologists such attention to textuality and rejection of old forms.[30]

One of the most important conditions for anthropological production has been the global structure of political and economic power. Despite a long history of self-conscious opposition to racism and a growing self-critical literature on anthropology's links to colonialism and imperialism (e.g., Asad 1973; Clifford 1983; Fabian 1983; Hymes 1969; Kuper 1988), anthropologists have not rushed to confront the implications for their work of their own location in this structure. Working in support of political movements to change that structure has been one response, but it is not particularly anthropological. Experimentation with techniques of ethnographic writing to relieve anthropologists' discomforts about their power over their subjects has been another response. Yet refiguring informants as consultants or "letting the other speak" in dialogic (Tedlock 1987) or polyvocal texts—decolonizations on the level of the text—leaves intact the basic configuration of global power on which anthropology is based. Other intriguing suggestions, such as "indigenizing" anthropology (Fahim 1982; Altorki and El-Solh 1988) or encouraging Third World anthropologists to bypass the West and travel to each others' countries (Scott 1989), confront other limits. As Mudimbe (1988, 19) writes in *The Invention of Africa,* "It seems impossible to imagine any anthropology without a Western epistemological link."

Until we decide—or are forced—to move anthropology to new "shop floors" (in Fox's phrase), or to abandon it altogether, we should perhaps be more modest in our claims to radicalism. At best

30. Lutz (forthcoming) suggests that one consider carefully the social contexts of postmodernism, noting three relevant features: late capitalism (building on Jameson's views [1984]), North-South relations, and the state of the academy. Sangren's (1988) broadside focuses on the academy; Said's (1989) address to the American Anthropological Association focuses on imperialism.

we are talking about reform—undertaken with as good a sense as we can develop of the world context in which we work. As long as anthropologists are in the business of representing others, the ethnographies through which they do so will likely remain a primary mode of anthropological production. Without pretending to master the determinations of our ethnographies (Clifford [1986a, 6] gives a nice list of these) or their reception, we can nevertheless be aware that the degree to which people in the communities anthropologists study appear "other" is in part a function of how we write about them.

By insistently focusing on individuals and the particularities of their lives, we may be better able to perceive similarities in all our lives. Of course, to say that we all live in the particular is not to say that for any of us the particulars are the same. Indeed, even in looking at the everyday we might well discover fundamental differences, such as those between everyday experience in a world set up to produce the effect of structures, institutions, or other abstractions (as T. Mitchell [1988] argues the modern West has been) versus worlds that have not. Yet the dailiness, by breaking coherence and introducing time, trains our gaze on flux and contradiction; and the particulars suggest that others live as we perceive ourselves living—not as automatons programmed according to "cultural" rules or acting out social roles, but as people going through life wondering what they should do, making mistakes, being opinionated, vacillating, trying to make themselves look good, enduring tragic personal losses, enjoying others, and finding moments of laughter.

It is hard for the language of generalization to convey these sorts of experiences and activities. In our own lives, we balance the accounts of ourselves purveyed by social science with the ordinary language we use in personal conversations to discuss our lives, our friends and family, and our world. For those who live "outside" our world, however, we have no immediate discourse of familiarity to counteract the distancing discourses of anthropology and other social sciences, discourses that also serve development experts, governments, journalists, and others who deal with the Third World. Ethnographies of the particular made up of everyday stories—that is, use of humanist conventions of writing, the same conventions favored by popular writers and a whole alternative (though devalued because largely nonprofessional) tradition of women's ethnographic writing[31]—go far toward providing this discourse of familiarity.

Why invoke humanism when it has been so discredited in post-structural and postmodernist circles?[32] There are certainly good reasons to be wary of this philosophy that has masked the persistence of systematic social differences by appealing to an allegedly universal individual as hero and autonomous subject; that has allowed us to assume that the domination and exploitation of nature by man was justified by his place at the center of the universe; that has failed to see that its "essential human" has culturally and socially specific characteristics and in fact excludes most humans; and that refuses to understand how we as subjects are constructed in discourses attached to power. Yet because humanism continues to be in the West the language of human equality with the greatest moral force, I do not think we can abandon it. In advocating new forms of writing (pastiche, dialogue, collage, and so forth) that break up narrative and subject identities and interfere with identification, posthumanists ask their readers to adopt sophisticated reading strategies along with social critique. Does this make sense for anthropologists writing in a world still full of prejudice against

31. I have written elsewhere (1990a, 1991) on why this alternative tradition of ethnographic writing, often by the "untrained" wives of professional anthropologists (best exemplified by the superb and informative ethnographies of Fernea 1969; Wolf 1968; and Turner 1987) but also by professional anthropologists writing under pseudonyms (e.g., Bowen [1954] 1964; Cesara 1982), was not recognized by Clifford (1986a) as a form of textual innovation.

32. So damning is an association with humanism that Said's lapse into it is the crux of Clifford's (1980) critique of *Orientalism*. For an analysis of Said's work that follows similar lines, see Young 1990.

those about whom they write? If experimental ethnographies are criticized for being solipsistic or hard to read, how can their theoretical, political, or human messages get through? What may be required is a tactical humanism, made politically useful but also limited in its effects by anthropology's location on the side of power in a world organized unequally along lines of "cultural" difference.

I therefore have adopted many of the techniques of humanistic writing. First, I have not shied away from leaving traces of myself throughout. I assume, however, that readers are less interested in me than in the stories I tell, and so I have tried not to be intrusive. Thus, while I did not make the encounter between myself and these "others" central, I also did not remove questions I asked or pretend that certain discussions were not directed specifically at me.[33] I also comment sometimes on what is happening. In short, I have sought a presence somewhere between the extremes of total erasure of the ethnographer's self (e.g., Atiya 1982; Friedl 1989; and Munson 1984) and imposition of his or her presence as an equal participant (e.g., Dwyer 1982, Lavie 1990, or even Jackson 1986, dialogic accounts in which the authors present themselves in the third person).

Second, I have constructed each chapter loosely around an individual woman or two. As I noted above, focusing on individuals encourages familiarity rather than distance and helps to break down "otherness," for it not only corresponds to the way we ordinarily

33. Works like Briggs 1970; Brown 1991; Crapanzano 1980; Dumont 1978; Favret-Saada 1980; Friedrich 1986; Rabinow 1977; Riesman 1977; D. Rose 1987; Stoller and Olkes 1987; and Trawick 1990 that have focused more specifically on the fieldwork encounter and have been more self-revealing have been extremely useful in bringing out the ways in which our knowledge about others is constructed out of particular experiences. B. Tedlock's (1991) comprehensive assessment of what she calls a major shift "from participant observation to the observation of participation" provides a much more detailed account of this literature. It came to my attention as *Writing Women's Worlds* was going to press.

think about those close to us in our everyday world, but also actively facilitates identification with and sympathy toward others.[34]

I have not, however, followed the life history genre, perhaps the most popular humanistic form, for several reasons. This genre, represented by such engaging works on women as Atiya's *Khul Khaal: Five Egyptian Women Tell Their Stories* (1982), Brettel's *We Have Already Cried Many Tears: Portuguese Women and Migration* (1982), Kendall's *The Life and Hard Times of a Korean Shaman* (1988), Shostak's *Nisa: The Life and Words of a !Kung Woman* (1981), and M. Smith's classic *Baba of Karo, a Woman of the Muslim Hausa* ([1954] 1981), has long been important for anthropology, but its limitations have recently begun to receive attention. Crapanzano (1984), for example, has argued persuasively that the whole notion of "a life" may not be meaningful for everyone and that conventions for talking about oneself may differ radically.[35] In a perceptive reflection on the genre, Behar (1990), drawing on Frank (1979) and Benjamin (1968), has argued that we need to recognize that life histories are actually stories that people tell about themselves, texts requiring attention to the conventions of storytelling and the context of the elicitation.[36] Her own reading of the life story of a Mexican marketing woman makes her case compelling.

34. A collection of life stories like Burke's (in press) can indeed serve as a counterweight to the dehumanization of Middle Easterners that is so prevalent in the West, but the dangers of the genre are also worth examining. Shostak (1981) has been criticized by Clifford (1986b) for using Nisa to project her Western feminist message, and Critchfield (1978) has been shown by T. Mitchell (1990) to have abused the genre by plagiarizing from another work in his alleged portrait of an Upper Egyptian villager.

35. Weintraub (1978), for example, has traced the links between the concept of life as trajectory and the fairly recent historical development in the West of the associated genre of autobiography.

36. See also Langness and Frank 1981 and Watson and Watson-Franke 1985. The new work on personal narratives (Personal Narratives Group 1989 and Stahl 1989) also seems to move in a helpful direction.

What finally made me reluctant to adopt the form was the fact that the life story may contribute to a sense of the person at its center as an isolated individual. The women whose stories are told here neither live that way nor think of themselves as such. Representing three generations in one extended family, these women live in a close community made up of relatives and in-laws most of whom they see almost daily. Each chapter therefore centers on certain types of relationships between the key individual and others, and it is my hope that these women's continued reappearance in different chapters will bring the reader a sense of the networks and the closeness of family relations that are at work.

In writing this book I made use of a third humanistic convention: the narrative form. I did not construct plots or think of the women as characters, of course; rather, I tried to make the stories flow smoothly, convinced that, while literary theorists may have sensitized us to the bewitching effects of narrative, it remains the most familiar and satisfying of genres for readers. I could have distinguished between the women's words and my own commentaries, or interjected reminders of the ways I was using their narratives to produce certain effects. The latter technique might have made for more honesty but would have drawn attention away from the stories. The former would have set up the usual hierarchy between "informants' words" and expert's explanations, a construct that, even when unintended, is hard to resist because of habits of reading and the structures of authority. As Behar (1990, 226–27) remarked of life stories, while the women's words may not "speak for themselves," the kinds of commentaries that accompany them often speak past them or, as in the case of Oscar Lewis's works, do violence to them.

Committed to a rough (and, if you look too hard, indefensible) notion of fidelity to what I heard and saw, and perhaps lacking the requisite literary talents, I have been unwilling to wander into the realm of ethnographic fiction with these stories. There, license to play with dialogue and story allows for evocative, sometimes powerful, works that may convey different sorts of "truths," but ones harder to evaluate in the customary terms of anthropology as an empirical venture.[37] J. Stewart's (1989, 8–12) argument that ethnographic fiction is ideal for plumbing the subjective or for "dealing with the inner lives of people" begs the question of how one can know such things. I preferred a more conservative approach, recognizing that any piece of writing by a scholar at an academic institution and published by a university press would be granted the status of authoritative account. Even though, as I will describe below, I have made the words of those I quote speak to issues they could not anticipate and have edited their conversations, I have reserved the use of quotation marks for that which I tape-recorded or wrote verbatim in my notes. And although we may always be inventing culture (Wagner 1981) and every interpretation itself is a fiction of sorts (Geertz 1973b), I have not deliberately fabricated any incidents.

I have, however, played with narrative to explore some of its possibilities. I have taken a variety of Bedouin women's talk—stories of everyday life, arguments, reminiscences, folktales, poems, songs, and even a written letter and an essay with oral commentary—and made them into five different sorts of narra-

37. This problem of fictions, "factions," and other serious questioning of what constitutes "truth" about other cultures is deeply vexing and cannot be dismissed lightly. It is the subject of a good deal of critical reflection in anthropology today and is related closely to the insight that the realist ethnography is itself a literary genre (Marcus and Cushman 1982; Clifford and Marcus 1986). A number of recent and successful works self-consciously embrace the values of this other form of writing (Jackson 1986; J. Stewart 1989), joining classics like Bowen's ethnographic novel *Return to Laughter* ([1954] 1964). Many anthropologists whose work is not yet in print—Barbara Tedlock, for example—have been trying their hands at this form. The popularity and new legitimacy of this sort of literary enterprise is reflected and reinforced by initiatives like the annual competition the *Anthropology and Humanism Quarterly* now sponsors for the best ethnographic short story.

tives. Chapter 1 comes closest to being the story of a life with key memories and incidents woven together to give a sense of time passing and the changing struggles of a woman and her family. The second narrative portrays a set of relationships that constitute a marriage, mostly from the point of view of a senior wife. Chapter 3 shifts like a kaleidoscope from mother to mother, revealing different views of children and parenting; no one mother or family could begin to represent this relationship. At the center of chapter 4 is the single event of a wedding. The final chapter takes its shape from a young woman's essay, which, like this introductory essay, was written and formal. Unlike this introduction, however, her essay was also commented on orally, and I include this commentary in parentheses. The life stages of the central figures of the five chapters suggest a movement from the past to the future.

The major editorial work I did was to compose the women's stories into narratives about patrilineality, polygyny, reproduction, patrilateral parallel-cousin marriage, and honor and shame. No less important was the minor work required to make these stories readable, even after I had translated them. On occasion I felt I had to cut uninteresting, repetitive, or excessively complicating sections. I hesitated most over the repetitions, since they seemed to be such a feature of storytelling style. But in translating repeated words and phrases, one risks giving the impression in written and much spoken English of a childishness not evoked for participants.[38] I also was forced sometimes to simplify stories to make them intelligible to outsiders. When women talked to each other and even when they told me tales after our shared years, they could assume a common knowledge of hundreds of individuals, tribal affiliations, and places. In cases where the person mentioned would not appear again in any stories, I have substituted the (understood)

---

38. Although Tannen (1989) shows that repetition is a part of everyday conversation, the preservation of this stylistic convention in the translation of a San woman's words in Marjorie Shostak's *Nisa* (1981) had, I believe, the effect of suggesting such a childlike simplicity.

---

kinship term—for example, "her uncle," "her daughter-in-law"—
for real names, something women might do themselves if telling
the story to a person outside the immediate community. I also have
deleted references to little-known places that are not significant for
the story, even though for the usual listeners they have dense
associations.

These editorial decisions are related to a much larger problem.
There seems to be no way to convey to outsiders the significance
of many of the details contained in the stories. Indeed, the speci-
fication of detail is always abundant: not just the people present on
a certain occasion, but the color of the dress, the food eaten, the
time of day, and the exact amount of money paid find their way
into these stories. Even when the events are fifty years old and such
details might be thought surely to have vanished, they remain fixed
in the narratives, which are told time and again. Every detail carries
meaning in a world that is so largely shared. When a woman
curious to know about another asks, "What does she have?" she
means "How many children?" From the answer she can grasp
immediately an enormous amount about the contours of the woman's life and her prospects. There is all the world of difference
between the answers "Two daughters" and "Five sons and two
daughters." To the outside reader, however, they are just facts.

However much one might want to preserve the actual words
and narrative structures of the Bedouin stories to give a more vivid
sense of the way these women live, one is confronted with the most
basic problems of translatability. No story can move between such
different contexts without some loss in meaning. Many details not
at all trivial to life as lived in this Bedouin community are hard to
convey in a written text in English. It is not just a matter of what
is lost in the transformation from oral to written language, although this is a serious issue that others (e.g., Tedlock 1983; Tyler
1986, 1987) have explored with insight. Nor is the problem simply
that inevitable shifts of meaning occur when one moves between
languages in which expressions have no precise equivalents and
words have varying connotations. Rather, it seemed that a number

of essential qualities of everyday conversation and narrative just could not gracefully be carried over into English.

Two habits of speech are illustrative. First, women's language, especially in storytelling, is rich in little affections so routine as to be hardly noticed: "So then, my little sister/my little mother/my dear one, he said . . . ," the listener is addressed. In stories about the community, most people are referred to by nicknames, diminutive forms of their names if nothing else. Diminutives are always affectionate, their proper application to children giving their use for adults a special sweetness. Because they sound a bit silly in English, where instead of the inflection of the name itself one must say, for example, "Little Ali," I have left only a few such cases in the texts. The sense of affection within the community that these references carry is therefore, unfortunately, largely absent.

Second, religious references saturate women's language as well. Some women use oaths almost unthinkingly to strengthen the effect of their stories, swearing by God and by local saints whose tombs are well known. Most women use standard religious phrases at appropriate moments. Common expressions are "Blessings on the Prophet" for admiration, "How Great God is!" for surprise, and "In the Name of God" at hearing something strange or beginning any act. Women cannot mention deaths, illnesses, or misfortunes without prefacing their remarks with phrases like "[May God come] between you and me [and evil]," "[May it be] far from you," and "[May it happen to] your enemy." The power of speech is evident in this habit, but so is the constancy of God's presence in the everyday. I have left most of these religious phrases in place, but not without some discomfort; they are so little a part of everyday language in my own circles that I fear they will be more noticeable than they actually are in the Bedouin context.

Through all these compromises of translation and humanistic conventions of writing I have struggled to make these women and their stories accessible to the educated, mostly Western, readers of this book. I have no illusions that my choice of a tactical humanism through ethnographic writing might contribute to some universal good. I recognize humanism as a local and historically specific language of the post-Enlightenment West. Yet it is a useful language because from our positions as anthropologists we work as Westerners (however tenuous our identification) and we contribute to a Western discourse. Positionality cannot be escaped. Nor can we escape the fact, as Riesman (1982) bluntly put it in his critical response to proposals for dialogic anthropology, "that we are using other people for our own purposes all the time" and "using the knowledge they give us for goals they would never imagine themselves." That does not mean that the goals are not provisionally worth pursuing or that working within Western discourse is not crucial. As Said (1989, 224) notes, "Anthropological representations bear as much on the representer's world as on who or what is represented." The world from which I write still has tremendous discursive, military, and economic power. My writing can either sustain it or work against its grain.

For Whom?

In an age when the boundaries of "culture" have become difficult to keep in place, when books travel, and when global politics appear increasingly uncertain, we have to anticipate the uncomfortable irony that our most enlightened endeavors might not be received as such by the subjects of our writings. Even when they can read what we write, they do not necessarily share our conventions. From where they stand, the power issues may look very different.

In a sad way the women whose stories I retell here are not the audience of this book. For the most part, the words I have fixed here are not the kinds of words they consider worthy of being written down. Men sometimes told me not to waste my time with women because "their talk is closed-minded"; some women agreed. One man said folktales were not worth recording; they were just "little somethings" told to children to keep them quiet.

Poetry preserving events that really happened, old words carrying the wisdom of predecessors, the history of the tribes of the Awlad 'Ali, the songs that no one knows how to compose anymore—these are what should be preserved. I ignored these men and do not apologize for that. I worry about something else. I have made public the narratives that women told only to specific others and have made permanent what was meant to be fleeting. Occasionally I have censored myself, knowing, for example, that certain women would be offended if I published sexually crude wedding songs; sometimes they censored me, as when some girls told me to cross out a wedding rhyme disrespectful of the Egyptian president. In general, however, I have proceeded with my own vision of what I wanted.

Curiously, I now realize that a more conventional and less personal ethnography might have been more innocuous. At best, people of the community would think it a general description of what everyone already knew; at worst, they would judge it an offensive misrepresentation of themselves as a group. But how can they respond to the specific and personal tales that make up this book? They might appreciate reading now, many years later, the stories they told and the conversations they had then. Like a snapshot, the book might stir memory and a nostalgic remembrance of people and times now gone. They might feel, as they do about those who have camped with them in past years, the same wistful affection apparent in the formula with which they often end stories about those acquaintances: "May God have mercy on them."

Yet the photographs people in this community really prefer are those in which they or those they love pose stiffly, unsmiling, in their best clothes; they always told me to keep the candid shots for myself. Like nomads, these formal portraits migrated over great distances, passing quickly from hand to hand. Certain words travel in the same way—the words of poems and songs worth fixing through memory and repetition. Women were always delighted when I read back to them poems and songs I had recorded in previous years. Yet it is not clear that they would appreciate the words of the personal and everyday stories I have written down here any more than the candid photographs they reject.

This makes me uneasy. My excuse for fixing and making public these stories is the "higher good" of critical ethnography working in the service of "writing against culture." But critical ethnography, as I have described, is a project for the West. What good does it do my subjects? Do the ends of undermining anthropological generalizations, questioning feminist interpretations, and shaking up assumptions about the Middle East justify the means? Oblivious to the anti-Arab sentiment that prevails where this book will be read, my friends would hardly be fazed by it anyway, since they are so confident of their moral and religious superiority. I can try to explain to them the context of my work, but is this sufficient?

People told me stories, talked in front of me, and even let me record, because over the years we had developed personal relationships of varying degrees of closeness. I had come to know some women quite well, our feelings of friendship having been forged as all bonds are in that community: through shared memories. When I returned in 1985, for example, the woman who had been a bride wanting to escape her husband was now the mother of several children, comfortably settled in the household. All it took was a word, however, to remind ourselves and her what trouble she had given us at first. When I came back in 1986, the sickly young man who had had open heart surgery while I was first living in the household was now a healthy married man, the proud father of a baby boy. I remembered beloved old aunts now passed away and neighbors who had moved. I recalled with affection, as they did too, cute things little children had said and done, children now serious in their school uniforms or, by 1989, tall young men with deep voices. I also remembered, with embarrassment, incidents in which my behavior was less than exemplary.

The closeness, defined always by them in terms of 'ishra (living together), was tempered with the recognition that I was an outsider, related by neither kinship nor marriage, and that I was there for a purpose, however ambiguous. Over a decade, as we came to know one another better and even to change as we grew older, our senses of one another became more precise. We had never confronted one another as Western self and non-Western other, or vice versa. I have reflected elsewhere (Abu-Lughod 1988b) on how my relationships to people in the community were affected by aspects of who I was when I first came to stay: young, unmarried, female, and, most important, of Arab background and Muslim. Being a "halfie," participating in both American and Arab identities, was both important in determining what I sought to do in my writing and crucial to them in their acceptance of me.[39]

As time went on, however, their sense of just what kind of "halfie" I was became more precise. They began to focus on the fact that I was part Palestinian. The women with whom I spent most of my time were more concerned with my marital and family situation than my Palestinian identity. They were glad when I married so they could share with me more easily the jokes about what goes on between husbands and wives. Yet they also pitied me for the unaccountable delay in having children. They, like the Bedouin men I knew well, could not understand what satisfaction writing books and articles or teaching might have. They knew it was good to get degrees and a job, but was the point not simply to make a good salary? The real part of life was family, and I seemed to them to be living in a strangely lonesome world, just myself and my husband. They prayed for me and implored God to grant me children.

The men, though, talked more and more about Palestine. Once or twice when I came back after being away, they would proudly tell me they had heard my father interviewed on the radio. One time they brought a poet to recite before me a poem he had

39. I have discussed in Abu-Lughod 1991 the issue of "halfies" (a term I picked up from Kirin Narayan) and the work of others like Kondo (1986) who have written eloquently on the experience of doing fieldwork as insider-outsiders.

composed about the Israeli invasion of Lebanon and the tragedy of Palestine. I was intrigued when, in a conversation between two tribal leaders about the loss of their coastal land through confiscation and sales and the influx of urban Egyptians and peasants to traditional Awlad ʿAli territory, the men agreed that they were being "Palestinianized." Most recently, with the publicity about the Palestinian *intifada,* people impressed with the courage of the young boys throwing rocks at soldiers began to ask me more about the Palestinians. Why did they not use guns? Why does the United States help Israel? As this latter question showed, my North American identity was not ignored either. After the U.S. bombing in 1986 of Libya, the country from which Awlad ʿAli say they originate and to which they still have strong ties, they challenged me about the American position. I can only imagine what they will ask when I next return, after the war in the Gulf.

Like other scholars critical of the notion of "objectivity" in social science, I have argued (1989, 1991) that we need to take greater account of the specific relations of the researcher to the object of study. Being a Palestinian American woman who chooses to live with a group of people who define themselves as a minority of Muslim Arabs living in Egypt (because tribal Bedouin) and then writes books for a scholarly Western audience seems a very particular kind of situation. Yet in the end, every situation is particular. I have criticized Bourdieu (1977, 1–2), who otherwise perceptively analyzed the effects of the outsider stance on the anthropologist's (mis)understanding of social life, for failing to break with the doxa that the anthropologist *is* an outsider. The obvious point he ignores is that the outsider self never simply stands outside; he or she always stands in a definite relation with the "other" of the study, not just as a Westerner or even halfie, but as a Frenchman in Algeria during the war of independence, an American in Morocco during the 1967 Arab-Israeli war, or an Englishwoman in postcolonial India. What we call the outside, or even the partial outside, is always a position *within* a larger political-historical complex.

The question that remains, however, is the one I began with: Does using my knowledge of individuals for purposes beyond friendship and shared memories by fixing their words and lives for disclosure to a world beyond the one they live in constitute some sort of betrayal? As someone who moves between worlds, I feel that confronting the negative images I know to exist in the United States toward Arabs is one way to honor the kindness they have shown me. So is challenging stereotypical generalizations that ultimately make them seem more "other." Yet how will my critical ethnography be received? This is the dilemma all those of us who move back and forth between worlds must face as we juggle speaking for, speaking to, and, when we are "halfies," speaking from.

I can only surmise from the reception of my first book how complex the local readings will be. My revelation, in *Veiled Sentiments,* of Bedouin individuals' attachments and vulnerabilities through their poetry was intended to inspire among Westerners a recognition of these people's everyday humanity; it met with another response in Egypt. When one woman heard someone read from the book a few of the poems she had recited years earlier, she exclaimed, half joking, "You've scandalized us!" For her, a book about particular people and everyday life in her community might seem little more than a public display of family secrets.

My presentation of the way ideals of personal autonomy and independence were manifested in men's lives took on complex and different meanings in Egypt as well. A copy of a long review (in Arabic) of my book came to the attention of a local Awlad 'Ali man who was a civil servant and aspiring official in the Egyptian government. He confronted my host with the article, angry that I had reported that they liked to carry guns, evade taxes, and guard their rights to settle their own disputes rather than let the government interfere. "This is your girl who wrote this!" the man accused. What happened then I will never know, since I was not there and heard only my host's version. He was, as usual, defiant, retorting that he had taught me everything I knew. And in any case, wasn't it true? Didn't the official have unlicensed guns? Did he report all his sheep for tax purposes? The man admitted these facts but still wondered if it was right to publicize the situation.

My host told me he wanted my book translated into Arabic so that Egyptians would come to understand and appreciate the superior moral standards of his community (of which many Egyptians are contemptuous). He thought to use my prestige to challenge Egyptian condescension and ignorance. Yet as the incident about the report of guns and taxes showed, he was only one voice in the Bedouin community. His ideas about what would gain his people respect were different from those of someone loyal to the government, even though both were sensitive to their position and identity as marginals in the nation-state. My work, though intended for a different audience, had entered a local political field where the relationship between Awlad 'Ali Bedouins and the Egyptian state was a contested issue.

The only aspect of these stories that I know will not seem inappropriate to those who told them to me is the larger way they are framed: by reference to Muslim discursive traditions.[40] Whether or not people actually live up to the Muslim ideals they set for themselves, they have no doubts that being Muslim draws for them the boundaries of the moral universe and shapes its features. Even if they recognize the tensions between some of their practices and those prescribed for them, they will be proud to see reproduced in these tales the constant invocations of God and the Prophet that are critical to their self-definition in the community. Although I intended this religious frame, like the social scientific chapter titles with which they are paired, to suggest disjunctions, my Bedouin friends would not be wrong to understand it as also conveying a deep truth about their lives—lives indeed imbued with faith in God, rich in practices that reinforce their sense of God's constant presence, and colored by a confident sense of belonging to a community of Muslims.

40. This is a phrase Asad (1986) advocates as central to developing an anthropology of Islam.

Chapter 1

PATRILINEALITY

A man came to God's Messenger and said, "O Messenger
of God, who is most entitled to the best of my friendship?"
The Prophet said, "Your mother." The man said, "Then who?"
The Prophet said, "Your mother." The man further said,
"Then who?" The Prophet said, "Your mother." The man
said again, "Then who?" The Prophet said,
"Then your father."

Tradition of the Prophet Muhammad

On a quiet day toward the end of 1979, the second year I had been
living in the community, I asked Migdim whether she would tell
me her life story. She said, "When you get old you think only of
God, of prayer, and of the oneness of God. What happened has
passed, you don't think about it. You don't think about anything
but God." And she refused to say any more. Then, as now, the
only decoration on the walls of her one-room house was a faded
black-and-white photograph behind finger-printed glass. It showed
her as a younger, upright woman standing proudly next to her
eldest son, now called Haj Sagr to recognize his status as someone
who has made the pilgrimage, both wearing the distinctive white
clothing of Meccan pilgrims. Although she was now bent nearly
double and walked only with the help of a stick, she still had the

many social duties of a world where the mutual visits of relatives and friends are the stuff of social relations. As the matriarch of one large family and the oldest sister in another, she was expected at weddings, sickbeds, and funerals, as well as at feasts to welcome home those who had been released from prison or had returned from the pilgrimage to Mecca. Even when she was at home she was always busy with something—spinning, winding yarn, sewing burlap sacks together to patch the old summer tent, seeing to the goats, giving advice, or bouncing a grandchild on her lap.

By the time I returned in 1986, seven years later, she could hardly stand and walked only to go outside to the bathroom or to do her ablutions for prayer. An eye operation had been unsuccessful, and she squinted to see people. She rubbed her red eyes and often kept them closed. Sitting hunched over all day, a blanket over her lap, she had more time for me. When I asked her to tell me her life story she said, "I've forgotten all of that. I've got no mind to remember with any more." But then she went on, "We used to milk the sheep. We used to pack up and leave here and set up camp out west. And there we would milk the goats and milk the sheep and churn butter, and we'd melt it and we'd put the clarified butter in the goatskin bag and we'd cook wheat until it was done and we'd make dried barley cheese."

She laughed, knowing how formulaic this "story of her life" was. That was all I got, though, from my direct questions. For her, like the other women I knew in this community, the conventional form of "a life" as a self-centered passage through time was not familiar. Instead there were memorable events, fixed into dramatic stories with fine details. One of the most vivid I heard from Migdim was the tale of how she had resisted marriages her father had tried to arrange for her. I even heard more than once, nearly word for word, the same tale of how she had ended up marrying Jawwad, the father of all her children. I heard it for the first time one evening that winter; she told it for the benefit of her sons' wives, Gateefa and Fayga, and some of her granddaughters.

She explained that the first person whom she was to have married was a paternal first cousin. His relatives came to her household and conducted the negotiations and even went as far as to slaughter some sheep, the practice that seals the marriage agreement. But things did not work out. The time was over fifty years ago, just after the death of her mother.

"He was a first cousin, and I didn't want him. He was old and he lived with us. We ate out of one bowl. His relatives came and slaughtered a sheep and I started screaming, I started crying. My father had bought a new gun, a cartridge gun. He said, 'If you don't shut up I'll send you flying with this gun.'

"Well, there was a ravine and I would go over and sit there all day. I sat next to it saying, 'Possess me, spirits, possess me.' I wanted the spirits to possess me, I wanted to go crazy. Half the night would pass, and I'd be sitting there. I'd be sitting there, until my cousin Brayka came. And she'd cry with me and then drag me home by force and I'd go sleep in her tent. After twelve days of this, my cousin's female relatives were dyeing the black strip for the top of the tent—they were about to finish sewing the tent I'd live in. And they had brought my trousseau. 'I'll go get the dye for you,' I said. I went and found they had ground the black powder and it was soaking in the pot, the last of the dye, and I flipped it over—POW! on my face, on my hair, on my hands, until I was completely black.

"My father came back and said, 'What's happened here? What's the matter with this girl? Hey you, what's the matter?' The women explained. He went and got a pot of water and a piece of soap and said, 'If you don't wash your hands and your face I'll . . .' So I wash my hands, but only the palms, and I wipe my face, but I only get a little off from here and there. And I'm crying the whole time. All I did was cry. Then they went and put some supper in front of me. He said, 'Come here and eat dinner.' I'd eat and my tears were salting each mouthful. For twelve days nothing had entered my mouth.

"The next afternoon my brother came by and said to me, 'I'm hungry, can you make me a snack?' I went to make it for him, some fresh flatbread, and I was hungry. I had taken a loaf and I put a bit of honey and a bit of winter oil in a bowl. I wanted to eat, I who hadn't eaten a thing in twelve days. But then he said, 'What do you think of this? On Friday they're doing the wedding and today is Thursday and there aren't even two days between now and then.' I found that the loaf I was going to eat I'd dropped. 'Well,' he asked, 'do you want to go to So-and-so's or do you want to go to your mother's brother's?' I said, 'I'll . . .' There was an eclipse; the sun went out, and nothing was visible. I said, 'I'll go to my maternal uncle's.' I put on my old shoes and my shawl on my head and started running. I ran on foot until I got to my uncle's. . . . I was in bad shape, a mess."

Migdim praised her uncle's wife for giving her refuge and explaining to her uncle what the problem was. "May God have mercy on her, she was a good woman." But her uncle sent her back the next morning, with instructions to his son to accompany her and to deliver greetings to her father and to ask him to oblige him since he had comforted his niece. If he were to delay a bit, perhaps she would come around.

"So I went home. After that I didn't hear another word. The trousseau just sat there in the chest, and the tent—they sewed it and got it all ready and then put it away in their tent. And autumn came and we migrated west, and we came back again. When we came back, they said, 'We want to have the wedding.' I began screaming. They stopped. No one spoke about it again."

Grandma Migdim's story had two more episodes of failed attempts to arrange marriage for her, episodes in which she did more of the same. She cried, protested, threw bowls of fresh food, and went to bed without eating. In the first instance her father's new wife intervened, so her father refused the proposal claiming that Migdim's little sister was too attached to her and their mother's death was too recent.

Then came a group of men who arrived in the morning and waited all day for her father to come home. He refused them, calling them stingy. Migdim explained what happened then. "Jawwad's aunt, married to my uncle, ran over to her brother's camp and told him, 'Come on, come on. The others have given up their claim to the woman. They came to ask for her and he refused them.' Her brother, the old man, came right away and asked for me for his son. My father agreed. Then the women came singing with the men who brought the sheep for the engagement. They had paid bridewealth of fifty Egyptian pounds for Jawwad's aunt Mastura, so my father said, 'We don't want to do anything different. What we gave you give us.' But one of their relatives said 'No, we should increase it by twenty Egyptian pounds.' But by God they never did give those extra twenty pounds. My father never did see them. Whenever I used to come home for visits riding on a donkey my father would say, 'Hey, why don't you give me that donkey? They promised it to me but never gave it.' "

Remembering the previous engagements, one of her granddaughters interrupted her to ask, "Grandma Migdim, did you eat and drink at that engagement?"

She answered, "Yes, I ate and drank." But then, as if to assure us of her virtue, she added, "Although I swear by my soul that it wasn't in my thoughts nor was it in his. Not at all. It was his father who'd seen me when I was young. I was energetic, really smart. He'd say, 'That girl, if only my son could have her.' "

Fayga, her youngest son's new wife, commented, "Bread and salt." God wills certain people to share meals and life.

Migdim agreed. "Yes, it was bread and salt."

With a smile, Migdim's son's wife (and cousin) Gateefa asked, perhaps for my benefit, "And what did they give you for your trousseau, my grandfather's family?"

Migdim itemized: "They gave me, my dear, a shawl, and a red belt, and a silk belt, and a white blanket, and a black headscarf, and large rice platters."

I interrupted to ask whether she had been brought in a bridal litter on the back of a camel, and she answered, "Yes, it wasn't far. I rode in the litter. It had a woven blanket over it with an entrance at the front. I was young and I was scared I'd fall off."

Gateefa returned to her teasing about the trousseau. "And didn't they bring you a washtub?" Everyone laughed about the new utilitarian objects brides now bring with them.

"No washtub, no cooking pot, nothing. There weren't such things. The old ones were poor. Nowadays women's brideprices aren't what brideprices were, and trousseaus aren't what trousseaus were. Now they bring teapots and kettles and kerosene burners and cakes and cookies and candy."

"And washtubs and pots and wooden chests and towels and . . . ," continued Gateefa.

They laughed at themselves and then went quiet. Suddenly Grandma Migdim referred to my tape recorder with its red light glowing in the kerosene-lit room. "Your friend there, doesn't he talk?"

The girls laughed and said knowledgeably, "No, this one just listens to the talk, grandmother. It doesn't speak." Then they begged her to sing.

> "Far away, no news of you comes
> even if you come to mind, O beloved . . .*
>
> Dear one, who in sleep comes near
> is distant on the earth . . ."

Were these songs about her husband, long dead? Or about the past? Or was she perhaps thinking of me, whose loved ones were far away?

*(Transcriptions of the Arabic poems can be found starting on p. 243.)

Patrilineality

Having Sons and Daughters

By Jawwad, Migdim had seven children who lived, four boys and three girls. Her four sons and their families now make up "the camp." One daughter lives nearby. The other two are married to men from distant areas and only come for visits on the major religious holidays, when they hear someone is ill, or to attend weddings and funerals. Migdim's daily life revolves around her sons, their wives, their children, and their grandchildren.

I asked Migdim where her children had been born. Most had been born in this camp or further west, near Alamein, at their spring pastures. A single daughter had been born east of the camp, and it was through her story that I later began to hear about the family's experiences during the Second World War. Some births were memorable for Migdim. She had never had a doctor attend her deliveries; she even maintained that she never had other women hold her.

"I always gave birth by myself," she said, illustrating with the story of her second-to-last son. "I gave birth to him alone. I had no one with me but God. We were out west, inland from Alamein. That day I did the wash. I washed up everything. In the morning I had washed my hair and braided it with henna and cloves. I cooked too—a pot of rice with yoghurt sprinkled with some butter from the goatskin bag. . . . My sister-in-law and my husband's aunt were visiting, and they asked for lentils. So the other women started making some flatbread and cooking the lentils. It got to be sunset—the days were short at that time of year.

"My husband had gone to sleep in the tent, taking the two older children. . . . I went to sit with the old women for a while as the girl cooked the lentils. My little boy fell asleep in my lap, so I said, 'I'll go put my son to bed.' They said, 'Stay until we eat supper, then we'll all go to bed.' I said, 'I'll come back soon. But if I don't come it means I don't feel like eating.' We'd had something to eat in the afternoon, and in those days people didn't used to eat much.

"I went off to put the boy to bed. I had three cramps while I was putting him down. I never came back for the supper. I circled around the tent, tightening the guy ropes. They called to me, 'Come have dinner, come have dinner.' The sun had gone down and they called out, 'Come have dinner.' But I didn't want any. I scooped out a hole in the sand and went to sit by it. I brought out a straw mat and a donkey's burlap pack-saddle and I put them down and sat on them, outside by the corner of the tent. When the labor pains hit, I'd hold on to the guy rope's tension bar. One hand between my legs, and one holding on to the rope above. The sheep came home after sunset, close to the time of the evening prayers, just as the child was coming out. . . . When the child broke through I lifted myself up by the pole, lifted my clothes up until the child dropped.

"When my sister-in-law came out to pee she heard. She ran into the tent and told the women, 'Migdim has given birth!' They came running. 'Where? Where?' they asked, and I told them, 'The child has a forelock [a boy]. The child with its forelock dropped.' So they lit a fire and wrapped the boy and they moved me inside. They cooked a pot of special food that night, and made tea. And the man was sleeping near us, in the corner, and didn't wake up. The women set up a compartment for me in the middle of the tent. He was sleeping with the children in the corner and didn't wake up.

"In the morning my mother-in-law killed a chicken for me and was cooking it when a woman neighbor of ours came over. 'Poor dear! Poor dear! When did she deliver? Why, just yesterday she was doing her wash and there was nothing wrong. Poor thing!' I tell you, from the minute the old woman said, 'Poor thing'—God protect me, God protect me—I was seized by cramps. Something (may it be far away from you), something rang in my ears. And something covered my eyes so I couldn't see. I prayed, 'There is no god but God, there is no god but God,' until my mouth went dry. That was all the woman had said when they had to come running. Something blinded me, blinded me and knocked me out. My mother-in-law came and started moving my head, she made me sniff a burning rag. Well, I tell you, I didn't taste that chicken she was cooking. I never even saw it. I always have bad cramps after I give birth. My cramps are bad then.

"I delivered my other children alone," she added. "I had no one with me but God." When I asked Migdim why, she answered, "The women laugh and they talk and they bother you. You'll be as sick as can be and they'll be making a lot of noise around you. I don't like them around." When I asked if she would also cut the umbilical cord herself she said, "No, after the baby has dropped they come. They come and they cut the cord." Then I asked why it was said that the woman who has just delivered is close to God. She laughed at my piece of knowledge. "Yes, people say that. By God, it's difficult. Ask the woman who has given birth, ask her about death. She has seen it."

Four more times Migdim "saw death." One child died. Of the last three, two were born in Alamein. The third, a daughter, was born southeast of where they now lived permanently. I wondered what they were doing there. "We had set up camp there," she explained. "The Germans had come. Airplanes came and started bombing. They moved us there, south of the railroad tracks, and told us to set up very small tents. 'Don't make the tents big, keep them small!' " she remembers them saying.

"They moved the whole camp; everyone had to move south of the railroad tracks. The English had come to Alamein. The Germans and English started fighting. . . . A plane started flying over the army camp, and they hit it with their artillery. It headed south and went to bits and caught fire. It was on fire until it landed way over there, in the desert south, and burned up."

A niece of hers elaborated on these events, their experiences of the battles of the European war fought on their soil. "I'll tell you about the war. One day, it was midafternoon, and we were in our camp south of Alamein. Grandma Migdim saw it first—the smoke. Smoke high in the sky. I don't know if they had set fire to something or what. And the airplanes—Duw! Duw! Duw!—the planes would strike. It seems there were tents or something, a military camp. We listened for a while, and then we packed up and moved. At dawn we moved. And when the planes came we would go into the caves. We'd sleep there and leave the camp. The airplanes would attack and make noise. And the English would shoot at them with big guns and hit them. It was the Italians' planes that circled.

"When there was an attack there would be something that made a horrible sound: 'Waaa! Waaaa! Waaaaa!' it would wail. They called it an attack. An attack, an attack. Two or three hours before, they knew the airplanes were planning to come. It would go on for two hours like that, 'Waaaaa!' Then they would raise the danger flag. A red flag. And the planes would come, circling around and then hitting them. Then they would strike. The airplane would swoop down and they would fire at it. It would go off and then come back and fire. And then parachutes would come out."

A younger woman listening interjected with excitement, "The parachutes were like the material of our new headscarves."

"No," Migdim's niece corrected, "they are like the nylon we make slips out of. . . . The women used to make them into dresses, red and yellow and white. . . . Dresses and slips and bloomers. And they used it for the patchwork of the tent walls."

She continued the story of their first encounter with the war. "So, the smoke was everywhere. This was in the afternoon. Early the next morning—we didn't sleep that night—at dawn we prayed and packed up the camels and migrated back. We traveled three or four days and set up camp near here, a place they call Jazeera. And we stayed there until the planes started coming there. We began sleeping in the caves and spending our days in the tents.

"And then, one afternoon when we were at the well, we saw an airplane circling, circling. Around the camp of the Snaagra tribe, east of the town. They had pitched their white tents, and the plane must have thought it was a military camp. They wouldn't have touched them if they thought they were Bedouins. It circled and hit them, hit them. It killed many. They still talk about it, 'the year the Snaagra were wiped out.' Men and children and women, in one afternoon.

"A day or two later the army came to our camp. They came carrying whole camps. And they made us leave. They made us ride in their trucks. They moved us, even our cooking stones. 'Pick them up, pick them up!' They moved us and set us down on a hill near Sidi Dmayn. What a great place! There was nothing good we didn't have. There were guavas and dates, tomatoes and cucumbers, watermelons and oranges . . . everything. We were in the gardens. They would come around on donkeys selling. And we would buy. We were happy. We didn't hear any more planes droning. After hearing them droning and circling, droning and circling."

It was at that camp, during the days of the war, that Migdim gave birth to her daughter Ngawa. She was a sickly child. Migdim says she wouldn't even nurse. She used to feed her drops of olive oil, dribbled into her mouth. A woman neighbor yelled at Migdim, told her she had to nurse the baby and that she should milk her own breasts to feed her. She did. And then she forced the girl to drink. Then one day, as the baby lay on the ground, her eyelids fluttered and she began shaking. It was her father who noticed. Migdim says Jawwad told her, "Your daughter's about to die." But then instead she vomited—it was bright green, Migdim swears. After that she started getting better, although she never got plump. She was skinny and often sick and her relatives were sad for her, even though she was energetic.

In the end Ngawa was married to a poor relation who lived nearby. Because of her health her mother thought this arrangement a good idea. In general, though, and using this example, Migdim defends marriage to close relatives—marriage within the camp, as they say. "If they are close by, daughters can eat with you and come visit you often. If they give birth, their mothers are near them. If they get sick, they're near their mothers. If you get sick they come. . . . If you marry far away someone can die and you won't hear about it. You don't hear about weddings, you don't hear about deaths. You're not there when anything happens."

We often talked about the differences between having sons and having daughters. Once when I was talking to Migdim about what

Bedouin women, in the days before doctors, did for women in labor, she described only the foods and soothing drinks that were prepared. "We would make ʿaṣiida [a cooked dough] for her and we'd cook eggs for her and we'd boil fenugreek. After she had delivered she would drink two or three cups of it so she wouldn't have cramps."

Migdim's daughter-in-law Azza, who was from a town, not the desert, interrupted, "And they bring the new mother meat."

"Yes, meat," continued Grandma Migdim. "And they slaughter chickens for her, to make her strong."

I added, "But only if it is a boy, right?"

She laughed. "No, they bring meat if it's a girl. If it's a boy they slaughter a sheep for him. The boy, you see, his name is exalted. He has a little pisser that dangles."

Her daughter-in-law again broke in, "And the girl—well, her father will be sad and her relatives will be sad and they won't cook at all for her."

Migdim was agitated. "No, the girl . . ."

But her daughter-in-law charged on, "The girl, poor thing, her mother is sad. That's how it is."

Migdim firmly finished, "No, the girl makes your heart happy. She's the one who should have a sheep slaughtered to celebrate her. It's just that people don't understand."

Another time, though, she made clear why people preferred sons. Looking out at a group of her little granddaughters playing, she sighed. "Little girls are nice. This one goes to get water, that one helps you. But in a week they can leave you and their place will be empty. . . . Daughters aren't yours. When they marry, that's it. They stay with their families and that's that. They leave you with nothing. But boys, they stay."

Losing Men

That sons do stay becomes especially important when a woman's husband dies. Migdim lost her husband, Jawwad, quite young. She

blamed his death on the death of his younger brother, killed by an exploding mine about seven years after what she knew as "the war between the Germans and the English." This kind of death was not uncommon after the battles of the Second World War had ended and the armies departed. In their desperate poverty the Bedouins had survived by scavenging scrap metal, an activity they called "rabbasha"—a verb made from the English word *rubbish.*

Migdim did not like telling the story of her brother-in-law's death. When I asked about it one day, she was terse. "We had migrated out west that spring. He went rubbishing, riding on a donkey with a friend. I didn't believe he was dead because when he left the camp he had been heading east. And he had money; he had no need to scavenge. But he ran into friends who persuaded him to go. They came across a mound and found a bomb. The other man started taking it apart. My brother-in-law said, 'I won't work on it.' But instead of moving far away, he sat near him. The man kept trying to take it apart, but it exploded.

"The bomb exploded and killed the man. He flew, who knows where he landed. Who knows where it threw him. But my brother-in-law, all that came his way was a small bit that landed (May it be far from you), landed in his chest. That year part of the family was camped near the train station at Alamein. They hadn't come with us. People brought him to them at night, in a car, and he died that night. They brought him in a car from the desert, from the camp of the man who had been rubbishing.

"We had all migrated from here and had set up camp way up in the desert south of Alamein. Someone soon came—the one who brought us the news came in the morning. He ran into the camp shouting his name, told us that he had died and was at the camp in Alamein. When he told us we jumped up and began running northward. My sons were young then, and they started running on foot, so I put on my belt and started running with them, wailing. We found everything in chaos. People came from everywhere. I found him wrapped in a blanket and wailed his name.

"When Jawwad went in to see him, he shuddered. He told me, 'I trembled and something pounded me from head to foot.'. . . He got sick, Jawwad, and he remained ill after the death. Ill for a year. And then a year after his brother had died, he died. And the old man, their father, died between them in the month of 'Ashura.

"My younger son wasn't very old then—he was still small. But he sang about his kinsmen who had died:

> He took away those around you,
> oh eyes, despair hasn't been easy on you . . ."

As her son, the Haj Sagr, now describes it, this dangerous business of "rubbishing" occupied many people after their return from the Nile Valley camps to which the British had evacuated them. "After they drove the Germans out, the English left. Then the Arabs could return to their territory. They went back as soon as they could. But they found that the armies had left the area covered with mines and bombs and big guns that had not gone off. We found hand grenades, some that had been tossed but had not exploded, some that were untouched. They had left everything: mines, broken tanks, cars, even whole garages with their dead in them. For six or seven years they were collecting their dead. . . ."

Migdim's niece tells a similar story of those early days after the war. Their wells had been destroyed, they had lost much of what they had. And they had not been able to plant barley for their bread. They had nothing. "When the Germans came to Alamein the English stopped them. They pushed them back. So we came back to our land. We found the world in chaos. There were broken airplanes, ruined cars, and broken big guns. And big tins of biscuits. We used to find spoons and forks, rope, nice shoes, and burlap sacks from the sandbags. And nice bottles, great little glass bottles. We used to collect them. White and green and red. Just lying around. . . . The boys would collect them and sell them. And there were tires, you wouldn't believe the new tires! They used to carry them off on camels and go to sell them.

"Later there was the work in iron. The flints of big guns. They started gathering that. Iron. And the copper, it was everywhere.

They began collecting that. . . . But the bombs, they got aluminum from those. At the time it was worth a lot, so they started digging in the ground to get out the mines. They would collect four or five detonators, five or six detonators, and they'd take them far into the desert. Then they would light a fire and set them off. They would explode. When they'd cooled, they'd come and collect the stuff and sell it. Many of them got hurt. There are poems about that."

The Haj Sagr elaborated. "Dealers from Alexandria and Cairo came to buy the copper, one kind yellow and another red, and the gunpowder. . . . People would go into the desert in cars and on foot, any way they could. One time someone would pick up a mine and it would explode in his hands. Another time someone would touch a bomb and it would explode. Another time someone would try to undo a detonator, to get out its cartridges or gunpowder, and it would blow up. Then five or six people would die together. It became like a war—explosions all the time. . . . A car would stray from the track and a mine would go off and blow it up with whoever was in it. It was like a war."

Migdim tells of her son's close call with these mines, before the tragedies of her brother-in-law's death and then her husband's. As she told it, Sagr had gone off scavenging with his older brother. They took a long time getting back, and she became quite worried. When she finally saw them returning she ran out to greet them. Her older son arrived, walking with his arms folded. "Show me your hands!" she demanded. "Are you all right?" He showed her his hands and there was nothing wrong. She was relieved but then they said, "Get Sagr down from the donkey." She cried out, "What's wrong, what's wrong?" They lifted his robe and it was all bloody. It was bandaged.

He had stepped on a mine. "Watch out, watch out, they are in front of you!"—that is what Sagr had shouted to his older brother. On the way home they had run across an Englishman whose plane had crashed. The man had bandaged Sagr so the blood would stop flowing. The boy had been hit in three places. In two of these—the thigh and the calf—what had gone in had come out the other side. The third place he had been struck was his heel. That bit was still in. All night long she stayed up with him while he cried out in pain. She massaged his foot until morning, when finally the thing, black and the size of a fly, fell out, "Tack!"—she heard the metal fall to the ground. Then they brought a doctor, who scraped and cut and stuffed the wounds to his screams of pain.

Haj Sagr himself told me the story in much more detail and with a different emphasis. Migdim, who remembers staying up all night to nurse him and massage his foot, barely figures in this account; his story has become fixed instead as an illustration of the mutual generosity of the English and the Arabs. His father, Jawwad, not his mother, is the central character. The date he puts at 1944 or 1945, when he was no more than fifteen years old, and about two years after the Awlad ʿAli had returned to their territory.

"We used to go out and collect copper," he began. "I went out with my older brother, Hamid, and two others. . . . We had some donkeys and bags to carry the stuff out with, to the cars that came into the desert. The four of us went on foot into the desert. We walked separately because we were afraid of the mines. Each person had to be paying attention. I was walking and my thoughts were on the big mines. I was afraid of the big mines. But there is a mine called 'One with the Little Mustache,' which has three prongs, even finer than needles, that go into the detonator. . . .

"I was walking along when I found that my shoe wouldn't go down. Of course, these prongs are very thin, and if you don't go right up to the mine you don't see them. And so my shoe . . . I tried to put my foot down but it wouldn't go—something stopped my foot, but I couldn't see anything. So I pulled my foot back. I lifted my foot and looked and then, Duvv! It moved before it exploded. It blasted me twenty-two meters. I had been walking westward, and I was hurled away and found myself facing east. I had been carrying a knapsack with copper in it, and I was wearing a woolen vest under that. It scattered all of this. And my clothes, there was nothing left. All I had left on me was my shredded undershirt. It had blown them up until they ripped. And my shoes—gone. They flew off and I couldn't find them at all. It was that powerful.

"It was hissing and there was smoke and after that it went 'Tub Tub Tub Tub.' I looked and saw my brother shouting and wailing. They couldn't see me because I was in a low spot. I tried to stand up, but my legs couldn't. I shouted, 'Watch out for the mines! Watch out for the mines! The mines!' They started running, but by then you could see them: every four meters was a mine. I could see them at intervals. One here and one there. 'Be careful!'

"I told them at the time, 'I'm safe.' After I'd felt around my stomach, my chest, my head, and found nothing I told them it wasn't serious. 'It's only something in my legs and it's not bad. But I can't stand up.' So I said to them, 'Just wrap up what's here.' It was really bleeding. . . . They had to carry me.

"I saw that they were frightened, afraid that I would die. So I said, 'There's nothing wrong with me. Let's just make some tea.' We had tea, but I only drank a cup. Then I told them to make me a saddle—a donkey's saddle is not like a horse's—and rope the saddle on and make me some stirrups in the middle so I could put my legs in. The blood, the blood was flowing and I was getting dizzy. It was a long way, about thirty-five kilometers to Alamein, and I was worried about the blood.

"We got on the donkeys, and when we reached the rise to the north of us we saw someone. He was not an Arab; we could tell from his clothes. There was an asphalt road that the army, the English, had made. And there was a pipeline that brought water, dug in the sand. He had left the road and was walking along the pipeline because the sand there was soft. He couldn't walk on the hard surface. When we got near him, Hamid whistled at him. He stopped. He stopped and started mumbling. He tried to talk, but he was really tired, completely wiped out. 'Hey, hey—bomb.' He'd seen the bomb and had heard it. He'd been close by, but we hadn't noticed him.

"Then he looked at me and saw the blood. He took off his backpack and took out a box with three pills—one small pill, one grey one, and a third capsule with each half a different color. He opened my mouth and put the medicine in it. Then he got his water flask—there was only a tiny amount in it—and he held me like this and made me swallow the pill with the water. He had hung on to this one last sip, the one I drank. Then he opened his bag and got out some dyed bandages with two ties. . . . He took off all the headcloths and rags they had used to bandage me. The wounds were bleeding, and he rubbed the yellow ointment on and wiped it. It was as if he'd put fire on them, and I let out some screams. He wrapped them with the bandages.

"We looked at this Englishman. He had headphones and was wearing only trousers. He had a sack with an aerial, like a walkie-talkie. And that's all. His body was burnt. His skin was peeling, exactly like a snakeskin. His shoes had fallen apart, and he had tied the torn tops on with what must have been a strip of his shirt so he could walk on them. His legs looked as if he'd put them over a fire: they were burnt and bleeding. His lips were cracked. And when he looked down you'd see that his eyelids were very white, just as if they had been painted white. He was young, about twenty-eight or twenty-seven years old. He said, 'Wadiwaant, waadiwij wij blayn. Duvv! Cairo, Cairo.' His plane had crashed. I don't know what he said, but we understood that his plane had crashed three hundred kilometers from Cairo. There had been maneuvers where the armies had been and something had gone wrong with his plane. It went down and he had left it. . . .

"He had been walking for seven days. He had with him a little water, which he drank bit by bit. And he had a pill to keep going, something to make him strong. He had gone on like this, walking a lot at night. In the daytime during the heat he sat in the shade— maybe he'd find a tree or he'd find a mountain with rocks to go between. But he was near the end. If he hadn't come upon us he would have died. He could barely talk—he just kept saying, 'Blayn.'

"When we got home my father came out and met us. When he first saw me he asked where I had been hit. When he found out where the wounds were, he said it wasn't serous. But if it had not been for that medicine and the bandaging of this Englishman, I would have bled to death. So he didn't attend to me but went and got water for the Englishman. He warmed the water and put the man's legs in the water, water and salt. And he massaged his legs and brought him two spoonfuls of butter and put them in his mouth and made him swallow them. Then he made him a pot of tea, and he drank the tea, and then he brought him a loaf of bread and some boiled milk and broke up the bread in the milk. My father took care of the Englishman. He fed him, cooked a little milk for him, and then boiled him some eggs and fed him, bit by bit. He made him drink a light cup of tea, sip by sip. From sunset to ten o'clock at night he fed him, first a bite, and then a sip of tea. He put a little butter on the tea and told him to drink this. And the man would look at my father and the tears would flow. He couldn't talk from the thirst and the sun and the wind. But he had courage, and a compass.

"When he fell asleep my father covered him. I swear to God he even slept next to him. My father really was kind and compassionate. All he'd said to me was, 'It's nothing serious.' "

"Did this bother you?" I pressed.

"Of course not." Sagr was quick. He mentioned his mother Migdim then, but only briefly. "My mother and the whole camp were feeding me and around me. . . . But my father was a doctor, he knew how to set bones and do everything. He was courageous and strong in everything. He said there was no big injury when I was able to stand up when he asked. 'The bones are fine, and the muscles are fine. The cuts don't worry me. Blood spilled, and that's all.'

"So, in the morning my father attended to the Englishman, made him a glass of tea with milk. The man started trying to say something, something about Alamein. He wanted to go to their headquarters. At the time there were British intelligence people in Alamein, with their radios, still there. So Hamid and two others took him. It was a long way. When they arrived, they were met by an armed guard outside. After the Englishman talked with him for six or seven minutes the guard put his gun on his shoulder, saluted, and ran inside. He came out with two officers. . . . They had an Egyptian with them who translated. He told them, 'These people here saved my life. If not for them I wouldn't have come back. They had someone with them who was hit by a mine. Before anything I want the English doctor to go and take a look at him. If it is serious he should bring him back to the hospital. If he can treat him there, he should. This is the first thing I request.'

" 'Right away,' they said. My brother said they took them inside to the mess hall and brought them breakfast. Then they got the car ready and loaded some jerrycans of water. The doctor got his bag. And then a major came and greeted the man. They talked a long while and the Englishman said to him, 'Those people saved my life. They must have a certificate.' So the officer wrote something saying that the British government should grant their requests because they helped the pilot So-and-so. He sealed it and then gave each of them ten pounds.

"They all rode in the car bringing the doctor. 'Hey howaayi,' he said to me. And he took some twisted gauze over cotton on the end of a scissors and put this inside the wounds. He'd open the wounds slowly and then push this through with one shove. I'd scream. I'd howl. He's stick it in and pull it out the other end. Every morning, after the sun had come up, he was there at the tent. He'd change my bandages, and he'd put this red medicine in some water and wash the wounds. Then he put medicine on them. For twenty-one days I couldn't stand up. On the twenty-first day I finally stood up. The Englishman came himself to see how I was getting along."

Unlike Migdim, who cared only about her son's injury, Sagr ended his story with praise for the British: "Those were real men. They are the real men among the Europeans. The English know about friendship. Like us, they have courage, stamina, and generosity." Yet he also estimates that twelve thousand Bedouins have been killed through accidents like his with unexploded mines left by the British and Germans during the war. To this day people and camels are being killed by mines, even though no one works in scrap metal anymore. Reflecting on the earlier period of "rubbish-ing," Haj Sagr concludes, "Some people got rich. People got rich, but it destroyed families."

Words That Scatter

After Migdim nearly lost her son through this dangerous business, she lost her brother-in-law and then her husband. That left re-sponsibility for the family in the hands of her sons. To get the family back on its feet after the devastations of the war they worked in smuggling (between Libya and Egypt), began to acquire land, and increased their sheep and camel herds. Many decisions had to be made, and they usually consulted with their mother. When they were in the camp, they spent their evenings with Migdim, talking in her room by the light of a kerosene lantern. During the day, if they found themselves free, they would stop by. Even when they had gotten older, her sons were relaxed in her company. As she aged, they became more solicitous. They had learned to trust her to run things in the household, among the women. She organized the work that needed doing and she divided up the goods, from food to dress fabric, that they brought home for the family.

But Migdim complained about her sons. They sometimes made her angry—when they would not take her advice, when they put themselves in danger by getting involved in arguments with other families, when they made bad decisions about women. She re-members, for example, refusing to sing or ululate at the wedding of her youngest daughter, Lawz. The girl's brothers had agreed to give her in marriage to their first cousin, on the same day as her brother Sagr's wedding to Gateefa, his cousin of twelve or thirteen, who was the same age as Migdim's daughter. Still, Migdim felt that Lawz was too young. "I was opposed to it," she asserted. "It was against my will.

"We had their weddings on the same day and we put them in our old house, together. But it didn't work out. I said they wouldn't manage, but the boys didn't follow my wishes. . . . The girls used to escape. We had a goatpen a little east of the house. My daughter would go and sleep among the goats, wrapping herself up in a straw mat. I'd find her sleeping there but wouldn't say a word. They'd look everywhere, but they couldn't find her.

"In the end they just didn't have bread to share, by God. Her mother-in-law didn't like her. She set up a tiny tent for her, put a bit of tattered mat down. She made her life miserable. . . . So Lawz came back and stayed with us.

"Then someone else came to ask for her. He had a wife and wanted her as a second wife. I said, 'I won't ever put her somewhere as a second wife.' Even her present husband—I didn't want her to marry into his family. I said, 'I swear to God I won't give her to them.' He was young, a kid. And his father was away in Libya. I thought the boy would just be in the camp alone. Well, it happened anyway. Her brother Sagr agreed to it, and we took her to them and they held the wedding. As you see, though, it worked out well between them."

That time she had been upset with her sons for what they had done to their sister. More often she was angry with her sons because of their behavior toward their wives. Her daughters-in-law often came to her with their grievances. If she thought her sons were treating them unfairly or poorly, she would speak to the men. On the other hand, her daughters-in-law praised her for being discreet about conflicts that arose strictly between women of the community and not involving the men. Most of her daughters-in-law appreciated how often she took their side and looked out for them in situations where they had little say.

As her sons grew older and became wealthier through their hard work in business and their good investments in land, orchards, and sheep, they began to take second and even third wives. Migdim insists that in her day it had been rare for men to have more than one wife. Later it was still unusual, except for those who were rich and important. She yelled at her sons each time they decided to marry again, even as she recognized that men wanted to marry women so they could have more sons, men to make the family strong. One evening Sagr tried to provoke her. If death didn't beat him to it, he said, he would build a new house and get another wife. She had a fit. "You fool! It's not good to bring together several women. Look at your household. Everything is left spilled, everything is a mess. That's because you have too many women. Each one says, 'It's not my responsibility. I won't pick it up. Let someone else do it.' " She had objected to his decision to take a third wife and had done her best to discourage the woman from marrying her son. She did not succeed that time, although she had managed earlier to frighten off the parents of another girl her son had wished to marry.

Her youngest son took a second wife after his first wife suffered a serious illness and several miscarriages and was forbidden by the doctor to have more children. When he started spending time at the household he had set up for his new wife, away from his mother, Migdim complained. She moaned that it was terrible to be alone, not to have a man in the house anymore; no one to say good morning to, no one to say good night to, no light in the men's guest room. The women would not let her get away with this. How often, they demanded, had Migdim's husband, Jawwad, slept at his mother's home instead of with her?

It was not just because her sons neglected her when they married new wives that she objected. She was protective of the mothers of their children, the women who had been there for years, and of the children themselves. This complex mixture of jealousy and protectiveness toward her daughters-in-law and grandchildren figured clearly in a conflict Migdim had with her sons in the summer of 1987, a conflict over a piece of family land that they gave to a long-time neighbor who wanted to build a new house.

She told her side of the story. "My sons came here and I told them I wouldn't give them a piece. But as soon as they left they went right over and signed it over to her. I had told them, 'My sons, don't sign it over to her. Let her keep what she's built and let her stay. No one will bother her. But as for a new house, no, she shouldn't build. If you sign it over, you won't have my blessings.' But they left here and went and signed it over to her. This made me sick. What kind of behavior is this? They do this for that other woman, when I'm their mother?"

I asked Migdim whether her sons had informed her that they were signing over the land. "No, they didn't come back here. Other people told me they had signed it over. . . . Sagr and Hamid drove the boys away saying, 'I swear to God if one of them opens his mouth I'll drink his blood.' That's what the old one said. They're pimps, the two of them. Ugh!"

I thought she must be joking. "How can you say that about your sons?"

Her response was sharp. "They're not my sons. I'm not their mother, nor are they my sons. Sons who crumble what I say and go along with what that woman says? They're not my sons at all."

Then furiously, almost incoherently, she began to explain what had happened. The problem started with goats. The old man next door had gone to the fathers of the young men of the camp to complain that they had tried to beat up his sons and drive them out. "The old man said they had done this and that and this and that, until Hamid began to act possessed. He started hitting his own sons, shouting at them. He almost killed them. What's this? You beat your own sons for the sake of that woman next door? Our boys had neither hit nor spoken to her boys. All they said was 'You shouldn't let the goats pass through here after grazing.'

"Nowadays there's an orchard on either side. And when three hundred goats pass through the fig orchards and graze . . . , they'll eat the figs. . . . There's no open land anymore. But then if we ever want to get some milk from our goats, they [the neighbors] won't let us. We have goats in their herd, you know, but they won't bring them by here so we can milk them. And then the billy goats get loose. I swear I spend the whole day going 'kh, kh, kh, kh' to keep them away. If we put fodder out for the cow, they eat it. If we put fodder out for the donkey, they eat it. If we put water out for the chickens, they drink it. I told my sons to tell them to tie up the goats. Hamid said he would, but he's a liar. I doubt he did."

I tried to reason with Migdim, suggesting that maybe her sons figured there was plenty of land. She was not convinced.

"Is there lots of land? Where is all that land? When their sons get older they'll start fighting. I told them that. I'm really mad at them, my sons, because I love them. They're my sons and I love them, but they shouldn't thwart me. Why does he ignore what I've said and go sign it over to that woman? No! He's not my son at all. He's not my son, nor will I bless him."

What had disturbed her most was an incident a couple of evenings earlier when her oldest son, Hamid, had chased after his sons and nephews, believing, despite their denials, that the boys had tried to beat up the shepherd's son. "I said to my son, 'They didn't want to kill him! They just wanted to say to him, "Listen, if your family wants to build you shouldn't. You've already built a house and you're living in it." ' But the old guy starts screaming, 'They wanted to kill the boy. They tried to beat the boy! May I be forced to divorce my wife if I don't kill them. God damn their father, their father who gave birth to them! Gypsies! Bastards! Good-for-nothings!' " Her voice was shrill as she imitated him.

I tried to calm Migdim down, but she insisted, "Those grown men, they're imbeciles!"

I told her that her son Sagr had planned to come by to see her that day but had gotten caught up in a dispute elsewhere. She knew about it already, about the land and the groups fighting over it. She had her opinion, too, about who was in the right. Like all the women in the community, she was worried about her sons who had gone off to the fight. She prayed for their safe return. But that did not stop her from going on about her own feelings. "My son, may he be safe, I don't want him to come by anyway. Let him stay away. I'm upset. I'm upset that he ignored what I said. He threw my words into the air. It is our land, and all of our boys are going to want some. Even the little ones said, 'It's our land. Tomorrow we're going to grow up and marry and we won't find anywhere to build.' They are shameless. If they had sense and understood anything, they would have said, 'Our mother says that maybe later this will create problems that get worse.' "

She then muttered, "Those people aren't kin, you know. They're not from our tribe."

I interjected, "But everyone says they've lived with you for so long."

"So what if we've been together for a long time? Does that mean they should let their goats destroy our crops? Let them move west, to Alamein. There's lots of land there and no orchards. Or why doesn't he go live with his brothers out west, west of Matruh? There's lots of land out there. The other day I went out to pee, near the barrel over there and I heard them laughing at me because I had to pull up my dress. I'm afraid to wet myself and I can't squat now. I heard them laughing at me, I swear to God. I can't even go out to pee now. No, I don't want them around. They're weighing on me.

"My son should respect my wishes. . . . He's my son. He came out of me. Who could be closer to me? Yet he goes and signs it over to that family when I said not to. By the Prophet, isn't that wrong? Given that I said not to?"

Suddenly a new element was interjected into the story. "And the old woman had the nerve to tell my granddaughter that the boys smoke and get high. She told her they spend all night in the men's guest room playing. 'You'd better not sleep at your grandmother's anymore. Watch out, maybe the boys will come in,' she told her. But I don't sleep at night. I swear sleep doesn't enter my eyes. Does she think I'll fall asleep and one of the boys will come in and rape them? I don't sleep. She told the old men that the boys get drunk and smoke hashish. What rotten lies. Do they have a café to smoke at? They don't have a café, and they don't have hashish. She's just causing trouble.

"Well, now Hamid won't let his daughter come sleep with me anymore. For three nights she hasn't come. I don't want them. God bless those who are with me. I have my water and my things here. As long as her father thinks his daughter is too good for me I don't need them."

It was becoming clear to me that Migdim's worries about the land had something to do with her feelings about her neighbor, feelings that seemed tinged with jealousy. She continued, "And yesterday, he was over there until midnight. He goes over there and he laughs over there and he talks. He never laughs with his sons. He never talks with his sons. He never says, 'My sons, what should we do about this and what should we do about that?' And when he comes over here he's like a stranger, weighing on me. Over there it's laughter and talk. May he lick their asses. I don't want them—as long as he cares about what the other women want and ignores my concerns. He has no sense. No, sister, I don't want him to come talk over here, I don't want him or anyone. Anyone who throws away his mother's words and cares about those of outsiders—he's no good."

When I first had asked her why the men listened to the shepherd's wife, she had shrugged. The second time I asked, when she was talking about how much her son enjoyed visiting with the old woman, she laughed and asked, "Who knows what she did to him? Maybe she had a charm written. May God protect me from her sins. I swear to God she has sucked the sense of the old ones, Sagr and Hamid. Sucked both of their minds."

She ended our conversation with a poem:

"The heart is a fool
it sowed words the wind scattered . . .

God damn them. They ignore my words and make hers come true?"

Son's Marriages

This was not just an argument about a piece of land. For Migdim, the matter concerned the entire women's community. The problem was that about eight years earlier, her neighbor's youngest daughter had become Hamid's third wife. And just a few weeks before the incident over the land, this young woman had decided to go against the usual arrangements for the sharing of domestic work among the wives, daughters, and daughters-in-law of the household. Her husband had agreed that she could separate from the others and begin to cook and bake just enough for herself and her five small children. She claimed her work load was too heavy and that labor was unfairly split among the twenty-five household members. Her withdrawal had been much discussed in the women's community, defensively by the other two wives, who feared being blamed for having been unfair, and angrily by Migdim and the mother and sisters of the senior wife (who was also Hamid's first cousin), not to mention the other women in the community, who took sides with the older wives.

Migdim had opposed the marriage. Her son had arranged this third match while she was staying with her sick brother. Upon her return she blew up, insulting Hamid and calling him names. His first wife was a close cousin who had not wanted to marry him; she had stayed, however, and produced a line of sons. The two, now like brother and sister, had long since stopped sleeping together. Hamid's second wife was the daughter of a shepherd's family that had lived near them for a while, herding their sheep. He had fallen in love with her and married her. As Migdim reminded him one day when he complained about the lousy bread this poor woman had baked, he had raved, in the days before he married her, about how delicious her bread was—and that was when they used only coarse brown barley, not fine white flour. Migdim sympathized with both these wives, but especially with this good simple woman.

Haj Sagr certainly believed this new marriage was a factor in Migdim's rage. A few days after my visit with his mother he asked me if she was seriously angry with him. Should he go make peace with her? He knew she was angry that they had beaten their own sons for the sake of an outside family. He also knew she feared that the split in his brother's household meant the young wife had her husband under her control. The Haj explained, though, that it was not his brother's land they were signing over but his own. In his presence, Sagr's senior wife supported their decision. The two concurred that Migdim was acting badly. What was the transaction costing her? Both her husband, Jawwad, and his father before him had always generously given people things they asked for.

One other woman, a visiting aunt, took their side and tried to calm Migdim. She counseled Migdim to keep quiet, arguing that silence was the best policy. After all, the world would go on a long time. Later, later when the men were dead, their signatures and their papers would carry no weight; it would be another generation. She also offered some pious phrases. She complimented the men, saying there were so few generous people anymore. They were merely following the model of the Prophet. The Prophet (God bless him and save him), she reminded Migdim, said that we must care for our neighbors, up to the seventh neighbor. The Prophet almost left an inheritance to a neighbor.

At this Sagr's wife retorted, "But we have actually *given* an inheritance to a neighbor. Are we supposed to be better than the Prophet?" Quickly, though, she added, "May God forgive me."

Most others in the community, however, found fault with the old shepherd's wife. They were worried about Migdim, who had been crying her eyes out, hurt by the accusations that her grandsons smoked hashish at her house and miserable because her granddaughter was forbidden from spending the night with her. This was the granddaughter, Migdim claimed, who woke up before dawn to heat the water for her so she could wash for the early prayers. (The girl herself complained that she was very attached to her grandmother and was used to sleeping at her house. She argued with her father and swore that she would not abandon her grandmother. Although she could no longer sleep there, she said she still went to her grandmother's every day to shake out her mat, sweep her room, and groom her.) Many shared Migdim's conviction that this was the work of bad magic. After all, remarked one woman, the shepherd's wife is an old woman and gets around to markets and things. Another whispered, "They say she gives the charms to them to drink. All of the men eat and drink at her house. Yes, the old woman gives the magic to them to drink, and they sign all the papers."

Each offered evidence of strange behavior. One described how Hamid had mercilessly hit the little daughter of his senior wife because she had been fighting with her new half-sister. The man's second wife had also complained of being beaten one day and accused of stealing a ten-pound note from the pocket of his robe hanging in her room. She defended herself by saying she had never even asked him for a ten-piaster coin to take as a gift to a new mother. The cloves and henna and money she needed she always got from her own family. She had wanted to go home to her relatives, angry at being accused of stealing his money; but she dared not, she said, because she knew everyone would say she was just angry because he was taking another wife.

Migdim had tried to intervene, but Hamid just brushed her off, as he always did when she interfered. I remember a day, a couple of months after his marriage to this new, eighteen-year-old bride, when he stopped by his mother's house, trailed by several of his little children. Migdim began to complain about the number of children in the camp. She criticized her son because his children had just accidentally smothered a small goat with which they were playing, and she had only barely rescued a lamb that four of them were trying to ride.

Then she told him she disapproved of the amount of gold he had bought for his new wife. "Her mother just buys and buys, and you pay." The least he could do, she argued, was to buy his senior wife a little ring or something. "Shame on you," she said.

"Gold isn't everything" was Hamid's mumbled response.

She warned him, "A holyman said the man with many wives will go to hell—if he doesn't treat them exactly alike, if he brings something to one and not the other, even if he looks at one and not the other. It's a sin, sin, sin."

Her son rejected this view. He joked, "No, it's the man with only one wife who will go to hell."

Migdim returned to the problem of children. Who is going to feed them? Where will they all live?

Hamid came back with the standard line. "He who created them will provide for them. Every being on this earth is born with his God-given livelihood. God will provide for them."

She grumbled, but he just smiled.

Pity the Women

If the conflict was over loyalty to kin versus generosity to longtime friends, over new wives against old, and exacerbated by the jealousy of an aging and grumpy matriarch, it also had to do with land itself. Land was becoming scarcer and more valuable now that the Egyptian government had begun to reclaim the desert through irrigation projects. What had once been good only for growing barley or grazing sheep could now be planted with other crops, especially fruit orchards. These brought in money. The government had therefore decreed that anyone who wanted title to land they had held traditionally had to purchase it formally. Disputes over land and goats eating fig saplings had thus become common.

These changes in the area had affected women's lives, and Migdim bemoaned their loss of freedom. She reminisced about the conditions that prevailed for most of her life. The whole area, she said, was sown with barley and wheat. In the spring, if there was rain, it turned so green there was no place to set up the tents, so they left with the herds to find pastures. Out west they would milk the sheep and store up butter to last the year. It was a good life. "The old ones," she commented, speaking of the last generation, "were blessed, really fortunate. They were happy. They had camels and sheep. They lacked nothing. . . . My sons, though, they say the old ones did the wrong thing by sticking with herding. But all that we have now is due to them. Then the government came and took their land, and so these young men had to buy it back from the government. This business of agriculture they're now in, may God release them from its troubles."

They had planted their land slowly. Migdim had brought a few cuttings from her father's olive trees. He'd been one of the first to follow the advice of the local British administrator they called "Brumly," who recommended planting. With watering, the cuttings grew. Yet the olive orchards that now take up much of the land were planted only in 1960. That year, an Egyptian man who worked for the government came and told them he wanted their acreage: it was a good site for a house. They did not want to give up their land, of course; moreover, they had heard that if the land were planted, no one could seize it. Day and night they worked, digging holes in the daytime and planting trees from Migdim's father's olive grove by night. In fifteen days they had planted the whole orchard, with the help of many neighbors, relatives, and friends, and had surrounded it with high posts strung with barbed wire. When the government people came to inspect the land they found it all planted, and so said the man could not have it. Migdim remembers that day well. The man left in his car, followed all the way back to town by Migdim's sons on horseback, firing their guns into the air in celebration. It was the first time a Bedouin had won a land claim against the Egyptian government.

Like most of the rest of the camp, Migdim's one-room house sits on a ridge that affords a wide view of these olive groves, their new fig and guava orchards, and the scattered clumps of houses that extend to the horizon. There are many people and houses now, but she remembers when the land was empty: nothing between hers and her relatives' houses. This crowding means that the girls no longer go off to gather firewood—because there isn't any; and their trips to get water are short because their kinsmen worry about them passing by the houses of so many nonrelatives.

When she gets together with other women, Migdim rails against the younger men of the community for being so strict about the movements of their young sisters, cousins, and wives. "The boys are terrible now," she said once.

Her daughter Ngawa agreed. "The boys are terrible. I swear by my father we have one son who's black in word and deed. And he's so young. You know the shiny material the girls like for dresses? Once my daughter's maternal uncle bought her a dress. I swear by Saint ʿAbd ar-Rahman, her brother spilled kerosene on it and tried to set it on fire. He said, 'What's this? She wants to wear a dress that sparkles? And she's wearing bobby pins and gold fringe? She's got complete freedom!' "

"Hey Migdim, I heard that your other grandson yells at the girls and won't let them go to get water," interjected a visitor.

"The boys are terrible."

A neighbor added, "Why, when we were young, remember, we used to go off to herd the goats on our own. Not anymore!"

Migdim's daughter continued: "Yes, that's how things were, may God have mercy on past generations. They weren't like this new generation. . . . The men now are awful."

Migdim talked about a young man who was working for them. "He's a good boy who took care of the herds and never argued with the women or bothered them. My youngest son came and found him sitting in the tent with my two daughters-in-law. He was keeping them company, he and my grandsons. . . . My son came in and said, 'What are you sitting here for? Why are you sitting here?' "

"I tell you, girls, we were just sitting there, that night, and the boy had just finished eating supper," confirmed Migdim's daughter-in-law.

Migdim continued: "My son came in and slapped him [the herdsman], shouting, 'God damn your father! Get out! Why are you sitting with the women?' I started yelling from my room, and he came over here. I said to him, 'My son, why were you hitting the man? You fool! When we were young, when we were young women, we always had three or four young men working with us, living with us. The old ones never said anything.'"

"Dark disgrace! Damn him." Her daughter-in-law was indignant.

Migdim produced a fragment of an old song:

"You who guards the female, you're fatigued
You who guards the female, you're fatigued
One time she'll go to milk the herd and rendezvous
One time she'll get up at night to tie up the goats."

The women explained to me, since I had not understood the words: "A woman can't be governed—anyone who tries to guard her will just get tired." "Whatever a woman wants to she can do. She's smart and she can think."

As if to show, however, that women are capable and eager to protect their virtue, Migdim launched into an anecdote. To much laughter, she recounted a trip she had taken to accompany a daughter-in-law on a visit home. As they sat in a crowded taxi, a man leaned against her legs. She warned, "Don't ride on my legs! Pull yourself over." She gave him a good pinch in the ass, as she said, and he flew forward. " 'Get back to your place,' I said to him. And I pinched him right on his ass," she repeated.

I'm confused by Migdim. She defends her granddaughters and grandnieces and even her daughters-in-law when the young men, and sometimes the older ones, criticize them or accuse them of talking to men or going places. But then she complains that the young women of today have no modesty. When she was young, she claims, they used to veil with heavy black shawls, not today's flimsy pieces of cloth that don't even hide women's faces. When a great-granddaughter of hers came in crying because she had lost her hairclip, Migdim scolded her. "It's shameful for girls to wear hairclips. Why do you want a hairclip? Are you looking for a husband?"

Yet the world she remembers is one in which certain things that would today be considered scandalous were perfectly acceptable.

Wedding celebrations, she complains, have lost their appeal. She tells Fayga, her newest daughter-in-law, that they celebrated her sons' circumcision with twenty nights of singing and dancing. At weddings in the past, young women, including her husband's sisters and nieces, had danced, veiled, in front of semicircles of young men who serenaded them. It was all "stuff that couldn't happen now!" they agreed, thinking of the sex-segregated affairs that weddings have become since the group's settlement into houses.

Young men and women at weddings used to exchange love songs, songs that Migdim often recites. Even more intriguing are the songs she remembers now with wonderment at how things have changed: the young men's shearing songs. In the days when they lived mostly by herding, groups of young men would travel from camp to camp shearing the patriarchs' herds. Shearings were like weddings, everyone was fond of explaining. People enjoyed themselves and had complete license to sing what they wanted.

Migdim found it comical to remember who had sung particular songs because these men had grown old and were now either distinguished or dead. The words of a shearing song are about sheep, but their meaning is about love. Young men sang as young women listened, occasionally coming out among the exhausted young men to bring them meals. The butt of many of these crude songs was the old herd owner, the "ram" who took offense only on pain of losing the services of these shearers.

The songs were so explicit and immodest that I had a hard task finding anyone willing to explain them to me. The women simply giggled when I looked at them questioningly. Even when the bemused Haj Sagr agreed to explain a few to me, his eyes twinkling as I wrote in embarrassment, he fell silent if anyone approached.

Some songs were transparent twists on ordinary love songs. Words like "the beloved" were replaced with ones like "goats" that rhymed with them. So a song like the following, which depends on knowing that sheep and goats must be herded together because sheep frighten easily and won't move at night without goats, is suggestive:

> Praise be to He who made you
> without goats patient, O sheep . . .

Other songs were more outrageous and testify to a time when, at least on these restricted occasions, talking about sexual relations under the patriarchs' very noses was possible. A song addressed to the head of the family warns him that his daughter has already had a rendezvous with her lover:

> He's lifted the back of your tent
> the wolf has already come, O shepherd . . .

Another song addresses an old man who has married a young woman against her will, making fun of him for losing his young wife to a young lover with whom she has eloped:

> The sheep drank at the well and took off
> and the ram he's the one who died of thirst . . .

Since young men were usually responsible for the herding, the singers usually identified themselves as shepherds. A young man who knows of a rendezvous his friend has had with a sweetheart might sing:

> In a late night sheep-milking
> the shepherd drank her milk . . .

Not all the songs Migdim remembered were so scandalous. Some might be sung by, or on behalf of, a young man who had either lost or gained a loved one. A young man angry that the family he worked for had given their daughter away in marriage to someone else might play with the fact that a shepherd is given, as his right, five sheep in the herd to use for milking for his own needs:

> He struck his tent in anger
> They'd taken away from the shepherd
> what they owed him . . .

Migdim was one of the few who remembered these poems. She
also chanted long lullabies that none of the young mothers knew.
Whenever her great-grandson wandered into her room she would
greet him as she did all her little grandchildren and great grandchildren, with a warm "Welcome, welcome, welcome!" A chubby
blond boy, he had become steady on his feet and would wander
around her room getting into things.

To distract him she would sing to him, holding his little hands
in her own wrinkled and tattooed ones to teach him to clap. She
sang about little boys who will grow up to ride horses, carry guns,
and become tribal leaders. Sometimes she bounced him up and
down and sang the kinds of songs sung at circumcisions. He was
happy to hear his name.

> Little Kafy, after the circumcision
> he'll ride on a horse with a gold saddle . . .

She teased the little boy too, in ways that suggest either the license
of old age or, judging by her granddaughters' reactions, a different
standard of prudishness in the past. Her favorite game was to call
out to him, "Come here, my little Kafy. Come gimme some snuff.
I want to sniff some snuff. Where's the wild parsnip?" He would
toddle over to her, lifting up his robe, whereupon she would
pretend to sniff and then sneeze, the way she and the other old
women do when they have taken snuff.

When I asked what a wild parsnip was, some girls ran up the hill
to dig one up for me. But when a granddaughter of Migdim's came
by to visit, she was horrified. "What a black scandal!" she exclaimed. She scolded the boy, "Go put on your underpants!"
Migdim just smiled and did it again.

Hyenas and Sons

Migdim is getting old. She is diabetic but does not know what to do about it except to avoid rice and fried foods. When she has a fever, cries because her head hurts or her eyes burn, loses her appetite, or can't sit up, everyone rushes to visit. Sometimes her nearby daughter moves in with her to bathe and feed her and to wash her clothes for her. As she begins to feel better, the mood lightens. All day her room will be packed with women and children, who, however, disappear or grow quiet when one of her sons comes in. Otherwise, even if her grandsons or great-nephews stop by, things are lively.

The women may entertain Migdim and one another with old folktales about the sexual desires of old women. They laugh at the shamelessness of such women, and perhaps at themselves, these women, some widowed, some divorced, with grown sons. On one occasion Migdim's daughter-in-law told a disturbing tale whose beginning I missed. "A man asked his elderly mother, 'Mom, do you want me to get you a husband?' She said, 'No, no, my son. That would be shameful. No, that's shameful.' But he said, 'No it's not. He'll keep you company.' So she said, 'May God grant you success if you do. If you do it, may God bless you.' "

The storyteller found this funny and went on. "He went off and killed a hyena. He killed the poor thing and wrapped it in a white shroud. And he brought the hyena to her—she was blind—and he put it down next to her saying, 'Mother, be careful. His name is Hassan. He's sleeping now, don't waken him. He was up late last night. Let him wake up on his own first. And don't move him. Let him sleep until he's slept enough.' And he put the bundle down next to her and left.

"She started shaking him, trying to wake him up—her son was nearby, even though it was evening and she assumed he had gone—she tried to wake him up. She said to him, 'Hey handsome! Hey handsome! Sit up handsome. Look, here's a jar and here's another jar. There are some more as well that are hidden.' She was talking about jars she had filled with gold and buried. She had buried them all over, and she was showing him, the hyena, as her son watched!"

This reminded Migdim of another story; she called up a few lines from it, and her daughter-in-law picked up the tale. "She would always say, 'May God grant you success, if only.' Any time her son talked to her she said, 'May God grant you success, if only.' The young man went and asked someone, 'Why does my mother only say, "May God grant you success, if only." What is this "if only"?' He was told she wanted a man. 'If only' just means if only you'd bring me a man.

"So he went to her and said, 'Mother, I've gotten you a man and he wants you to come to him. I'll take you to his house.' 'His house?' she says, 'May God grant you success my son. Let's go.' So he brings her to a hyena's lair and leaves her there. It was rainy and cold and when she heard the wind in the night whistling and going 'OOOH!' and 'RRRRR!' she thought this was the noise of the celebration of her wedding night. She thought she was going to get married and that soon her groom would come to her.

"Well," the storyteller continued, "he came to her. The hyena came and wanted to eat her."

Migdim interrupted, "Yes, he started eating her."

Imitating the old woman's high voice, but laughing as she tried to finish, the storyteller trilled, " 'Ooh! Ooh! O God, O God, the groom is licking and stroking, licking and caressing me.' "

A younger woman burst out, "Damn these Bedouin stories!"

Migdim repeated, again imitating the old woman, " 'The groom, he's licking and caressing!' He gnawed on her until he ate her up! (May it be far from you!) She assumed he was really her bridegroom, curse her! He came in the morning, her son, and found her dead."

"Shame on him," commented a visitor.

Migdim chuckled as she gave the basic plot: "Her son had gone everywhere with her and done everything for her but still she would never say to him, 'May God grant you success.' All she'd say was 'If only.' So he put her in with the hyena. 'I'll get you an old man,' her son said. 'And here's his house.' 'His house?' the old woman said. 'God grant you success my son.' "

She saw my tape recorder, resting discreetly near her. "Lila's machine is working now," she announced, "taping our words." She chanted a rhyme to it:

> "A pity, you who this cap belongs to
> A pity, you who this cap belongs to
> A pity, you who this cap belongs to
> They said you were a man among men
> He died without me laying eyes on him
> A pity, you who this cap belongs to."

From the commotion I gathered that the other women had never heard this rhyme before. Migdim told us the story: "The old woman is lamenting the old man. Her son is a joker! He was teasing her. He said to his mother, 'I found'—what he found was a cap, a cap in a room on the floor, and he brought it to her and said—'I found you a husband, but as we were leaving the market he dropped dead. Here's his cap!' "

"What a bastard!"

"What a joker!" The women laughed.

Migdim laughed too. "So she started lamenting: 'Woe is me, such a pity . . .' "

My tape went on recording the laughter and repetitions of the rhyme, the comments on the son, and one woman's comment, "Hey, if he'd said the old man was alive she would have gone off to look for him!"

One by one, the women sighed, chuckled, and got up to leave. They had things to do—cooking, baking, weaving, washing, children needing care.

Like the women in the stories, Migdim is almost blind now. She has to ask whether it is time for prayers. When I am there I tell her by looking at my watch. "Yes, it's after three o'clock, time for afternoon prayers," I say now. She positions herself to face south-east, unrolls her prayer rug in front of her, and, without standing, because she can't, she begins her prayers. When she finishes she feels around under her blanket until she finds her prayer beads. She starts counting off on them the names of God. As she folds up her prayer mat she ends, as she often does, with "Praise be to God. Praise be to God. May God keep evil away from us. May God keep weddings going forever among Muslims. May God always bless Muslims with celebrations."

She is happiest at the weddings of her many grandsons. What-ever disappointment or anger she may sometimes feel toward her sons, it seems to disappear as she sings songs praising them as fathers of these boys. At the last wedding I attended in the com-munity she sang a song that placed her where she wanted to be: at the center of her family.

> May they always be blessed with happiness
> the sons of my sons with me in their midst . . .

Chapter 2

POLYGYNY

If you fear that you shall not be able to deal justly with the
orphans, marry women of your choice, two or three or four;
but if you fear that you shall not be able to deal justly (with
them), then only one . . .

Qur'an 4:3

Co-Wives

Migdim's son Sagr sat with two of his best friends in an office in
Alexandria. They were waiting for a phone call about some business venture, and I was waiting to be driven to Cairo. I would leave
for the United States the next day, after a stay of four months with
Haj Sagr's family.

Sagr's two friends, one dressed in "Western" or city clothes—
trousers and a shirt—the other, like Sagr, in the long white robes
distinctive of the Awlad 'Ali, began teasing him, perhaps for my
benefit. They criticized him for having more than one wife. He
wanted to know what was wrong with that. One said, "How
would you feel if it were reversed and your wife had another
husband?" The other pulled from his wallet a photograph of his
wife to show me, proudly saying they had been together for forty
years. Sagr laughed when he saw the photo. "But she's old!" The

man replied, "So am I." Back and forth they went, the old man saying he wouldn't be able to face his wife if he married again. He wouldn't even be able to face his young bride. Finally Sagr said conspiratorially to me, "They're not Muslims. This is Christian stuff, to stay with just one woman." Expecting me to back him he charged, "Lila, you've seen my wives. Are there any problems?"

I had just left his co-wives Gateefa and Azza sitting together in a room at the back of the house where Gateefa had given birth. Azza had washed her co-wife's bloody clothes for her and hung them on the line to dry. She had helped her get dressed, brought her food and the things she needed for her new baby. When she was done, she had come to sit with her and the women who had come to visit. She had teased Gateefa about her reaction to the labor pains, imitating her moans and prayers. The visitors, who included their third co-wife, Safiyya, a woman who lived in a separate household with her grown son, swore they would not want Azza to help when they delivered—she always mimicked the poor mother.

I had been glad Azza was there because she knew what to do. The other time I had been with Gateefa when she gave birth I was frightened. There had been no other women in the household at the time, Azza being away at her brothers' house. Gateefa had begged for some sand from the nearby saint's tomb. I had run with her ten-year-old daughter to get it and had cried, as the girl did, when she kissed the tomb and implored the saint to keep her mother safe. When Sagr's brother finally passed by the house I demanded he fetch the doctor from town. It had seemed to take forever.

This time, I had not felt so responsible. Just as the sun was setting and we sat in the courtyard having tea we had wondered where Gateefa had gone. She had been uncomfortable that day, even though she had managed to make it to a neighbor's wedding. In fact, I had joked with her for days that she'd better hurry: I wanted to see the new baby before I left. She just kept asking God to relieve her of this burden. It was her eleventh pregnancy, and for months she had worried about the swelling in her legs and the ache in her back. Whenever she sighed, her husband would comment, "This will be the last."

I now waited with Azza, her sister-in-law Fayga, and Gateefa's older daughters as the younger girls went into the house to look for their mother. When she did not come, Azza, without a word, followed them. Gateefa was wandering from room to room, distracted, her waters broken and her green silk dress stained. She put her arm in Azza's and walked slowly back to the west room; this was where she liked to give birth because it was away from the men and their guests. It was also sheltered from the wind. Azza had been comforting. "Just walk slowly. Hold on to me."

By then the sun had gone down. We ran around in the dark looking for pillows, old blankets, and burlap sacks to place under her. Where is the kerosene lantern? Where are the matches? The boys were instructed to go into the house and keep the little ones with them. Gateefa's three teen-age daughters and I set off into the night to bring a neighbor who was a healer and midwife. There was no moon and I stumbled on the rocks in our path, but we were guided by electric lights and jumping television shadows in a few of the still-unfinished houses that had been built nearby in the last couple of years. The girls picked up some rocks, as did I, in case we encountered dogs.

We arrived home to find the baby born. I caught a glimpse of it by the kerosene lantern, lying quiet on the ground waiting for its umbilical cord to be cut. Gateefa was leaning back against the wall thanking God. The midwife entered the room whispering, "In the Name of God the Merciful, the Compassionate." There was incense burning.

Meanwhile the men had come home, and Gateefa's brother-in-law shouted for a bowl of buttermilk. His wife went to get it from the goatskin bag and I, annoyed, told him the women were busy right now. He asked what was going on. I wouldn't say because I presumed he knew. Then I was called to the men's guest room, where I found seated on cushions around the edge of the room a big group of visitors. The men's voices were loud, the smoke from their cigarettes filled the air. Sagr introduced me to the men, one of whom was a well-known poet whose poetry he wanted to tape-record with my machine. Gateefa's husband could not let his guests know that anything was going on, so all he did was ask me, in a low voice and with a knowing smile, "What's their news? Is the business finished?"

It was not until the next morning that anyone was willing to announce that the baby was a girl, Gateefa's ninth. She had told our neighbor, the first woman in her network to visit her, that her eight-year-old son had come in to see her and said, "Why didn't you give us a brother? There are only two of us and we wanted a boy." The neighbor had responded, "God keep her relatives and her brothers safe." Gateefa's husband, too, had stopped by to greet her in the morning, saying, as one of his daughters reported, "Thank God you're safe."

For the other women who came to visit, including the third co-wife, Safiyya, Azza answered questions about what had happened. I wanted to know exactly what she had done for Gateefa. She demonstrated the squatting position a mother should take while giving birth and told how she had held Gateefa from behind while her sister-in-law had held her from the front. Suddenly wiping away some tears, she described to us how Gateefa had cried and prayed to God to protect her daughters, sure that she was dying. The two co-wives, sitting cross-legged on the freshly laid bedding, their knees almost touching, and the tiny swaddled infant lying between them, looked long at each other. In that moment I saw something about these two women that I had not grasped before, although I had known them for many years. Despite their difficulties with each other—and they had many—there was between them a closeness and dependency, perhaps as women who give birth (indeed, other women remarked that day, "Men experience nothing compared to women—do they think giving birth is easy? It is as hard as war"), perhaps as women bound together by sharing a household, daily life, and a history. Fourteen years of shared history made for a bond, even if life together was often tense.

Cousins

Their most recent argument had been bad. It had begun during Ramadan, the month of fasting, just before I had arrived more than four months earlier. I had heard occasional references to it, in passing and always in humor, but did not ask Gateefa about it until her husband mentioned the argument at the end of a long conversation about the early days of their marriage.

We had been sitting in Gateefa's room on a quiet afternoon. I was trying to sound disinterested as I asked Sagr about his plans for the marriages of his daughters. This started him talking about a favorite subject: the benefits of marrying relatives. Gateefa had come in and sat down, with a groan about her aching shoulders. He had imitated her, "Oh my shoulders, Oh my knees, Oh my . . . ," rhyming this with a line of poetry. But then he said, "That's the reason you should marry relatives, Lila."

"What is?" asked Gateefa.

Looking at her, this beautiful plump woman with smooth olive skin, refined tattoos on her forehead and chin, and dark smiling eyes, he explained: "This one, of course, she was young when I married her. She has spent all her adult years, ever since she began fasting, with me. I was already fifteen when she was born; there are fifteen years between us. She was born the first year I fasted Ramadan. I never gave her a thought, though. Not at all. Even though her father—he was my father's brother—the day she was born we had planned to go with him to spend the evening in town. It was Ramadan and we used to go spend the evenings in the market because at the time we were camped in Alamein. Her father said, 'Come on, let's go.' They were waiting for me to come with them, but her mother was giving birth to this one. And when I came from the tent they asked, 'What kept you?' I came and told them, 'She has given birth.'

"My uncle, he was young then—he still used to sing with us young guys at weddings. They asked, 'What did she have?' There was a group of men there, and it wasn't him who asked me but the others. 'She had a girl,' I said. Then he said to me, 'She's your chance. This one I'll give to you. That's done.' The others said to him, 'Tomorrow she'll grow up and they'll come to you offering who knows how many she-camels and you'll give her away. You won't even give your nephew the time of day.' He said, 'No, I swear to God, I won't ask for any brideprice from him.'

"Five years later, when she was only five years old, he died when that mine exploded. You know that story about rubbishing. She was too young to remember. And she left. Her mother didn't have any other children. She had given birth to two other kids, boys, but they didn't live. In that period—he died in 1950, in the eleventh month of 1950, and my grandfather died in the sixth month of 1951, and then my father died in the eleventh month of 1951— within a year—I had to take over the family. A year after Gateefa's father's death, exactly a year, her mother left to go back to her relatives."

"And she took Gateefa with her," I added, knowing this part of the story well.

"Yes, she took Gateefa with her. We took them and all her stuff there, but I would go to visit every two or three months. I'd give them money, for her and her mother." Sagr smiled as he remembered. "At the time she was young. I was the only one who would come to visit. She was so young that when I arrived she'd come running up to me and I'd pick her up and hug her. I'd bring her gifts. When she got a bit older I'd take her back with me to stay with her grandmother. But her maternal grandmother really loved Gateefa, so when she'd come to stay with us here only a week would go by before one of her maternal aunts would come to take her back."

I wondered aloud how old she was then. He thought twelve. It was about then that Sagr began trying to make arrangements to marry. Three of the arrangements fell through because the girls' male cousins claimed the would-be brides away from him. The fourth arrangement was for Safiyya, the woman he eventually married as his second wife. But initially, after he had asked for her hand and paid the brideprice to her father, once again a cousin had asserted his prior claim and Sagr had been forced to look elsewhere.

Haj Sagr complained, "Really! I swear to God, I tried to marry more than seven women. But no matter what, it didn't work out. So then one day my father's cousin came to me—at the time I used to make money by going back and forth to Benghazi to buy goods and to sell camels and sheep and cows; all my brothers except the youngest had married—he came to see us at the household I shared with my older brother.

"He said, 'You don't see or understand anything.' He started scolding us loudly, 'Look, you've asked for five or six women now, and then people have withheld them from you. Don't you see the tribes won't give you their girls? But you've got a cousin who's not so little anymore. Are you going to leave her to others?' He swore, 'May I be forced to divorce my wife if I don't bring some sheep to offer them. I'm going right now to take them the brideprice. She's our girl and no one can take her.' He was a tough man; he had his gun. And he swore, 'May I be divorced if I don't go there today.'

"We protested that she was too young. He threatened, 'Oh really! Well, if that's what you think, then here, here's some money for the brideprice. You go look for a woman!'

"So they went, taking some sheep. And they agreed on the marriage and paid the brideprice. He paid them. And we also arranged to marry my sister Lawz to my cousin on the same day. On the wedding day, though, the men from the other tribe came— Safiyya's brothers. They didn't know any of this and came and found the wedding in progress. 'What do you want?' we asked. 'Well,' they answered, 'we had agreed to give our sister to our kinsmen but now they've released her.' So I said to them, 'Okay, I'll come for her in a few weeks.' I'd already paid the brideprice for Safiyya and everything. A bit later, I told the family what had happened. To celebrate we brought candy and cookies for the children. Gateefa at the time used to like cookies."

At this Gateefa laughed.

"It's true," he went on, laughing, "she'd stand there with the little kids and I'd bring them all cookies. We didn't sleep together. We had held the wedding, but she just ran around the camp as she wished. At least no one else could marry her. She was young, not really a woman, and for two years she lived in the camp not knowing a thing. She'd just play and hang about. I had brought the other woman about three months after the first wedding. After two years or so, Gateefa started thinking about things. She saw what the other woman did and started dressing nicely, pulling herself together. Bit by bit."

He looked at Gateefa, and she laughed with him, mumbling something I couldn't understand. Then he teased, "And then she agreed to me. And the older she got the more beautiful she got."

"Oh, and wasn't she beautiful when she was young?" I asked.

"No," she laughed, "I was ugly."

Sagr began to tease. "She got better and better the more I hugged her. I wouldn't ever scold her. She was important to me. Until then there had been nothing sexual between us. Then she began to know a little bit. And then she had the girls. Finally I said I'll bring another wife. So I brought the other [third] one."

Gateefa pitched in, "He wanted to get a woman who would have sons."

He defended himself. "I wanted sons, do you hear me? No, that's not exactly it."

His senior wife repeated to him what I had once said: that even his third wife, Azza, had not just produced sons. She, too, gave him daughters.

He was impatient. "But I'm telling you the truth, Lila. Everything is hers [Gateefa's]. To this day she's the mistress of my house, she's the one with the last word, her requests are the ones honored. And it will be this way until she dies, until she dies."

Gateefa looked embarrassed.

"No one dares upset her," he added.

I protested. In her defense, I argued that it was just that she bore patiently what came her way.

"I don't mean the kids making her angry. What can I do about that? I mean something else," he said. "Why, just a little while ago Azza came to me, complaining about her. And what did I say? I

said, 'You go ask her forgiveness. You must go kiss the top of her head.' She went and kissed her on her head. Isn't that true? See? Gateefa had hit her."

Gateefa smiled defiantly. "I hit her with a wooden spoon."

When I asked why, she said, "Because she insulted me."

"Listen, Lila," Sagr said, "when Azza came to complain about her I said, 'You go to her room and make up and kiss her on her head.' I said, 'Either you go or I'll divorce you. I'll write your divorce papers and take you home to your relatives.' She went, then and there, although she dragged her heels. Azza went to her and kissed her on her head. What more does she want from me?"

Again Gateefa said something to him that I didn't catch. Then she accused, "But aren't you the one that brought her here?"

"So what? She can't do anything to you, can she?"

But Gateefa wouldn't let him off.

"All of my brothers are married," he protested. "What am I supposed to do? It's not just me—everyone has two or three wives."

Gateefa snorted, "But they're not like this one." When I asked how, she explained, "The other women are decent, they're respectful." Sagr had to agree.

Aren't We All the Same?

That evening, when we were alone, Gateefa reflected on her co-wife Azza. When the Haj had first married Azza, she said, his mother had criticized him for spending so much time with her and putting her in such luxury, setting her up in a separate apartment in Alexandria. He had quipped back that his two other wives were just old donkeys—they'd eat anything, and their clothing was full of fleas. Why worry about them?

Upon hearing about his plan to marry again, Migdim had admonished her son not to. But he had already made the arrangements and paid the brideprice without telling anyone. He reassured

his mother, "She's sweet and pious." I had heard from one of Gateefa's daughters that Migdim had also gone to Azza to warn her against marrying Haj Sagr. "Grandma told her the man was tough, his wives were difficult, and he had lots of children. But my father's wife assured her she'd cherish his children."

But as Gateefa commented, "She was as you see her now."

I knew what she meant. Azza was loud, often swore, and never prayed. She was not unkind, but she was also not always easy to get along with. Stubborn and overworked, she sometimes lost her temper and sometimes withdrew to her room, forcing her children to come with her.

"From the moment she arrived," explained Gateefa, "she couldn't stand it. The first time she came here she only stayed four days. This was twenty days after she married him. Even when she was a bride she had no modesty. She'd wander around the camp talking to people. When she saw him coming home she'd run back excited, 'Sagr has come! Sagr has come!' Why, in those days we women in the camp were so respectful of him that we couldn't even say his name."

That Azza had been treated differently from Gateefa and Safiyya, the other wives, was a strong theme in descriptions of the tensions among them. On my first day in Sagr's household, in October 1978, I'd been told that Azza was different. She was estranged from her husband at the time and living with her brothers, but her co-wives spoke about her. They said she was from Tunisia— meaning, it turned out, that her ancestors came from there. Unlike them, they each told me, she did not veil or wear a red belt, something every married woman in the camp did.

Over the years I would hear Gateefa complain that town women (which Azza was) were not like Bedouin women. Telling a story, in 1980, about the early days of her husband's marriage to Azza, Gateefa commented that he had mellowed after marrying Azza. "She did things," Gateefa explained, "that were unheard of. After that he left us alone. When he first married, he was away a lot,

spending time in Alexandria. Every day or two he'd come home and take one or two hundred pounds to spend on her. There she was, just one woman alone in a house, and yet he would bring three kilos of meat every time he went. Your grandmother Migdim went crazy. She was furious. She yelled that it was not fair, that his children didn't get to see him. 'You spend lots of money on *her* and your children don't get to taste a thing.'

"She scolded and scolded until he finally brought Azza to the camp. Azza stayed with us for thirteen months, and then he said he was taking her home to her family to have her baby. But instead he went and put her in a new house he bought in town. We didn't know about it. When we found out we were angry. All those sheep people bring as gifts for slaughter, and all that money, and your children don't get any?

"Well, Azza had her baby about a week later, and Migdim and I agreed that we had to go pay a visit. We took the children and went in the car. We found Aunt Fatma there. She had heard the news of the baby and figured we would be there, but all she found were Azza's relatives. A house full of them! Her sister, that gypsy, 'giggle giggle,' flirting and laughing all night, playing cards with him [Sagr] in the men's guest room, just the two of them. She'd sit right next to him and 'giggle giggle.' This was something we'd never seen. Even Azza used to talk with him all the time and laugh with him. All that stuff, nightgowns and slips—we didn't know any of it.

"Migdim spent one night there. It was clear that Azza didn't want us there. She insulted us. I had always treated her well, like a person. I had cooked rabbits for her and everything. She treated us badly, and I was furious. The Haj had asked me for my rugs to put in the guest room. When I got there and saw the guest room, I couldn't believe it: pillows and cushions and pads, two couches. Stuff worth six hundred Egyptian pounds. He hadn't told us about any of this. At that time we didn't even own pillows: we used to stuff straw into old burlap sacks—those were our pillows! We had nothing. And the number of sheep they had cooked! We went into the kitchen and found cartons and cartons of dried fat and the sheepskins piled high. A woman alone and all that stuff?

"The next morning when Aunt Fatma and Migdim were leaving, we snuck into the kitchen and gave Fatma a bag full of dried fat to take home with her. Migdim too, she wanted some skins. Later when Azza came in she screamed at me, 'This is mine, he brought it for me!' I yelled back, 'If it wasn't for her you wouldn't have him. You want to deny his mother a few sheepskins?' Even her sister came in and told her to be ashamed of herself, to be quiet. Other things happened, worse and worse things. She was nasty, and my blood was boiling. I felt I was going to explode. My heart got this big!"

As she made a gesture to suggest something enormous, I asked an obvious question. "Were you jealous?"

"No, I wasn't jealous," she insisted. "I was angry that we were being treated unfairly. Aren't we all the same? She had all of this. And food—halva and cheese and bread from the market, when we had hardly ever seen a tin of halva and had to go out and collect every stick of wood for the oven so we could bake a loaf of bread! And she was terrible, insulting. 'This is mine, this is mine,' she'd say.

"In the end I fought with her about the rugs. I had lent him my woven rugs to put down for the guests, but I was angry that they hadn't put ashtrays down. The men had spilled things all over them and the rugs were filthy. Azza fought with me then: 'Take your rugs back. Who needs them? I don't want them in my guest room!' The lady with her bed and her nightgowns and her nice soft blankets.

"I was so furious I wanted to leave that night. If I'd had anywhere else to sleep I would have left that night. . . . I didn't eat at all. First thing in the morning, I demanded that the Haj take me home. He tried to get out of it. He had important business in the market, he argued. 'No, I must go right now. You can take me home first and then go to the market. And I'm taking my rugs,' I said. He agreed to take me home but begged me to leave the rugs for two weeks until the guests stopped coming.

"In the car ride home I really let him have it: for the money spent on her while the rest of his family didn't have anything, a woman who isn't worth even a shoe, and on and on. 'I'm not a real woman if I don't get a house like that myself,' I swore. 'You will see,' I warned him."

"What did he say?" I asked.

"He didn't say a word all the way home. When we got back everyone asked me what was the matter. 'You haven't eaten,' they said. It was true, I had eaten neither dinner nor breakfast, and my face was pale. But I didn't tell them what had happened."

Rivals

This was only the beginning of Gateefa's troubles with her co-wife. Even Sagr found it difficult to live peacefully with his third wife. Of the fourteen years of their marriage, Azza has spent at least four living back with her own relatives. Three of her children were born during these times away, yet the children were also the reason Sagr always decided to take her back.

Gateefa once mused about why Sagr had married Azza: "He saw that she was fat and strong, and that's all. He didn't know what kind of person she was." The problem was her behavior. She did things everyone associated with peasants or townspeople. Once, for instance, some neighbors had scolded her son for something, and Azza set off with barely her hair covered to swear at them. When she got back to the house Sagr came out after her, furious that she had disgraced him by showing herself in such an unseemly way in public and by using such foul language. As she escaped into her room he called out after her, "Shame on you," and spat in her trail.

Azza admits she is stubborn. When she tells the stories of the last two times she fought with Sagr and almost divorced, it is clear how impossible both of them are. It is also clear how far she has fallen from the grace of those first years of special treatment, extra food, nightgowns, and a separate house. Of the second-to-last time she stayed away she says: "I went home the second day of the religious feast. I didn't find my mother at home because she was in Matruh: my sister had just given birth there. The Haj came to pick me up the next day. He said, 'Come home.' I said, 'I won't go.' He said, 'Come.' I said, 'I won't go.' He yelled at my son to get into the car, and I yelled back. Then he said, 'You'll find yourself divorced.' He gave me a slap, but I didn't budge. And he left. He went to find my brother and talked to him about what had happened. My brother came home but didn't say anything. He came bringing chickens. We slaughtered them and I made rice with tomato sauce. My brother came in and asked, 'Are you going to have lunch with us?' I said, 'I'll eat lunch.' He said, 'Don't be upset. Just forget him.' "

Azza gave birth to a daughter at her brother's. After three months her husband sent word that either she should return with the children or he would divorce her and take the children. She agreed to go back, but only for the sake of her children. Because she and Sagr were not sleeping together, she says she was not obligated to cook for her husband or share in any of the household work. Yet she pulled her weight anyway. This changed when a religious authority told Sagr, who wanted to go on the pilgrimage, that he was wrong to eat food cooked by a woman he was no longer married to. His pilgrimage would not be accepted unless he took her back as a wife. So he did, and she got pregnant again, although the boy died.

Another religious feast came around and Azza wanted to go home to see her mother. Everyone in the camp tells a version of the story. Her sister-in-law Fayga tells it this way: "Azza said to him, 'My mother's sick and I want to go see her.' He said no. 'All the women want to go home and see their mothers for the feast—you can't all go at once.' But then he changed his mind. He said, 'I'll take you. The three of you—Gateefa, Azza, and Fayga.' I went and got my bag ready and got dressed, and your Aunt Azza here went and got her bag ready and got dressed. Gateefa said, 'I'll skip this trip.' She knew he was angry. Then he said to Azza, 'If you go, you can consider yourself divorced. If you go now, you'll just be hurting yourself.' But she said, 'I want to go to my mother. I'll just go and come back tomorrow.' He grabbed her and hit her and divorced her. Well, your Aunt Fayga here returned to her room. I didn't go. And your Aunt Azza they took to her relatives, and she didn't come back for nearly a year."

Azza added, "I stayed with my mother for nine months."

Her sister-in-law picked up her sadness. "But now the mother she used to go to has passed away."

Azza never tired of contrasting her husband's home with that of her father. At her family's home they had fruit and meat every day. They had a washing machine and refrigerator. Her brothers bought clothes and nice things for the children. They took them to doctors when they were sick. "Here," she once said, "they let the children run around in rags. They don't pay any attention to them. If they live, they live; if not, so what?"

Sagr's view of her family was quite different, and he was not shy about insulting them, as I discovered one day while sitting with him.

Azza's son came and stood bashfully in the doorway. His father said, "Come sit down with Lila. What did I tell you the other night?" Acting pleased with himself, he said to me, "It was great— you'd like to hear this old poetry."

Azza, it seems, had come to Sagr the other day and told him that her brother had suggested she take her son out of school, since he wasn't doing well. Her brother was willing to offer the boy a chance to work by his side until he learned his uncle's trade; Azza's brother would teach his nephew the skills of a butcher. Sagr had answered angrily: "That's not the work of his father." Whereupon the boy had asked, "What *is* your work, Dad?"

In answer Sagr had told a long tale about the days when the Awlad ʿAli tribes were at war with the tribes of Libya. The fighting was serious at the time—around 1929 or 1930, when Sagr was born. The Sanussi family—good pious people and reciters of the Qur'an who were never involved in fighting—had finally agreed to arrange a peace. The tribes assembled, tribe by tribe, each with its "colonel" and twenty horsemen, at a huge tent (actually four tents sewn together) pitched at the border of their territories.

The Libyan tribes wanted to start the proceedings, but the Awlad 'Ali tribesmen objected: Said Hafyaan had not yet arrived. Finally he rode up. So far, as each of the other men had arrived, some had stood up to greet them and some had remained seated. But when this man arrived, even before he had dismounted, all had risen in respect. He left his horse, came in, and shook hands with the men one by one.

One man, however, did not rise. This was 'Abd as-Salaam Bu-l-Kizza, a Libyan pasha dressed in decorated robes of the highest-quality baize. Said went around the circle greeting everyone in turn but passed by the seated one.

When he got all the way around they said to him, "You didn't greet 'Abd as-Salaam."

"I greeted those who troubled themselves to stand up. He's comfortably seated, so I thought I'd greet him once I got comfortable too." Once he had sat down, he shouted across the tent, "Hey, how are you, 'Abd as-Salaam, you Tightwad" (mispronouncing and thus changing the meaning of his surname).

The man, who did not know him, answered, "Hey you, what do you do where you come from?"

Said Hafyaan's answer surprised him:

> "My work is a strong steed
> that rides alone at the head of an army.
> When he approaches the gathered tents
> he bursts apart his harness.
> The noble invite and are generous;
> they are accustomed to giving,
> while the lowly begin to fret
> even over the smallest biteful."

Sagr eagerly explained. The Libyan had expected to hear what kind of leader he was; instead, through poetry, Said Hafyaan showed what the work of great men was: generosity and respect. He was insulting the pasha.

After this answer, 'Abd as-Salaam stood up and walked all the way across the tent, just to shake his hand. He knew Said Hafyaan to be a real man.

"So," Sagr finished with a smile, his green eyes flashing, "I said to my son here, 'Your mother's relatives may do that kind of work, but that's not the work of your father.'"

Despite his feelings toward Azza and her family, Sagr kept agreeing to take Azza back because he wanted all his children together with him. Yet he found it hard to live with her, and he knew that Gateefa did not sympathize. Once, after an argument with Azza, he sat fuming in Gateefa's room. He turned to me and complained that Gateefa made his life difficult for him. She was like a press, he said: she turned the screw just when he had managed to forget how rotten his home life was. Yes, he admitted, he knew well enough that he had two wives who hadn't worked out. That was bad enough. But she never let him forget. "She's angry," he went on, "because I married other wives after her."

Although she said it with humor, her retort was quick. "No one told you to do it. It's your own doing. You brought it on yourself."

The Haj conceded this. He had been fortunate to get a wife who was really special, he said. And he wasn't one of those ignorant men who don't understand things. But he lamely offered as his final excuse the religious saying "In the moment of God's power a man is blinded." He added, "One must bear patiently one's fate."

Gateefa was reluctant to absolve him of responsibility for his bad judgment. She had her own views on men's choices, modeled perhaps on two folktales she liked to tell. Both showed the difference between a good husband and a bad. In one story, the husband rewards the good and clever first wife and punishes the beautiful but idiotic second wife. In the other story, the good co-wife, who is also, perhaps significantly for Gateefa, a senior wife, does not fare so well. But this time it is because the man is of bad stock.

The first tale goes something like this:

There was a man who had two wives. One was beautiful, ample, and fair-skinned; she was also stupid. The other was small, clever, and energetic. After he sheared some sheep he said to them, "I'm going to Siwa to get dates. When I come back I'll bring the pack camels to the one who has woven a new tent. I'll unload only the small calf in front of anyone still in an old tent." And he left.

The clever one started spinning at night and during the day worked inside her tent. The other one, the beautiful one, did nothing. She was pleased with herself and didn't do a thing. And the small one was busy, busy, busy, every night. She set up a loom and wove the new tent.

When she saw this, the fat one came to the busy one and asked, "When did you do your spinning? What am I going to do?"

The clever wife answered, "I'd take my wool to the sea and say, 'Spin it.'"

The woman went off. She gathered together her wool and took it to the sea. She left it there by the sea. Fifteen days later she went back for it.

The clever one asked her, "Did you finish your spinning?"

"No," she said.

"Did you go to the sea?" the busy one then asked.

"Yes, but I found my wool just as I had left it. Except for some seaweed on it, nothing."

"What did you put with it?" asked the clever one. She suggested, "Put some rice and dates and flour and stuff and put the wool close to the water and say, 'O sea, spin,' and leave it. What if you tried putting it in the water?"

So the woman went off and put her wool in the sea. She stayed away, stayed away, stayed away, and then went back.

"Sister, did he take it?" her co-wife asked.

"Yes."

"And what did he say?"

The woman responded, "He said to me, 'Duvv, duvv, duvv,' " imitating the sound of waves.

"That's the way he spins and twines. Just be patient," said the clever one.

But the other one thought, "She's spun and woven her tent and twisted the ends and pitched it, and he's about to come back and I haven't made a tent." She asked her co-wife, "What should I do?"

The clever one suggested that she take a sackful of flour and make dough out of it and then cover the top of her old tent with the dough so it would be white and look new.

So the woman made some dough and slapped it on the tent. She plastered the whole top of the tent. But when the dough dried it started to crack and fall apart. Birds came and picked holes in it, and the chickens jumped on top of the tent and pecked at it.

One night after the two women had gone to sleep their husband came back. He circled around the tents. He saw the black stripes on the new tent of the quick wife. And he saw that the tent of the big beautiful wife had dough stuck on it. So he unloaded the pack camels in front of the clever one's tent and tied only the young calf in front of the other's.

A few days later he said to them, "Your relatives have sent for you. There's a wedding. What will you take with you as gifts?"

The clever one wanted to go. She thought, "What shall I take with me on the visit?" She got her load of dates and kneaded them with butter and made little date balls.

The other wife had only a small amount of dates. So she said, "I'll save up some shit and fill my sack." She began to shit each day and put the shit in the sack.

The clever one kneaded the dates with butter and made little balls and put them into her sack and then went to her husband. He asked, "Have you gathered everything together? What are you going to take with you when you go to visit your relatives?"

She said, "I'm ready and packed, but I don't know about her."

He went over and opened the other wife's sack and found it full of shit. He loaded it onto one camel. Then he put the clever wife's two sacks, one with dates and the other with date balls, on the other camel and they set off.

Then he asked them, "What will you ride on?" He told the beautiful one to take a palm stalk and ride on it until she reached her relatives. She got on her stick and rode off. The other one rode on the camel with him. The one ran and ran, and they rode and rode. The man and his clever wife arrived first, and the people asked, "Where's your other wife?"

The man said, "She's on her way. She's riding on her stick. Here are the sweets she's been saving for you."

Her mother opened the sack and found it full of shit. "Here's your daughter," the man said, "take her back. I won't stay married to her."

The second tale Gateefa told about co-wives ended differently. It began as the story of a young man who, with his brothers, had kicked out their mother. They were poor, and so he began to wander around looking for work. A rich family took him in, gave him animals to raise, found a wife for him, built him a house, and gave him a slave to herd for him. He became rich and proud and suddenly announced that he wanted to leave that household to live on his own. They were disturbed and didn't understand why, but he insisted and took his wife and slave away. Not satisfied with the wife they had arranged for him, he then married a second wife he chose himself.

One day he announced that he wanted to go on the pilgrimage to Mecca. He told his wives and slave to stay camped in the same place until he returned. He had the two women [their genitals] sewn up as a precaution to preserve their chastity.

Gateefa, for whom this detail was as unusual as it is for us, proceeded dramatically with the telling. "Every day, the slave went off to herd the camels and then came home to the camp where the two wives were. Now, the older wife, well, I guess she was pathetic, modest. And the wife that he took second, she was one of those who . . . Well, shortly after he left, the young wife said to the slave, 'Let's move camp.' The older wife said, 'No, we shouldn't move. He told us to stay here until he returned.' The young wife said, 'No, I want to set up my tent in a new place. Let's go to another area.' So they moved.

"The young wife had undone the stitches. Right away this woman said, 'Come here,' to the slave. The other one remained sewn up, the old one. So they moved and set up camp in an empty area. There was nothing to eat or drink there, and the camels and the sheep started going hungry and dying. The carcasses of the dead beasts lay there, and crows came to eat them. Then each day the crows would circle around the camp. As the slave was putting medicine on the camels he'd say:

> 'Crows make people happy but I'm afraid of crows
> they bring us the shadow of the one who's longing
> and blinded from missing us.'

The slave was afraid, and the old wife knew what the crows meant: they herald the arrival of people who have been away. The young one didn't know.

"Then one day, the man arrived home. He said to them, 'You moved camp. I wouldn't have found you if the crows hadn't brought me. I started walking in their trail, every night in a place, every night in a different place. I moved with the crows until I found you.'

"That one had met him, the young one. She had come running out to greet him saying,

> 'In my joy for you
> I undid it just for you
> but Ahmad's mother is still all sealed up.' "

At this Gateefa commented, "See what women are like!" Then she continued, "So he went to the old one and found her disgusting,

bound and putrid." She laughed again. "He said to her, go away.
I divorce you. And he returned and took back the young wife, and
they moved camp."

I wonder if Gateefa sometimes feels there is some of the same
injustice in her own world. Her husband, too, had found her grand
co-wife Azza attractive and, blind to her faults, married her se-
cretly, against the wishes of his mother. Unlike the good husband
in the first story, he had seemed to judge his wives not by their
virtues and their actions but by their looks and the life-style they
represented.

Gateefa presents herself as stoically putting up with what her
husband has imposed on her. Take, for example, her version of
what happened when Sagr married Safiyya as his second wife,
which differs from his. He presents himself as a victim of circumstances, a man with a child bride interested only in cookies. Gateefa
gives the same basic facts about the marriage: Sagr had planned to
marry Safiyya, but her cousins claimed her; he went around looking for a wife, but everywhere he went the girls were claimed away
from him; finally he ended up with her; after a while he ran into
Safiyya's brother in the market; her brother said, "If you still want
her, her cousin has released her."

But then she told her side of the story: "Right before the
wedding to Safiyya he took me home to visit my mother, just for
a visit. My mother had bought me a silk dress and a fancy slip, and
I came back with them. On the night before the wedding my aunts
dressed me up—they were furious with him—and they did my
hair. My hair was long and thick and my braided topknot *this
big*"—she gestured with her hands—"in those days. They hennaed
my feet and hands just like a bride. You should have seen me. I
wasn't upset. I didn't care about the man. They brought the bride,
and everyone was shocked. He had told everyone, 'She's like the
moon, wait till you see her!' But she was thin and yellow. She had
been sick before she came and was sick for fifteen days after she
came. And I was beautiful—healthy and plump and fair-skinned.
Everyone said I wouldn't stay—'She'll never put up with it,' they
said.

"I really didn't want the man. From the first night I used to escape and go wherever there were other women I could sleep behind. I'd climb into their midst to sleep. Especially our neighbor. She'd threaten him, 'I'll beat you if you come nearer.' "

Having heard a friend tease her with the same tale her husband had told about how she had come around to the idea of being married, I asked: "And so after Safiyya came you changed?"

Her answer was short. "I got a little more sensible."

By the time I came into their lives the Haj had separated from Safiyya, although he still supported her. He said it was by mutual consent, but I knew the situation was more complicated. The point was, she had eight children and was not about to go anywhere because it would mean leaving them. Bitter and sad though she was, she nevertheless did not question the justice of men marrying more than one wife. For her the problem felt like one of a preference for cousins over outsiders.

Still, she and Gateefa appeared to get along well. Gateefa says that Sagr had treated the two of them fairly in the days before he married Azza. Gateefa's daughters remember that their mother and Safiyya used to argue when they lived together but that the troubles lasted only a few days and the women never told their husband. Azza, of course, always tried to involve Sagr, even though her pleas to him had begun to backfire.

The Fight

Azza could be hurtful, as Gateefa had discovered. She told me, on a hot day in June, about their fight during Ramadan—a story I might not have heard if Gateefa had not been angry with her husband. When an unexpected respite from the stream of visitors left him alone he had gone, as usual, to rest in her room, and I went to sit with him. He apologized for being so busy that we hardly got a chance to talk. He wanted to recite some poetry for me. Poetry, in his view, was important because it was about events that really happened. Then he began a story about two paternal cousins, a tale that Gateefa would interrupt.

A young man from a poor family wanted to marry his cousin, whose family was rich. He went to her father, his uncle, to ask for her hand, but the man said, "Go ask her." When he did, she refused him saying:

"I'm not your prey and you aren't my falcon
nor will your [gun]barrel fit my riflebutt
God will be kind to you and you'll find someone else."

Rebuffed, the young man decided to leave the camp to find work. He warned his relatives that if anyone tried to marry this girl he would kill him. He left, and God opened the way for him and he found work. After five, six, or seven years he returned. He came back riding a beautiful horse. He had camels and money, but no wife. He threw a big party and everyone came, and they found him much changed. He had servants and offered a great feast. He had paid a call on everyone in the camp except his cousin. Everyone came bringing sheep to honor him. But they were surprised—"It's odd that he has servants but no wife," they said.

People went to tell his cousin all about him. They told her he was a real man now and they spoke highly of him. No one had dared to marry her because they had heard about his warning. She waited and waited but he never came to greet her, so she said, "I'll go say hello to my cousin." She dressed up and went over to where he was. He greeted her and then asked who she was. She told him and he said, "Welcome." He slaughtered a sheep for her and hosted her generously, and then he had his servant give her a gift, a pearl necklace. But he wanted her to know that it was not he but his servant who had given it.

She started thinking about the situation and got worked up. She said, "He's the one who prevented me from marrying and he won't say a word about it." So she sent an emissary who conveyed the message that it was his fault she was still unmarried.

He answered, "I treated her well when she came as a guest and I didn't get angry at what she once said. Get out of here—after what she said to me, what can I say?"

"I'll apologize," she said, and told the messenger to let the man know that she would be willing to marry him.

"Fine, if she's willing, I'm willing," he said. He was lying. "What does she demand for a brideprice? What about the trousseau?" He brought everything she demanded and held a wedding feast the likes of which no one had ever seen.

When the guests left he told her, "I swear by God, you must tell me again what it was you said to me then."

She pleaded, "I was young. I was wrong. I'll be like your servant now."

He repeated his question, "What did you say? Say it again."

"I've forgotten it."

So he recited her verse, and she hung her head. "I have something to say too," he then announced.

> "I forbid myself to touch you
> and forbid myself your bed and beddings
> bring the camel and gather your stuff on it
> and wander where you want to fly
> for I'm not your prey nor am I your falcon."

Haj Sagr explained this to me. The man forbade himself this woman and would not touch her because she had hurt him. He wanted to make her blood boil. He threw her out and proudly refused to accept any of the brideprice back, even the wedding gifts he had given her. And the next morning he held another wedding and married someone else.

Just as Sagr was reaching the end, Gateefa came in to tell us that lunch was ready. He ignored her, intent on finishing the story. He admired the young man for his response, commenting, "He really burned her!"

At this Gateefa said sharply, "He only felt the ways that she hurt him. He didn't feel what he did to her."

Sagr fell silent at this surprisingly pointed remark. She left the room. When I joined her later, I asked why she had said that. She repeated her remark, and this time there was no doubt that she had, as the Haj and I had both sensed at the time, meant that comment for him. She had accused him of insensitivity to the pain he caused others (herself?) and shown sympathy for women mistreated by men.

She may have been smarting from a remark Sagr had made a couple of days earlier as we drove back from their nephew's wedding. Both Gateefa and Azza were in the car, so he made a point of commenting on how many beautiful women he had seen when he went in to shake hands with his aunts. He didn't understand, he said, why all those men who were nobodies should have more beautiful wives than he had. Neither of his wives smiled. Nor did I. I saw tears welling in their eyes, but they said nothing. I protested, trying to look disapproving. I didn't want him (or them) to think he had an ally.

In our conversation Gateefa referred to this remark, saying that the point her husband seemed to have missed was that all those other women looked beautiful because they were comfortable. Unlike hers, their husbands didn't impose troubles and worries on them, troubles like Azza. To illustrate, she described the fight she had had with Azza during Ramadan, the one her husband had mentioned to demonstrate how well he treated her.

They had argued because of the children. She had been cooking dinner when Azza's son came and helped himself to a bowl of vegetable stew, even though it was barely cooked yet. His little brother and Gateefa's young daughter started crying because they wanted to share it with him. He wouldn't let them and then hit her daughter with a sandal, twice. She had yelled at him either to put the food back until it was cooked or to share it with them. He refused. She threw a plastic sandal at him.

Azza had shouted out, "Are you beating my son?"

Gateefa had answered, "What, it's hard on you when I hit your son but not hard on you when he hits my daughter?"

Azza threatened to go home to her family. Her brothers were alive, she added defiantly, implying that they would defend her.

Gateefa told her to go ahead. "Go home," she had said; "you're the one who came to me!"

Azza insulted her back, "You who don't have any kin."

Gateefa slapped her on the cheek. "These are my kin, and this is my house."

After Azza's son had eaten dinner and then eaten again with his father, he went to bang on his mother's door. But she was not there: she had gone across the road to the rest of the camp. When Gateefa reported to her husband what had happened he said, "Good riddance."

Azza returned the next day, brought back by the Haj's sister Lawz, visiting her mother Migdim at the time, who pleaded her case. Azza accused Gateefa of, among other things, hitting her and saying that she had chased after the Haj to marry him—half of it lies, according to Gateefa.

I interrupted here. "And is it true, as Haj Sagr said, that he forced Azza to go kiss you on the head and apologize?"

"Yes, it happened," Gateefa replied.

What had incensed Gateefa was the charge that she had no kin. To have no kin is to be vulnerable and isolated, since the family is such a crucial source of identity and of support. For a woman, having brothers behind you allows you to stand tall in the world, and especially in your husband's community. Gateefa kept saying, "God Bless my kin. These *are* my kin, and this is my house."

Isolation

Azza's insult had stung, though, because it held a half-truth. Although she was Haj Sagr's first cousin and a member of his kin group, Gateefa had no father and no brothers; and she was isolated in the women's community. The problem was not that she wasn't central to all family functions, including representing the family group to outsiders. Indeed, she was perhaps the most distinguished woman of her generation in this family, having always been a clever storyteller, a talented singer, and a moral woman with good judgment who had grown into her role as a senior wife and mother with grace and dignity. Her aunts were affectionate with this only child of a favorite brother killed so young in the rubbishing accident, and several cousins also obviously enjoyed her company. All of them liked to stay with her, spending happy hours talking, when they came home to the camp for visits.

The family was not the problem; rather, the women of the camp had isolated her. I had seen the split widen since first coming to live in the community and assumed that it was because Gateefa had moved with the Haj (about the time of my arrival) into his new house across the road. Absorbed in her own busy household, she saw less and less of the women with whom she had spent all her married life. So alienated was she that she refused to give her eldest daughter, Sabra, in marriage to one of the boys in the camp. Among the other families, though, ties multiplied as sisters agreed to let their children marry each other. Even some of the women from outside the community who had married in were related to each other and tried to have their children marry. With each intermarriage between households, Gateefa and her children became more cut off.

Yet she claimed that these women had always ganged up against her, an opinion that her maternal aunt confirmed. As we sat alone, this older woman lowered her voice to tell me that the others had never been good to Gateefa. She had recited some poems about this eight years earlier when she came to help her niece sew a huge new ceremonial tent. A woman starting such a large project expects other women in the community to help out when they can, but hardly anyone came to help. These poems, then, were about Gateefa's loneliness.

> Friends in times of ease
> I found out in need were enemies . . .

Your worries increased, my love
watch you don't pick up terrible illnesses . . .

They watered the loved one with a waterwheel
of bitterness until she was drenched . . .

Despair over them, oh loved one
made you a stranger even to those your father begot . . .

What lay behind Gateefa's isolation in the women's community I can never know fully, not least because my attachment to her is well known by the other women. The makeup of the community and the strength of some of the alliances and kinship ties among its core women are partial explanations. Gateefa herself, often in justifying why she did not feel it unfair to receive gifts from the Haj's wealthy friends, alluded to this fact when she pointed out that she, unlike those women, had no sisters.

There was also the problem of the matriarch Migdim. According to Gateefa, her mother-in-law had always sided with Safiyya. I knew from experience that Migdim in fact often did defend this co-wife and criticize her son for treating her unfairly; she also tried to make sure that Safiyya got attention and goods even though she was now separated from her husband. This favoritism was not a new thing, Gateefa confided as we walked home after a visit to her mother-in-law. She recalled how Safiyya's mother used to come to visit, staying for as long as a week or ten days; when it was time for her to go home, the two matriarchs (the Haj's mother, Migdim, and her niece, married to Migdim's husband's younger brother) would run around like mad gathering up good things with which to fill the visiting woman's bag—butter, henna, whatever they could find. When Gateefa's mother came to visit, in contrast, making a special point of complimenting them by announcing that she had come to pay a call on her relatives, she would arrive with her bag full of things to give away, but when she left the old women wouldn't budge. She had come with a full sack and they let her go home with it empty.

"Isn't this something that hurts?" Gateefa wanted to know. Her mother, though, would tell her not to worry, not to do anything. One should not respond to people with wrongs, she would say. Gateefa admires her mother. "That's the way she is. She even tells me not to hit the children. When I ask why, she says, 'God is with you. Don't be like the others.' She's never said an angry word."

I was surprised to hear about this rudeness to her mother and asked why it happened. Gateefa was bitter. "You've only seen my mother now that she's grown old. But if you'd seen her before. . . . Her brothers-in-law, my uncles, really liked her. They always went to see her, and she'd honor them, be respectful of them. They liked her a lot. The two women, their wives, used to say that she must have done magic because the men would always come and sit with her. And they were afraid that my uncle would marry her as a second wife."

Was it common for men to marry their brothers' widows?

"If the woman is willing," Gateefa answered. "They had sent someone to ask her if she'd be willing to marry him. She'd said, 'No, no, no!' But there is a hatred from way back. My mother-in-law is difficult."

To complicate matters, the Haj's eldest sister, Dhahab, had married a man whose badly treated senior wife was the sister of Gateefa's mother. Migdim would certainly have sided with her own daughter. I do not know if this situation affected relations because I never heard those stories. All I could gather was that Gateefa may have been made to suffer for having a beautiful and good mother who was a threat to her sisters-in-law. These rivalries were part of the past, but the present was also tied up in unspoken ways with jealousy over my special closeness to this woman with no sister of her own.

Outsiders

Gateefa's maternal aunt, to explain why things were so hard for her niece, once remarked that there was too much work to do and her co-wives would not relieve Gateefa of it. Further, she whispered, the women in the community were jealous because they felt Gateefa got things they didn't get. Outsiders always asked about Gateefa and liked her, she added. This made the others envious.

There was little doubt that I was part of this world of outsiders who liked Gateefa and brought her gifts. But I hardly felt that my small gifts even began to make up for what she gave me. She was indeed gentle and gracious to strangers. I still remember the kindness she showed me on my first visit alone to the community. She had looked at me warmly, concerned about my comfort. She spoke slowly and looked for words I would understand, asking me if I needed to go to the bathroom, if I wanted to rest. I was tired from the strain of sitting with people I did not know or much understand. She took me to her room, spread out a small mattress and pillow, and lay down on the floor next to me as I rested. I remember being so grateful to her as we lay in the cool semidarkness away from the sun and the crowd of women and children that had gathered around me asking questions, obviously talking about me, and wanting to look at everything in my bag.

On many other occasions I watched Gateefa graciously host guests, not just visiting Bedouin women (everyone knew the conventions for that encounter), but the families of Egyptian men who came to see her husband as well. She made special efforts to put them at ease, bringing them special food and sitting with them, suspending her own moral judgments to converse with them. An Egyptian friend of the Haj's once brought along his wife and college-age daughter. Gateefa politely ignored the shortness of the girl's dress and asked the mother and daughter all about the young woman's fiancé. The visitors enthusiastically talked about him and about the country clubs the couple went to and the things they did together. Gateefa smiled kindly and listened. She did not even hint at what her eavesdropping daughters were later to howl about: the sheer scandalousness of talking about a fiancé as if a girl were anxious to marry, not to mention admitting that she spent time with him.

Gateefa's dignity as a hostess, a role thrust upon her as senior wife, was often appreciated, and she and her children were sometimes sent gifts by the Haj's friends. One man who had built an extravagant villa on some land owned by Haj Sagr was particularly generous. In that case, however, Gateefa's sense of self-respect, and ultimately her pride, made her disinclined to be hospitable.

I had heard about these new neighbors when I came for a visit one winter. The man was reputed to be rich, originally from the Sudan but working in Saudi Arabia. His Egyptian wife, they said, had been an airline stewardess. I soon saw this woman for myself. One day, a Mercedes drove up to the house. Out stepped a woman with makeup, frosted hair, and large dangling earrings; she wore high-heeled black patent leather shoes and a long fashionable red sweater over black pants. When her husband was taken into the men's guest room she came with us into the house, where we put cushions down for her in Gateefa's room. Gateefa sat with her politely; the other women in the household came in to greet her. When they went off to prepare the food, I ended up alone with her.

She was curious about me and horrified that I was speaking the Bedouin dialect. She told me it was not proper Arabic and that I should not learn from these people. She let it drop that she had numerous American and English friends from her stewardess days and that she used to go to parties at an English language institute I knew about in Cairo. I was uncomfortable, resenting her assumption that I would share her sense of superiority or that we had any bond.

Haj Sagr came in after we had eaten. He sat close to her—too close—and teased her in a way I had never seen him treat any Bedouin woman. He joked with her about a land deal she wanted to make with him. Then quickly, and in dialect, he said something to me and Gateefa about her. He then made fun of the woman for not having understood what we said. Politely (and pointedly), he offered her cigarettes, which she willingly took and smoked in front of him, something no Bedouin woman her age would have done.

The couple had come to invite us to dinner in their villa, to eat the lamb the Haj had given them as the traditional welcome for new neighbors. That evening we prepared to go. Gateefa put on one of her good dresses, her best colorful gold-threaded socks, and doused herself with cologne. She dressed her youngest daughter, the two-year-old, in her only Western-style dress, torn though it was in the seams. The Haj, whose robes were always clean and pressed, put on a stunning white robe and draped his rich wool cloak around his shoulders. His sons begged to go too, and when he agreed they ran off to wash their faces and find their shoes. The little girls were crying as we piled into the car; they did not want to be left behind. So we grabbed them too and headed off.

The villa was large and indescribably lavish. Gateefa and the children stared. The boys touched the wall, papered with a life-size portrait of a horse. In the cavernous living room, draped with silky curtains that divided it into quadrants and covered the ceilings, one wall was decorated with a giant poster of a Caribbean beach scene. The elaborate moldings had been painted green, their shadows caught by the red lamps that lit the entire space. Leaving our shoes at the door, we padded in across yards of fake Oriental carpets and perched gingerly on the yellow satin banquettes that lined the walls.

The mixed-sex situation was unusual for Gateefa, who sat in silence. The children, too, were wide-eyed and quiet. Our host offered to bring a kerosene heater in and then the television. This they turned on and began to watch, the Haj and our host and hostess meanwhile making conversation. After about twenty minutes the Haj's brother arrived with a friend to join us for dinner. They were hurried into another quadrant and a curtain drawn on them, since as a nonkinsman Bedouin the friend could not politely mix with the Haj's wife. This was too much for Gateefa. After a few minutes she whispered to me that it wasn't right to draw the curtains on those men; she didn't feel comfortable watching television while they sat over there by themselves. She persuaded me to get up with her and, taking the girls with us, to move to the main bedroom down the hall.

Our hostess joined us there, still chain-smoking as she had done in front of her husband. She was relaxed with him, bantering with him in a public way that was unimaginable for Gateefa. The woman took us on a tour to show off the house. It was uncanny the way this family I felt so close to and who usually seemed so ordinary suddenly appeared, as I saw them through our hostess's eyes, like ragamuffins or Gypsies. They ranged through the house touching everything, looking wildly from one new object to the next. When our hostess left us alone again in the bedroom the children jumped up to touch the velvety blankets piled high on the bed, sprayed themselves from the five bottles of cologne arranged on the dressing table, ran into the bathroom to wash their faces and hands and arms with the brand-new bar of soap that lay on the sink. Their splashing resulted in a trail of mud on the ceramic floor tiles.

Everything in the house was new. To me the Italian lacquered bedroom set, the shiny mirrors, and the gleaming red porcelain bathroom fixtures looked grotesque. Was it because our mirrors back at the camp were plastic framed, hand held, and usually chipped in the corners? Was it because our bathroom had paint splattered all over it, fixtures that did not work, and no running water? Was it because the two beds in the Haj's house, a grand and foreign house compared to other families', were held together with rope and painted crudely with a simulated wood design? Was it because we kept our precious bars of soap hidden so people would not walk off with them, and our bottles of cologne locked in wooden chests, to be used only before going visiting or, for the boys, before going to the mosque on Friday? I felt caught in between: I knew how to live in such a house and they did not, but I also knew how to read such a house as the tasteless display of people who have suddenly acquired too much money. Gateefa and her children only saw clean, luxurious goods in quantities that awed them.

I was caught in between in an even more direct way later that evening when our hostess began to discuss veiling with me. She had pulled out a sequined cocktail dress to show me what she was going to wear to a party in Alexandria the following evening. This led to a discussion of what her life in Saudi Arabia was like and what she wore there. When Gateefa stepped out of the room she commented to me, "Their ways are certainly different."

I recommended, half-joking, that she read my book to find out more; in it I had explained why Bedouin women veiled and avoided men.

She cut me off, "Oh, I know them well. They veil their faces but do all sorts of things."

I disagreed. She insisted that in Saudi Arabia she knew it to be true, thereby implying that the same was true of Gateefa and the other Awlad 'Ali. I protested angrily that perhaps some were like that but certainly not most.

Weeks later, I reported this conversation to Gateefa. She was indignant. She countered with stories about the Egyptian stewardess. Gateefa had been embarrassed the first time the woman had visited their house because she had sat with the men in the guest room, leaning back in her short dress with her legs stretched out in front of her. Gateefa whispered that the woman drank liquor. She commented on what the woman had been wearing the day I met her. Making a suggestive hand gesture, she showed how the outlines of the woman's genitals pressed through her stretch pants.

Later, Gateefa would tell me that ever since I had passed on to her what the woman had said about them and their veils, she had felt sick even looking at her. There were, indeed, limits to her graciousness to outsiders.

Intimacy

Gateefa was somewhat more dependent on her husband than other women were. From the early days when her mother-in-law criticized her and defended her co-wife Safiyya, Haj Sagr had learned to guess where the truth lay. He never fought with her, she said, which made the others suspect her of having done magic. With a laugh she tossed aside that idea; it was just that unlike the others she never talked back, she was too afraid of his temper. When I came to live with them just after their move to the new house, set apart from the rest of the camp, she began to know her husband in a new way. "You know, Lila," she confided several years later, "before you came to live with us I'd never spent an evening with him. He always spent his evenings with his brothers in their mother's room." I had, in fact, noticed how quiet she was at first when we sat all together in the evenings.

She is still reserved with Sagr. "She won't talk to me," he complained once when I found them sitting silently, side by side, enjoying the breeze at sunset. For all his proud talk of honoring her as a sister, knowing her since she was a child, and trusting her, sometimes he seems to know her not at all. I saw them as well matched: both intelligent, articulate, insightful about people and knowledgeable about life, good at telling stories, fond of poetry, generous, and self-respecting. Yet he seemed to have no idea that she was a good poet and singer. She had shared with me hundreds of poems and had begun to teach me to appreciate them. But he was surprised once when, sitting in the back of the car he drove to pick up the bride, she sang the requisite wedding songs. "Hey, she's not half bad!" This was the first time he had ever heard her sing.

Another time, flipping through an article in *Natural History* I had written about them, Sagr had peered at the photographs. He didn't have his glasses on and asked, "Who's this?" about a photograph of Gateefa. She and I laughed. He looked closely and said, "She was a gazelle then." I sometimes sensed that he regretted not appreciating what he had, caught up as he had been for so long in making his family wealthy, building his reputation, and striving for sons.

When Gateefa gave birth to her ninth daughter, just before I left, he seemed to take it in stride. Although he spent the evening on which she had her baby listening to poetry with his male guests, this was not unusual; men always stay away from women's affairs like giving birth. But he went the next morning to see Gateefa, breaking the convention of a forty-day avoidance. Even though she had some women visitors from the community, he came in with his cassette player to share with her a tape he had just received from an old friend of theirs who had gone to Libya twenty years earlier. The young women with Gateefa all jumped up to leave, too modest to sit with, much less listen to a tape in the presence of, a man of his stature. Only one older cousin of theirs stayed to witness Haj Sagr affectionately offer his wife the cigarette he knew she desperately wanted. Later this woman would tell everyone how much this familiarity had impressed her.

Every day Haj Sagr spent time with his senior wife in her confinement. Their eldest daughter had once remarked how impossible her father was when Gateefa was away: it was bad enough when she left the house for a few hours; when she went away for days at a time—to visit her mother or to attend a wedding or funeral—the Haj just wandered around and didn't know what to do with himself. He would start picking on his children. That was why he always fetched her back from these visits sooner than most other women were brought back, and sooner than he would bring back his other wives. Indeed, it seemed to me that he did not feel truly comfortable anywhere but in her company.

The same could not be said of her, but perhaps I had this impression because she was so aware of the social impropriety of public affection. Also, she made no secret of her resentment of the burdens he placed on her everyday life. One day a friend who was grooming her commented on how grey her hair was getting. "It's the women who've made you go grey," she suggested in a loud voice. Looking over at Azza, Gateefa said, "It's Azza. She's the one who's made me go grey. She does things that hurt one's insides."

She took little consolation from being her husband's current favorite, expressed most openly in his favoritism toward her children. He was especially affectionate with the younger ones, even though most were girls. When he took his turn with Azza, spending the night in her section of the house, Gateefa's youngest daughter would go in to play with him first thing in the morning. She would pick up his plastic bag of medicines to bring back to her mother's section. He encouraged her in this and delighted in telling people about it. He would also play a game with her. Because she followed him everywhere and crawled on him looking for hugs and kisses, he would instruct her: "Hey Little Nura, go smell your mother's veil. Is it sweet?"

"Sweet," she'd whisper, and he would laugh.

"And what about Azza's veil?" Coaching her, he would turn up his nose and make a noise, "Peeuw!" Nura would imitate him and they would giggle.

Gateefa may resent what he has imposed on her, but she remains loyal to her husband, who is also, after all, her close relative. She takes responsibility for running his household, she protects his property, and she tries to uphold his reputation. She fears for him when he goes off to mediate disputes, knowing the dangers of angry men. She is proud of his standing in the world and his generosity to guests as well as to the women and children of the whole community, for whom he brings gifts when he goes on the pilgrimage or holds a celebration. She cares for all his children, sometimes protecting them from the wrath of their own mothers. She once took care of Azza's children for weeks when their mother left in anger. She would never disgrace him.

She worked hard at the wedding of her husband's oldest son, his son by Safiyya. She wanted it to be a success. Her women friends and relatives congratulated her and gave her as many gifts as they gave her co-wife, the boy's mother. As always at weddings, she sang many songs. To show her joy, she also danced. The family had much to celebrate. The boy had recovered from a heart condition that had troubled him for years, thanks to an expensive operation paid for by the Haj. He could now marry. Moreover, the family had just avenged after ten long and painful years the murder of a dear cousin. The anger and humiliation were over. Sagr's brothers and cousin had been detained for forty days, but the authorities had released them: no one was willing to testify against them. The wedding came at the end of these troubles.

Gateefa sang at this wedding two songs to encourage her husband's son as he went to his bride—a tense moment requiring, among other things, sheer courage.

> Son, be like your kin!
> strong willed and steady eyed . . .

Even facing the government of Egypt
their eyes were steady, they didn't falter . . .

Her songs were also songs of praise for her husband and his
brothers. The most touching of her songs was one her mother-
in-law recited to me later; it expressed an intimacy not of direct
affection but of understanding. On the night before the wedding
she sang about how her husband must have felt:

All of his desires achieved
on now calm seas he unfurled his sail . . .

Chapter 3

REPRODUCTION

Paradise lies under the feet of mothers.

Tradition of the Prophet Muhammad

It was a long walk, past fields of green barley shoots edged with daisies, poppies, and wildflowers—purple, orange, and pink. Ahead, the unplanted fields were a strangely soft blue, covered, as we would soon see, with a haze of tiny white flowers that extended even to the roots of the dusty olive trees. From the distant houses, their windows like black eyes in wide yellow faces, children came running to greet us.

We stepped over the door ledge into the darkened room, with the proper greeting, "Thank God you're safe!" In the corner we could make out Ngawa's form buried in blankets. The glint of a silver bracelet on her right wrist struck us when we leaned over to shake her hand and to place by her side a couple of bars of face soap, a little dress stitched together from bits of leftover fabric, and six eggs wrapped in tattered plastic.

Her last pregnancy had ended in a miscarriage. I had heard her melodramatic tales of the hemorrhaging and the three blobs she had expelled, one bloody, one white, and one pronged "like a rabbit's ears." When she had collapsed, "dizzy and up to my waist in blood," her brother had rushed her in his pickup truck to the clinic in town. First, she said, she went deaf. Then suddenly everything went blue, bright blue. "I've gone blind, my brother. I've gone blind! I can't see you!" she had screamed. They gave her an injection, and later she found herself hooked up to an intravenous feeder. She knew that many people thought she had lost her baby because she'd carried heavy loads. But what could she do? Stop working? Others had just said, "It was from God."

Ngawa tucked the soap and little dress under her pillow. The eggs went into an old tin can. She felt around and pulled out a small bottle of kohl. Then she signaled to her young daughter to look under the handwoven rugs folded neatly against the wall. "May God give you success, darling, if you find me the hair oil."

The girl produced a stained yellow plastic bottle of scented olive oil. Ngawa insisted we put some on. The women we had just then sat down with—Ngawa's mother, Migdim, her sister Lawz, and several of her brothers' wives—handed us a small mirror and the smoothed twig used for applying kohl to the eye.

Giving birth was expensive. Not only the kohl and hair oil had to be readied for the women who would visit, but also the fenugreek and *maghaath* (root of *Glossostemon brugieri*) for cramps; sulfur for fainting; *maḥalab* (*Prunus mahaleb*), musk, and cloves for a perfumed necklace; and incense for burning. A new mother does not bathe until seven days after the birth. In the old days, I had been told, when there was not much money around, each neighbor would come carrying on her head a small sack of milled barley flour, tea, and sugar in honor of the birth. The older women of the household would insist as she left that the visitor take back a share: three big handfuls of flour at the birth of a girl, five for a boy.

"In the name of God, in the name of God. Let me hold her," Gateefa murmured as Ngawa cautiously pulled out from under the blankets her swaddled newborn. The baby's cheeks were pink. Her eyes were shut tight but black-rimmed with kohl. Wisps of dark hair peeked out from under the handkerchief knotted around her head. "God keep her parents and her brothers safe," Gateefa blessed. "Girls are nice. I swear to God, daughters are caring. If I were alone, without my girls, I don't know what I'd do."

Ngawa's sister Lawz began teasing her, though. "I don't know what happened. Ngawa, didn't you have some camel fat for breakfast seven mornings in a row after your last baby?"

Migdim argued, "Daughter, if you wanted a boy you should have wrapped the bit of the umbilical cord that falls off and buried it. You bury it with barley, salt, and lentils, but you have to make sure that the umbilical cord is on the bottom."

Turning to me, Lawz explained, "You know, Arabs prefer boys."

Gateefa disagreed. "They are equal with God. And He even prefers girls. It is only the ignorant who prefer boys. Some daughters are worth a hundred sons."

Suddenly the children in the doorway scattered. "Move, move out the way," yelled Ngawa's sister-in-law as she came in carrying a large wooden bowl. She put down the special birth meal in front of us—cooked dough doused with butter and molasses—and greeted the new arrivals. "Greetings. How are you? How are your daughters? How is your family?"

"May God keep you. How are you? How's your father in his illness? How's your family?"

"Go ahead and eat," urged Ngawa's mother-in-law.

"Go play outside, outside!" Ngawa's sister-in-law shooed the children out. Only the visitors' youngest children ate by their mothers' sides. A child cried outside and was told to go over to the oven where his sisters were baking bread.

Migdim laughed at this and began to tell an old tale about a woman living alone with her children. They were so poor they had nothing to eat. Her little boy woke up in the middle of the night crying, "Mom, I'm hungry."

She said to him, "My son, go to sleep, go to sleep."

"Mom, I want a piece of bread. Mom, I want a piece of bread."

"Go to sleep my son," was all she could say. There was nothing in the house, nothing at all.

Then suddenly she looked up and saw a man rummaging through their stuff in the corner of the tent. "Even he wanted some bread, the thief!" interrupted Ngawa's mother-in-law.

Migdim continued, "Yes, he was looking around for some bread. I don't know what the woman was afraid of. She had absolutely nothing in the house. So when the boy cried again, she said to him in a loud voice, 'Son, go to sleep, go to sleep. I swear on my life, your uncle over there is looking for some food for you and if he finds some bread he'll give you a scrap!'"

A man's cough outside the door interrupted our laughter, alerting the younger women to pull their veils over their faces. Ngawa's husband poked his head in the door. "Welcome, welcome! How are you ladies?"

"Greetings," we responded.

One of the older visitors called out affectionately, "Congratulations on what you got!"

"May God bless you as well," he smiled as he left.

A woman teased Ngawa. How was it that she was the only one whose husband hadn't taken a second wife?

She laughed weakly. Women don't end up alone with their husbands unless the men are poor, "like my old man," she said. As soon as they get any wealth, men take second wives. Some women were clever, she added. They bathed and got perfumed each night. But not her. Making fun of herself, she said, "I'm filthy, as you see me. He has to take me as I am."

Unlike her wealthier sisters, Ngawa was always unkempt, her dresses caked with dirt or flour, her headcloth slipping off to expose thinning hair she had not had time to braid. She worked hard, but when she sat with you, her long thin legs stretched out before her, she talked fast, gesturing, smiling, frowning, poking, rushing from one topic to the next.

Lawz was fond of her sister. "Hey, did you hear what Ngawa's daughter told her father the other day? She said, 'When my mother stays over with her relatives, I have a happy night.'"

Ngawa protested that it was because the girl got to use her mother's warm blanket. The women were surprised. "She sleeps in your room with her father?" Ngawa explained that she had to take care of the little ones, who usually slept there.

Lawz went on with the story. "Do you know what the man said to the girl? He said, 'But my night isn't a happy one!' "

The women laughed, especially when Ngawa reported that her daughter had then quipped, "Yuck! What do you want with her anyways?"

Her sister Lawz agreed. "Indeed! What would he want with you in this cold anyway? It's hard on the knees!"

We knew Ngawa's daughter had filled two snail shells with blood from the umbilical cord of this new baby and then crushed them. She had also rubbed seven date pits in blood from the umbilical cord and buried them wrapped in a rag. This was to prevent pregnancy. She thought her mother had enough children. Three boys and four girls are enough if you're struggling.

God Rewards the Midwife

A small bowl with chicken and macaroni was brought in for Ngawa. A new mother must eat good food: chicken, eggs, but no fried vegetables or milk products. She should not drink anything cold. She should never be left alone, nor should anyone give her trouble. She is vulnerable.

I had once asked Ngawa's mother-in-law about birthing because she had acted as midwife for all her sons' children. Would she mind telling me how she did it? The women present had giggled and refused when she asked for a volunteer to demonstrate. So instead she made me squat facing her.

She began, "I sit in front of her and I look, like this. When the contractions come, I look. I put my finger against the opening and feel. When the child's head pushes my finger I know it is close to time. And I start widening the opening. If it is close and the child's head is stuck or is pressing but off-center, then I reach with my finger as far inside as I can and turn it, turn it, turn it until I straighten it out."

How had she learned?

"I've given birth before and I know."

The women asked for details. She continued, telling them how she pressed against the woman's anus to push the child forward. When she feels the time is near, she instructs the woman, "Push, push. Push, push!"

"Does the woman cry?" I had asked. "Does she scream?"

"If she has sense she doesn't cry. If she has a strong will, she doesn't scream. But if she's like these women," she had said, turning to her daughters-in-law, "she makes noise like this."

They had all laughed, these women who had given birth so often, as one of them mimicked for me the moans and screams of childbirth.

The old woman went on. "Then I say, 'Listen. Hold your breath.' This is so the kid comes out right away. When he comes out, I hold him face up. I hold the umbilical cord, like this"—she made the gesture of milking an udder and added, "If the afterbirth doesn't come out I gently massage the cord, with my hand. This is birth as we do it. The Egyptians are different."

When I asked if any of the other old women in the camp, Migdim for example, knew how to deliver babies, she snorted. "Once I came and found Migdim and the other old woman just sitting there with one of the twins lying on the floor next to its mother. I told them, 'Why don't you lend a hand? You've all given birth before. What's the matter with you? What are you being bashful about? Why don't you get close?' . . . Midwifing has great recompense, I mean God rewards it. I swear to God, these hands—it is righteous before God—these hands here and these legs strain. And I won't even talk about what sometimes comes down on my hands. My arms will be swimming in blood. Only after the woman finishes and is fine, only then do they get me soap and hot water. I wash my hands and my body and my hair. I take off everything I was wearing."

"There's lots of blood? You don't get disgusted?" I can't help asking.

"No. Because it is a righteous act, you don't get disgusted."

I had heard something similar from Ngawa's older sister, Dhahab. In the area where she lives, she helps women in labor because, as she explained, "God made me one of those who doesn't feel disgusted delivering babies. Some people can't stand it." She figures she has delivered a thousand infants. Although people offer, she never takes money for her services. "God rewards this," she says. "There is no reward like God's reward for those who midwife." But she doesn't say no to small gifts of soap or incense.

Searching for Children

A neighbor once remarked, "A woman gets anxious if she doesn't have many children. People talk. They say, 'Poor thing, she doesn't have any sons,' and so she goes searching for children. Even if a woman has four or even five kids she still says that's not enough. Don't you know the louse's lament?

> 'Every day you give birth to a hundred
> Alas, what a pathetic brood.' "

"Hey, that's not the louse but the bedbug," someone corrected.

The woman was serious. "There are people who've had children and people who are looking for children. People aren't the same. Some people have many children and still say, 'I don't have any.' That's the way the world is."

I had heard that she took a long time getting pregnant and asked her about it.

"By God," she swore, "I don't do anything about it. I wait for God's help. If it comes it comes, if not it doesn't. Some go to doctors or to the religious healers. The healers write them amulets. They have quill pens and write, and you soak the papers in water and bathe with them."

A woman listening to us laughed, noticing my questions. "If you are having trouble getting pregnant, Lila," she said to me, "you go to a woman healer who massages you, lays on hands, and ties little strings on your back. I'll take you. Or you go to a healer from the saintly lineages. He'll tell you to bring a goat to sacrifice—either red or blue. You slaughter it there and he and his family get themselves a good meal. You bring him rice, oil, sugar, and tea. And if you're really an idiot you bring flour too. They just take you for a ride. They walk the goat around you seven times and then kill it. And after he's nice and full of rice and meat, the man begins to drum and trance. It's all just a waste of money. Children are from God."

On one of my visits to the community, people were worried about a new bride who had not gotten pregnant yet. "May God grant him children," mumbled one of the aunts of the young husband.

Another whispered, "We heard people say her family is thinking of taking her back. Have you heard that?"

Migdim, the man's grandmother, confirmed this rumor. The bride's family had discovered only at the wedding that he was twice divorced, with no children. She also reported that at the wedding, her daughter Lawz had made sure the bride stepped back and forth seven times over an iron peg. And she was careful to make sure that the bride spoke first in the morning—no one came in on her and said anything. Others approved of these measures meant to ward off "blocking."

I asked if he had gone to any doctors to see what the problem might be. Migdim answered, "He's been to every doctor and every religious healer. And the doctor said go to the healer. The healer said go to the doctor. The healer said he should divorce that last wife and get a new one. Don't you remember? The last healer said to go to a certain area to get this one. 'She's got the crown of a baby already at the top of her womb,' he said."

"So we went to get her," an aunt added. "The doctor said go to the healer, and the healer, the last one, told him to divorce his wife and bring this new one. But he's still looking for the boy, still looking."

"May God grant him a son from this woman," wished Migdim.

"Even a girl, if God wills. Just so he has children," her daughter said.

The women began exchanging stories of people who had children after many years. "It is God the Glorious on High who grants it to them. Some people say a person who's thin and sickly doesn't have kids. Forget it. It's a matter of fortune. Some big strong men don't have kids."

"And there are some who sit ten years without having kids. Some wait eight years . . ."

Another woman in the community was encouraging. "You know," she said, "the other day my little girl hugged him and followed him around calling him Daddy."

"Maybe because she has called him 'father' that means . . ."

"Yes, maybe that means he'll conceive. So I said, 'Why don't they take this little one as a laying egg?' Maybe if the woman sleeps with the baby in her bed for a few nights she'll get pregnant."

The women laughed, but I was excited. I told them about how our newspapers at home reported often that people who adopted a child would suddenly have one of their own. Or sometimes even when they got a pet, a cat or dog.

The women thought this amusing, though the idea of adoption—parents giving up their own children—horrified them. "Protect us from evil and the flames! No, this baby, may God protect her, her mother and father are still alive. They'd borrow her only as a nesting egg. There's nothing shameful in that. They could take her for a little while and feed her good food and get her nice clothes."

They also argued about the wedding. Circumcisions are sometimes celebrated with weddings so that guests need attend only one festivity and give one gift. This had happened at the unfortunate couple's wedding. A neighbor said to Lawz, "Hey woman, I heard that someone entered the bride's room with some blood from the boy's circumcision on her dress. She's sure to have loused it up."

Lawz wouldn't accept this. "No, no, his mother said they had already put some of the blood inside the room before she arrived."

Migdim disagreed with her daughter. "They did not. They hadn't put any blood in the room."

"They said they had."

"We told her again and again not to do the circumcision at the same time."

They explained to me that you must put some of the blood from the circumcision in the bride's room before she arrives, otherwise it may block her. And she should be the first to go out in the morning: no one should enter her room before she comes out. But rumor had it that the bride's new sister-in-law had gone into her room in the morning. "Bad luck," someone said.

Advice was offered on what the young bride should do to undo the blockage. "She should wash with the virginity cloth of someone who has already gotten pregnant. Before a woman gets pregnant she must not wash the cloth; she should save it. But once she's gotten pregnant she doesn't have to keep it. The new bride should soak it in a pot of water and step back and forth over it seven times. Then she should wash herself with the water."

Another woman pitched in. "My daughter did that. When she didn't get pregnant at first, while her sister got pregnant right away, we thought, why not do the blood thing? She took her sister's virginity cloth and soaked it in water and bathed with it. She didn't see her menstrual blood again until she had the baby." I had heard long ago that this girl had been blocked by her own virginity cloth because she had refused to leave her room on the wedding day. What she should have done was go out and then follow the women back into her room when they brought in the blood-stained cloth at sunset after it had been taken out for public display.

Women often talk about how to undo blockages. One visitor from a town nearby told her daughter's story. After six years of marriage she still had no children. They took her to doctors and everywhere, and all of them told her, "You have lots of children in you." They went to a local woman healer. She said, "She's blocked. Go get some milk from a woman whose child has just died. Wash with it." A woman they knew sent over some milk. The daughter soaked a bit of wool in the milk and placed it inside, in her vagina. Three mornings in a row. She did not even get her period that month. And now she has three children. When the old mother had thanked the kind woman for giving the milk, she had prayed to God to be good to her and to reward her by making it possible for her to go on the pilgrimage to God's House. Shortly after, the woman received a small inheritance. Her brother said, "Here's your share. You can live on it or you can use it to make the pilgrimage to Mecca." She said, "I'll go on pilgrimage," and thanked her neighbor for the answered prayer.

It is said that if a woman who has just weaned a child, or a woman whose baby has just died, or even a woman who has just given birth enters the room, she may cause a blockage in the flow of a new mother's breast milk, if not conception altogether. Even animals—dogs, cats, and donkeys—who have just given birth can do this to a woman. Women returning from funerals are careful never to enter the room where a new mother sits; she must come out to greet them.

If the blockage is caused by a woman wearing a gold medallion necklace who enters the room of a new mother or bride who is not wearing her own gold, the necklace should be dunked seven times in a pot of water with which the blocked woman would then bathe on three successive Fridays. A certain black-and-white stone bead blocks nursing mothers. Yet this stone is good for fertility too if dipped in the bathing water seven times on three successive Fridays.

Haj Sagr's wife Azza had not had a child in many years. She had already tried undoing the blockage by stepping back and forth seven times over the afterbirth of a friend. And when a neighbor's donkey foaled, she had stepped seven times over its afterbirth. At first they had thought she was blocked because just after her youngest son had died a donkey that had just foaled had entered the courtyard where she was sitting. Now, though, there was another theory.

"She wants to go turn over her boy," her sister-in-law confided. "Her son must have turned over on his face. When a child dies, they put some stones under his head so he won't turn over. If he turns over on his face, the mother doesn't get pregnant. Until she sets him right, she won't be able to conceive."

"On a Friday," clarified a visitor. She should go to the cemetery and pick up a stone from someone's grave. At home she should bathe, three Fridays in a row, in water in which she has soaked the stone. Then she should return the stone to the cemetery, being careful to replace it upside down. She should wear her dress inside out and be sure not to leave the cemetery on the same path she used to enter.

These remedies do not always work. Sometimes matters are more serious, as a commotion one day in the camp showed. Two women were spotted heading for a neighbor's house. They turned out to be the former wife of our favorite neighbor and her mother. Ten years earlier, after a few years of marriage, the woman had sworn by the local saint that her husband was not a man and would never have children. She wanted a divorce and got it. She had remarried, and so had he. But she was never able to have children. She had gone everywhere for help. Now she had come to him. Perhaps if he forgave her for swearing falsely against him, God would grant her children. When she and her mother got to the door, they were met by the man's current wife who later whispered, "You should have seen her face when she saw me with my children there. She said, 'Blessings on the Prophet!' I said, 'And these are just some of them. The others are at school.' She came in and wept."

Children Keep You Company

Living near us was an intelligent and hard-working man from a poor branch of Haj Sagr's family. His two wives were both from the farming areas to the east—loud, amusing, and inseparable. The second wife, no younger than the first, had just had her third child. The first was childless and sometimes came by for consolation. "People always want what they don't have," others remarked. "There's no profit in having kids."

The haggard young mother argued that all children did was tire you out and give you headaches. She pointed out that her co-wife was comfortable; she could sleep through the night. With a baby you're up and down, up and down, your eyelids dropping as you try to manage. "Listen," she said to me, "I don't know why everyone tries so hard to have children. They suck your blood and sap your strength, and what do they do for you? Nothing. In the end you die and what good are they?"

Other tired mothers wonder if God could possibly call them to account on the Day of Judgment. After all this bitterness—children and work and exhaustion—could there be any more in the afterlife? There just couldn't be, argued one of them; women couldn't possibly have any sins counted against them. Some women took me aside to ask if I could get them "something" to stop them having children. "You're better off," they sometimes said to me. "Better to stay light."

Yet when someone like Ngawa would pick up her crying new-born, women watching always said, "Blessings on the Prophet!" They were careful to say this to protect the baby. Gateefa had told me once about her eldest son, now skinny and prone to colds. "You should have seen him when he was small. He was huge and fair. Then one day a neighbor came by and said, 'I never thought you could have a boy like this!' Well, the next day he woke up with a huge boil behind his ear. I sent someone to the Sudanese religious healer who used to live nearby to find out what had happened. The woman had entered on the boy and not asked for the Prophet's blessings. She'd given him the eye. The healer gave me an amulet, sewed something in a pouch, and said I should keep it and put it on each child I had. For forty days."

When I had asked what "the eye" was, Gateefa had answered, "Whatever pleases the eye." Then she told a story about the

Prophet's daughter. The Prophet told his doubting daughter, "You don't believe in envy? Do this: hide your baby and instead wrap a rock in its blanket when the women come to visit." After the women left—visitors who all had said admiringly, "What a big healthy baby!"—he told her to look at the stone. She found it smashed to bits. That's envy.

A newborn faces other dangers that were apparent when we sat with Ngawa and her new baby. Ngawa's youngest son, almost three and curious about his new sister, leaned over his mother and tried to kiss the baby, but he squeezed her a little roughly. And was he pulling her hair? The women nearby challenged him, "Hey, little Ramadan, where did your new sister come from?" "Hey, Ramadan, shall I take her home with me?" "Hey, Ramadan, shall we take the little girl and throw her in the irrigation ditch? What do you think?" He grew suddenly protective and began to cry as he shook his head. When his mother asked gently, "Then, shall we keep her?" he nodded. He watched intently when Ngawa pulled out her breast to try to nurse the infant. This had been his until eight months ago. Now the lap that had been his contained someone else. He pushed the baby. At this his grandmother hollered for his older sister. "Come here, Sultana." Silence. "Hey, you good-for-nothing. Get over here to take your little brother." Ngawa murmured, "May God keep you for me," as her daughter dragged him out.

Ngawa laughed and asked if we'd heard what her other son had said. He had challenged her: why was she still having children? "You're an old woman, Mom," he'd said. "There are women younger than you who've stopped having children."

"Who?" she had demanded. "Name me someone." When she tried to appease him with the offer to "do family planning," he'd been condescending. "It's too late to do family planning, Mom! If you wanted a planned family, you would have had to stop three kids ago."

Older women seem reluctant to do anything for birth control besides stepping on snail shells, burying date pits, or wearing on a string amulets made of salted goat's penis. As one woman put it: "Childbearing—both its good and its bad—is God-given. The other is the work of God's servants—that's different. If something goes wrong it is better to have it be between just you and God. That's better than if the servant had interfered." She followed this with the story of a woman who underwent four operations for a dislodged intrauterine device.

I was holding a visitor's child in my lap. Her mother said, "You'll like having babies. Having children is nice. They keep you company."

God Creates Them Good or Bad

"Welcome, welcome, welcome!" Several children dressed in their rumpled beige school uniforms tumbled in, smiling shyly. They shook hands with the women, tossed their schoolbags on top of the rug pile, and sat down next to their grandmother.

The mothers complained about the costs of school. Every day the children came wanting money—one day for books, one day for pencils, one day for food. And the teachers demanded fresh eggs to take back to their city homes.

One woman argued that the children hadn't learned a thing. It was just a waste of money sending them to school. A woman from the next village had all her daughters in school. She said school ruined them. They got lazy and did nothing around the house. They stopped listening to their mothers.

Migdim contrasted the old Bedouin teachers who educated her sons with today's Egyptian schools. "The Bedouin teacher," she said, "wrote on a wood slate. He made ink out of burnt sheep's wool. The children began by learning to read the letters. He would write in really big letters, *b, t, h, k, n.* When they had recited these, he would erase the board and write more letters for them. It was amazing how quickly one came to understand with him."

I asked if they didn't learn from the government schools.

"Not like with the Bedouin," she said. "The religious teacher would sort out the letters until they learned. Quickly they learned what he wrote. But in the schools, they give them a book to write from. They copy it, but they don't read it. They don't know what they're writing because they just copy what is written. They don't know what it is. They don't understand."

The schoolchildren did not protest. They were used to the women's blunt talk. They were used to being talked about: "Little Sayyid's ears are too big" (to which his mother retorts, "When he grows up the headdress will cover them"); "None of the girls in the camp are appealing except Fawzia"; "Little Ali is just like his father, always hanging his head"; "Hey, slave boy, how did you turn out so black?" (to which his mother answers, "When he grows up to be a man and goes to put his arm around you, I'll tell him what his aunt said about him!").

As the women talked, the room filled with more and more children. Their noise began to interfere with the women's conversation. When two who were chasing each other fell against me, Migdim cursed, "May pain take you! You beasts!" To her nine-year-old daughter, Safiyya shouted, "You're not little anymore. Go get your sister some clean clothes. Go feed your rabbits." To her little son and daughter she said gently, "Go, Mama's sweethearts, go with your sister." Then—"Oh, my head," she complained.

"There didn't used to be so many children in the old days," commented Migdim. "They were always outside, playing or herding the goats or sheep. Not like now. Then the kids didn't bother you; they didn't get into everything."

Gateefa was harsh. "Some people know how to raise their children. Ours, they're not afraid of anyone, not even their father."

Once I had asked, "What makes children turn out bad?"

She had answered, "It's from God. God creates some good and some bad."

"Not from their parents?"

"No, not from their parents."

I had tried to keep the topic going. "Do you know that in America parents blame themselves when their children turn out bad?"

"Yes, even here some do," Gateefa's sister-in-law nodded. "If a man does wrong—cheats in a hearing, lies, steals, kills people or wrongs them—his children will be bad. This is from God. But if a man is good, God rewards him with good sons. Look at Muftah Bu-Sultan. His uncles are all thieves and murderers and their sons are worthless. But *his* father was a good man. He never wronged anyone. And now look at his son—good, strong, healthy, and tall, and everyone respects him."

Someone brought up a contrary example. "But what about Hussein? He's a good man but all of his sons are lousy. Only one of them is worth anything—the son of the older wife."

"So is it thanks to the mother that a kid turns out well?" I asked.

Gateefa said, "No, they say it is the mother's brother. A person gets two-thirds from the mother's brother. If the mother's brother is good, the boy will be."

"But you know what else they say? If a mother is beautiful, her children will be awful. There is a proverb: The mother with snot in her nose, her children will be lovely."

"Why would that be?" I wondered.

"People would envy the beautiful one," was the answer.

No one mentioned training or molding children, although they sometimes pointed out that children imitated adults around them. I was confused by the way women disciplined children in my household. If two siblings began to quarrel and their exasperated mother, sitting on a mat trying to cook with an infant in her lap, warned them to stop and they didn't, she would grab whatever was handy, usually a plastic sandal, and hurl it. They'd duck and run off laughing. She would threaten to tell their father when he got home. She'd shout for their older brother, "Come here with a rod and hit these kids." But he wouldn't come, and the next thing you'd know she was finished cooking and listening adoringly to the children's excited stories as they lay with their heads in her lap.

When daughters reached eight or nine, discipline was imposed and they became mother's helpers. They would eventually grow up to be their mothers' closest friends, but now, accustomed to earlier freedoms, they often stubbornly refused to do what they were told. Then invectives would fly. "You slut! You willful girl! You're not a little girl anymore!" Later a mother would confide, "Girls are such a responsibility. You worry about them all your life."

Shock

Out of breath, children came running in to announce some visitors. The floor mat was swept quickly. It was the wives of old Migdim's brothers, and we stood up to greet them warmly. Come to ask after the health of their husbands' sister, the women sat awkwardly, asking after everyone they could think of. Migdim sat close to them and asked about her relatives. News was exchanged. After food was brought and tea poured, the women's stories got longer. One asked Migdim about a daughter-in-law: had she had any more children since the little girl she had seen on her last visit there?

"Yes," Migdim began, "She had another girl, but she died. And then her mother died. She'd given birth eight days earlier when her mother came east. Her family had set up camp on that southern ridge over there because they wanted to wean their lambs.

"The old woman's grandson, her daughter's boy, came along and reversed the car into her and killed her. They'd told him, 'Over there, stay far away, boy! Boy, don't come near, keep away. Son, the car doesn't have any brakes!' But he started rolling in it, rolling in it until he ran over his grandmother. She died instantly.

"At the time, my daughter-in-law had just given birth to this girl. Her husband was the one who told me. 'Her family just set up camp near here and her mother has been killed—her grandson ran her over. Go tell her, go tell.' I said, 'Oh my God, what can I say to her? What should I say to her? I can't . . .' Should we tell her this, or tell her that? Finally her older brother-in-law went in

and told her: 'Your family had set up camp here and now a car has
knocked over your mother. She's got a broken leg.'

"Well, the woman let out some wails. She said, 'God, she's
probably dead! God, it's none other than death!'

"He told her, 'Get into the car. I'll take you there.'

"They took her in her husband's car to where her family lives.
They had taken the old woman back immediately. She'd come in
the morning alive and went home dead. I rode with my son and his
wife, and we took the baby girl. I put her in my lap, and I took care
of her little son too. Until we got to Alamein. There they washed
the body and buried the old woman. There was nothing wrong
with her at all except that the car had run over her stomach. Killed
her right away.

"I stayed there eight days. But the children got sick; they got
measles, and I was taking care of the little baby and the boy. In the
end, I decided to take the boy and come home. We stopped at the
clinic on the way, and they gave the boy an injection. Then we
came home.

"She stayed there about fifteen days. When she came home, the
baby was sick. She brought the baby back, and four days later the
little girl died. After that she never got pregnant again."

"From shock," offered Ngawa.

"Shock is tough," she concurred.

They asked about our new bride. We quietly said she was still
"washing," or getting her period. Had a religious healer been
consulted? Had the young husband perhaps been frightened or
shocked? There were many stories about shocks, the most devas-
tating of which always involved the loss of those one loved—
especially one's own children.

Dhahab, the older sister of Lawz and Ngawa, had a husband
who was legendary. He had married thirty-one wives. As Dhahab
told it, "Every day he brought us a new bride. He'd leave us
feeding the animals and tending the orchards, harvesting the figs,
and working. He would come back with a bride. Every year he
married once."

I was confused. "You mean they would actually hold a wedding each year?"

"Yes," Dhahab laughed, "we'd hold a wedding and ululate. Some brides stayed a week, some stayed six months. There were those who stayed fifteen months, two months, a month, and sometimes only a week. My son asked me why, but I said I would not say anything. I told him, 'If only God had given him. Your father hasn't had children.'

"This is what happened. When my son was only one month in my womb, my co-wife's daughter was with me. One minute she was talking with me—she was so young and beautiful—and the next thing she had fallen in the well. Her father got shocked and went crazy. For a month he could not sit up without hauling himself up with a rope. After that he didn't have any more children. A healer came and wrote him some amulets, but he took a long time getting better. He was sick for three or four months after the girl died. He didn't have any more children, at all, after that. And me, I had my only son in my womb, and that was that. I'd had four daughters and then this son and then it ended. From shock.

"And my co-wife didn't get pregnant either. He had been shocked. And so, my dear, he'd bring a woman and she'd stay a year, stay a year and a half, she'd stay a month or two or three. She wouldn't get pregnant, and she'd leave. Until he got old. When he got old, his relatives told him he shouldn't keep marrying. His sister said, 'Go have yourself examined if you want to have children. Go find a doctor for yourself, or a religious healer. Go to someone. You're the one with the problem, it seems.' "

In a whisper she gave details of what happened. "His aunt, his father's sister, was an old woman, and she knew about men. She said to us, 'If a man doesn't have children, it is because of a shock. He must have been shocked. If a man doesn't have children, we must look at the cloth that he and his wife wipe themselves with.' She told us to hide it under the bed and bring it to her in the morning. We brought it to her in the morning, and when she looked at it she said, 'No, that one can't conceive. There's nothing there. Because of shock he's only producing water.'

"So she told him, 'You can't have children anymore.' 'How's that? But I've had all these children.' She said, 'You had the kids before. But after the girl fell in the well she gave you a shock and you haven't had any since then. Go find yourself a religious healer.'

"So finally a Sudanese healer started writing amulets for him. He'd gotten older and older, so when he went to try to arrange marriages people would turn him away. What young woman would want him when he was an old man? But finally he married the mother of the girls. She was very young. And then he married another wife. And both of them had children with him—one had two girls, and the other two boys."

Gateefa, who had heard the story from her maternal aunt, the girl's mother, told it with a different emphasis. She spoke of the beauty of the girl who had died, a young woman who had fasted only five Ramadans. She had just had a marriage request, and they were getting things ready. The day she died she was wearing a red dress. Her grandmother had just cut the fabric for the red-bordered white slip she would use on her wedding day. She was heading off somewhere, but her grandmother asked her first to fetch water from the well. Before she left, her father looked at her and said of his future in-laws, "By God, she's being wasted on them!"

She went off, carrying a water jar. She was wearing embroidered boots, and her legs were strong. Her hair came down to her waist, and her eyes . . . never mind her eyes. At the well she filled her jar, and then a neighbor of theirs, an old woman, came to fill hers. The girl offered to fill her containers for her and then sat on the edge to wash her feet. She put her boots back on, but as she rose to pick up her water jar her foot slipped on the side and she fell in. Straight in. She had nothing to grab on to. They sent for divers from Alexandria, but they could not get her out until late the next day. They dragged her up by her belt.

Shocks are said to make even stranger things happen than infertility. One woman said she'd had a fetus in her womb for thirteen years. When she had been four months pregnant she saw a train hit something. She feared it was her two sons because she knew they were out herding the sheep. As it turned out, the train had only hit a few ewes. But from that moment, she swore, what was in her womb stopped moving. She didn't want to do anything about it because she was embarrassed to be pregnant at all. She was already the mother of grown sons. Just as well, she thought. A local woman healer felt around and said the baby was parked in her side. For twelve years the baby girl remained parked there. Then, one day, in a sandstorm, the woman witnessed a train collision. When the trains crashed she felt something in her side, as if a stone had just been flipped over. This released it and the baby got better and she gave birth to a girl.

I asked how long she had carried the fetus after it had come to life again. Nine months was the answer. When a young woman disputed the story—"How can a baby be dead and then come to life? It would become putrid"—the woman swore it was true.

Since countershocks seem the best way to undo the damage of a first shock, whenever a large snake was found and killed in the area, women would insist that it be used to frighten someone who was having trouble conceiving. In our community, this was said to have worked with two people, one man and one woman. Cars turning over, mines exploding, or even loud noises can have the same effect.

Not all shocks that bring illness are bad. A former neighbor ("Many blessings upon her") had just celebrated the first annual festival in honor of the saint who had possessed her after the death of a son. She was now a healer. I had visited her once when she still lived nearby, in the company of Lawz, who was trying to wean a child. We had found the healer dressed in the white robe of the men; instead of the typical black headcloth, she wore a white headscarf over a green kerchief. About eight months pregnant, she sat cross-legged at a low table, her belly pressing tightly against the robe. Her voice was hoarse as she indicated we should sit and wait in the adjoining room. When we were invited in, she spoke in a deep voice. "What do you want?"

She asked Lawz's name and her mother's name (which she knew perfectly well in her ordinary state). She made a few scratches with a Bic pen in a child's notebook. These looked like numbers. She whispered, "In the name of God, in the name of God." She looked down at the paper, then at her upturned palm. She talked but didn't say much. "Are you dizzy?" she asked. "Tell me if what I'm saying is true or not." Lawz agreed, "Right, right. Right."

Then she scribbled, filling page after page of a notebook. She whispered as she wrote. After she had covered each page, she spat on it. Then she tore the pages out and folded some incense into them. Others she tore into scraps. "For burning with incense. For massaging your body. Bathe in the water in which you've soaked the papers. Right before dawn."

She sprayed Lawz's head and rubbed some of her spit (with its blessings) onto the suffering woman's chest. "How blessed she is," the women kept saying.

The story was that she had been an ordinary woman, just like the rest of them. Then one day, when she was away visiting maternal relatives, her ten-year-old son was hit by a car. It was dusk, and the two of them had been walking along the road. She tells people that when she wanted to cry out, two apparitions came before her, one with a beard. The bearded one put his hand over her mouth and sprayed her with water to stop her from crying or lamenting the boy. After that, all she would say about the death was, "His life came from God." A year later she fell ill. They took her to doctors and to local healers. Finally they took her to a woman healer who told her that she had been possessed by a saint. To cure herself, she would have to begin drumming and trancing to become a healer.

As Ngawa put it, after the woman's son was killed, "She fell ill and started going to doctors and going here and there. But she didn't get better. Finally she went to a woman healer. And when she went to her—this after what? After she had gotten worn out from going to all the doctors—she talked about the one who had possessed her. The healer said he had told her, 'I came to her because I was afraid for her. She would have gone mad if I had not. I have forbidden her to cry over her son.' He had also said, 'She should build me a tomb and make me a resting place.' What he said, the healer told her to do. And she did it. Then when she started to hold trance sessions, the saint would come to her. Her voice becomes the voice of an old man." Those who come to her God frees from illness.

Women say that it is a sin to cry over one's little children who die. It is said that for every tear you shed there will be one less drop of water in the jug your child brings to you in heaven. It is said that your dead children come running to greet you, carrying a jug of water. A woman, they say, should not get upset, because it comes from God. But their stories show the pain of shock.

"Tell Me a Story, Grandma"

The sun was getting low in the sky. Children lying on the floor, their schoolbooks spread before them, were trying to do their homework. Other children played nearby, sometimes taking a workbook on their laps and turning the pages to look at the illustrations. Older daughters were in and out, preparing for the evening. We thought about going, since it was a long walk home.

"Daddy's car! Daddy's car!" Little Mastura had spotted her father driving slowly over the rutted dirt approach. She ran out to hug him. His nephews went out to greet him and lead him into the men's guest room. We knew now that we would stay for supper while he spent a companionable evening with his brothers and their guests. Nice to catch a ride home.

In the stew were a few chunks of fatty meat from the market. These were placed before the guests. We ate, dipping the freshly baked bread in the bowls of vegetable stew. The kerosene burner was brought in and tea cooked slowly in an enamel teapot. The youngest children were already beginning to drop off to sleep, lying on the mat with their heads resting on a mother's or an aunt's leg. Mothers rubbed their sleeping children's hair, feeling for lice. One fussy child, crying and looking around while lying in his mother's lap, was suddenly covered with a blanket and rocked. "Hush, hush. Quiet! There's a dog trying to come in. Get out of here dog! You'd better go to sleep quick."

It was dark, despite the lantern. People drew closer and talked. Some of the children asked for stories. "Tell us a little story," they pleaded with their grandmother. I asked for the story of the old man and the old woman. They laughed. "You want to hear this one, Lila?"

Old Migdim told the story about the old woman and old man who traveled into the desert and set up camp in a lonely area where there were wolves. They had brought with them seven goats, a cow, a donkey, and a puppy. The first night, a wolf came to the tent. He called out:

> "Hey old man, Hey old woman
> O cow who's stopped milking
> O seven black goats
> O little braying donkey
> O little yelping puppy
> Give me someone for dinner tonight
> Or else, Humm, I'll eat you!"

So the old man and woman gave him a goat.

He came the next night and called out the same thing, asking, "Who will you give me to eat for dinner tonight?" They gave him another goat. This went on night after night until the old couple had given the wolf all seven goats, their donkey, their cow, and their puppy.

Then they realized that they had no more animals to give him and that he would eat them. The old man said to his wife, "Hide me in a basket and hang it from the tent pole. And you, hide in the big urn." So she hung up the basket with the old man in it, and she hid inside the pottery urn.

When the wolf came that night, no one answered his call. He came into the tent and sniffed around. Then he looked up. Now, the basket had a tear in it, and the old man's genitals were showing, they were dangling out of the hole in the basket. The wolf started jumping up trying to bite them. The old woman watching this started laughing so hard she farted. This split open the urn she was hiding in, and the wolf ate her. Then he nipped at the old man's genitals until he pulled down the basket and ate the old man too. And then he went to sleep in their little tent.

As with all stories, this one ended with "And they went far away and I came back." This time it was amid much laughter. One of the women commented, "She was laughing, the old woman was laughing at the wolf biting her husband's thing."

Then someone begged, "Grandma, tell us that story Aunt Dhahab told, the one with Bu-Taroori!" The women laughed again. Dhahab told good stories, unlike her younger sister Ngawa, who always lost the thread. Once when their brother Sagr had found us together trying to record stories, he'd made fun of Ngawa, saying, "My sister, you're not the right one to do this. Dhahab's the one with a clear mind. You, your mind's busy with children and how to make ends meet."

After some moments the various conversations stopped as the old woman struggled to recall the story her daughter had told them on her last visit.

"She said there was Khwayteela and Bu-Taroori, and they had three daughters. Bu-Taroori said, 'Come on, let's go visit our girls.' But then he said to his wife, 'Khwayteela, what are we going to take for them? What are we going to take?' She said to him, 'Don't worry, you take a sack and I'll take a sack and we'll fill them with shit and we'll go drop in on them.' "

A woman listening exclaimed, "What nerve!" The rest of the women and girls laughed. Then, with a look at my tape recorder, "And this is going to go all the way to America!"

"So, my dears," the old woman continued, "they went off to their daughters. They came to one and gave her the sack of shit. Seems she figured it was candy or cookies, and so she threw it in the corner and that was that. And they spent the night with her, they had dinner. In the morning she said to them, 'Why don't you stay here while I go to get water from the well.' Her house was full of containers of honey and oil. They must have been merchants. And who knows what their problem was, but they started spilling the oil, and spilling the honey. They'd yank open the tops—'Here

Khwayteela, hold this!' 'Grab this, Bu-Taroori . . .' When their daughter came back she yelled, 'What a rotten visit!'

"So they went off to see the other daughter. This one, they gave her a sack, and she threw it out. This one had a little baby. They spent the night with her, and in the morning she said to them, 'Here, hold my son while I get water from the well. I'll be back.' She left. The boy started crying and crying. The old man, with the help of his wife, killed the baby and it died. They covered him and put him to bed. The boy's mother came back and asked, 'How's the baby?' He said, 'The child is over there sleeping.'

"She found him dead and shouted, 'Rottenest of visits! Rottenest of visits! Get out of here, go before your friends [her in-laws] catch you. The people will kill you. Move, move! Run, run!'

"They got up and ran. They ran and ran. . . . They walked and walked until they came upon a house that had a dead sheep in it. They opened it up and cut out its stomach. Bu-Taroori pulled on the stomach and stretched it out and cut it and then wore it as a cap. And the old woman wound the intestines around her waist as a belt.

"He said to her, 'Hey Khwayteela, by the Prophet, aren't I handsome in this cap?' She said, 'You really are handsome! And me, aren't I beautiful in this belt?' He said, 'You'd be really beautiful if it weren't for that fly sitting on your nose!' A fly that was wandering through the filth had landed on her nose. She said, 'Smack it, Bu-Taroori.' Bu-Taroori whacked it with a stake. This smashed her nose and she died.

"He started jumping up and down and wailing. He started wailing and began to go fart, fart, fart, fart. 'What's this, you asshole?' he said. 'Farting when my sister's dead? By God, you're asking for fire.' So, my dears, he went and made a fire and shoved a metal pin in it, like this pestle we grind with. Then he rammed it in his asshole. He died."

Ngawa's sister-in-law objected that this wasn't a good story. "Has Lila heard the story of Ngaarij?" Yes, I had. "How about Rjuuˤ?" Yes, I'd heard that one. "Tell her the story of Slaysla," said one of the older girls. "That one's good." And so we heard the tale, which goes something like this:

> Once there was a boy and girl whose mother died. She left them a cow. Their father remarried, and the stepmother (their father's wife) had a girl and a boy.
>
> Every day the boy and girl would take the cow out to pasture. They'd come home and the stepmother wouldn't feed them—she'd mix a little flour in water and put that out for them to eat. But every day when they went out with the cow they would call to it, "We're feeling hungry," and the cow would come close and urinate milk and shit dates. They'd fill a whole bowl, and they would eat dates and milk until they were full.
>
> The stepmother began to wonder, "My son and daughter are dark and ugly and these two are beautiful. Why, if what they eat all day is grazing plants?" So she called her son to her and pointed this out. She told him to go out with them the next day to see what they ate.
>
> So the next day the boy went out with them. They called to him and said, "We'll show you something, but promise not to tell a soul?" He promised. They called the cow and said, "O cow of ours, we're hungry. Shit us some dates and urinate milk." They milked her, and they drank milk and ate dates until they were full. Then they went home. When his mother questioned the boy, he said indeed, they ate nothing but grass.
>
> So the next day she called her daughter to her and pointed out how lovely the other children were. She told her to go out with them and see what they ate. The same thing happened, but the girl came home and told her mother.
>
> This woman then pretended she was sick. She lay on her bedding, having put a sack of dry bread under her, complaining that her back hurt. She would move on her bedding and say the noise made by the dry bread came from her back. Then a peddler came by. She paid him a lot of money to pretend that he was a religious healer, and she told him to prescribe the sacrifice of a cow. He wrote her some amulets to rub herself with and then, when the husband came home,

told him he should sacrifice a cow. The husband said, "Oh, we have a cow." He called to his children to bring their cow.

Their half-brother came to find them and tell them to bring the cow for sacrifice. They sent him home, saying they would follow. Then they went to the cow and told her, "If they make you lie down, don't do it; and if they cut your throat, don't let them; and if they cut you up, don't let them; and if they cook you, don't let them; and if they eat you, don't let them."

With that they took the cow home. When their father tried to make the cow lie down, he couldn't. Finally he asked the children to make her. They said, "Lie down," and the cow did. Then, try as he might, he couldn't slaughter her until he asked the children to make her submit. They told her to let him sacrifice her. On and on, the same happened with the butchering, the cooking (the meat cooked for hours and hours and refused to be done), and the eating. When they came to eat the meat they couldn't, and so each person threw away his portion.

The girl and boy collected the pieces of meat in a sack and the next day took them far away. They buried each chunk and watered them separately. From each piece sprang a fruit tree—a date palm, an apple tree, an orange tree, and so forth. Every day they would go out to that place and call to the trees, "Lower yourself, our tree, we're hungry." The tree would bend over and they'd climb on, and then the tree would straighten up. They'd eat until full, then say, "Bend down, we're full now." And the tree would let them down.

Now, the stepmother began to wonder. She thought, I've killed their cow but here they are, beautiful and healthy, and I don't feed them. She sent her son out with them. He saw, but he didn't tell his mother. The next day she sent her daughter, who related what she had seen. So the mother went to get a woodcutter. But the woodcutter, when he got near the trees, found a big snake coiled around. He couldn't chop the tree down. She ordered him to, but he refused.

Frustrated, the stepmother devised a new scheme. She sent her stepdaughter, Slaysla, to borrow a sieve from the female ghoul.

The girl set off. She passed a tall tree and said, "Good morning!"

The tree greeted her, "May your length be in your braids, not in your legs."

She passed a horse and said, "Good morning!"

He responded, "May my whiteness be in your cheeks, not in your eyes."

She passed a crow and said, "Good morning!"

The crow answered, "May my blackness be in your eyes, not in your cheeks."

Then she passed a peddler and said, "Good morning."

He said, "Here, take these sesame seeds, and when the ghoul asks you to delouse her, pick out the lice and pop these sesame seeds into your mouth saying how delicious her lice are."

Finally she reached the tent of the old ghoul. "Good morning, Grandmother," she said to the old lady.

"Good morning," answered the ghoul.

"I came to borrow a sieve."

The ghoul said, "First knock down the tent."

So Slaysla tightened all the guy ropes, swept the tent, and got it all nice.

Then the ghoul said, "Break my dishes."

Slaysla washed all the dirty dishes and stacked them neatly.

The ghoul said, "Go shit outside my tent."

So the girl took a broom and swept all around the tent.

Then the ghoul said, "Come groom me."

The girl sat down, and the old ghoul put her head in her lap. Slaysla began to groom her, picking out the lice and throwing them away and eating the sesame seeds saying, "Your lice are delicious, Grandma." She did this until she had completely cleaned her scalp.

Then the ghoul said, "Come help me get water from the well. Which would you prefer—that I lower you with a thin or a thick rope?"

The girl chose the thin rope. The ghoul lowered her into the well saying, "O well, Slaysla has come; fill her with gold and silk."

The girl came up glimmering with gold and silver. When her stepmother saw her come home with all this gold she called her own daughter to her and said, "Go return the sieve to the old ghoul and come back with lots of gold like Slaysla."

So Umm Zabarbar headed off. She passed the peddler, but instead of saying "Good morning" she said, "Look at the man who's harvesting in the morning." To the tree she said, "Boy, what a tall tree!" On and on, insulting everyone. Finally she got to the old ghoul's. She said, "Good morning, old lady, I came to return the sieve."

The ghoul told her to knock down the tent, so she did. Then she told her to break the dishes, so Umm Zabarbar broke all the dishes. Then she told her to shit all over the yard, so she went from place to place defecating. Then she said, "Come delouse me." She put her head in the girl's lap and the girl started picking lice from her hair and eating them, saying how awful her lice tasted. Then the ghoul asked her to help get water. "Do you want a thin or a thick rope?" she asked. The girl said, "I want a thick rope." (She was afraid she'd fall in the well.)

As she lowered her into the well, the ghoul said, "O well, Umm Zabarbar has come; cover her with donkey hides and scorpions."

The girl came up screaming, covered with snakes and scorpions, donkey hides and dog skins. She ran screaming all the way home. Her mother was horrified when she saw her so hideous. She picked off all the scorpions and snakes and yelled at her.

Then one day some people came to ask for Slaysla in marriage. When they came to pick her up for the wedding, the stepmother put her own daughter in the covered litter. Slaysla she put in the oven room to bake bread. Each of the girls had a pet cat, and Slaysla's cat meowed: "Slaysla's sitting baking bread and Umm Zabarbar's in the carrier." Umm Zabarbar's cat meowed the opposite. The men overheard this and asked what was going on. "It's just the cats fighting," said the stepmother.

But the men listened. Then they went in and took the cloak off the bride in the litter. They said, "That's not our bride!" So they went to the oven and found their girl. They dressed her up, gave her clothes; she already had her gold from the ghoul. They carried her off on the camel to her husband's home. They had the wedding, the groom slept with her at night, and they celebrated in the morning.

Slaysla stayed with her husband's family for a long time without going to visit her own family. After a while her brother wondered why she hadn't come. Her stepmother volunteered to go pay a visit. She went. She told Slaysla her father was sick and that she should come with her. So Slaysla left with the woman.

They walked and walked and walked, into an area that had no one in it. The stepmother suggested they rest a bit and offered to delouse Slaysla. She groomed her until the girl fell asleep. Gently she lifted her head off her lap and took off running, abandoning her.

The sun was shining, and it heated the earring resting on Slaysla's cheek and woke her up. She looked around—north, south, east, west—but saw she was alone. She started crying. Then she started walking. In the distance she saw several tents, but when she approached she found them all closed, so she decided to keep going. When she looked back she saw that they were all tombs. She said God's name and kept walking.

She came upon another tent. She looked all around but didn't see anyone. She went in and saw tombs in the tent. Also, there was a pot of rice on the fire. There was also a big chest in the tent, and she decided to hide in it. Toward sunset she cooked some vegetable stew, baked some bread, ate dinner, and left the rest of the food out. She climbed into the box and shut herself in.

Shortly thereafter a man arrived. He found dinner ready and was surprised. Later his two brothers returned. There were three brothers living there, herding camels. They took turns with the cooking. The other two were surprised that he had made them dinner so early: usually he didn't get it ready so fast. But he decided to say nothing. They had dinner and stayed up talking.

The next day, the girl cooked rice, ate, and made herself a pot of tea. Then she got ready another pot of tea, put water, tea, and sugar in the pot, and left the rice on the fire. She climbed back in the chest. The second brother came home to make dinner and was shocked to find it all ready. When the brothers returned he told them what had happened. They decided that one of them should stay home the next day. He would hide and find out who was cooking for them. So the next day, one of them hid.

When she thought everyone was gone, the girl got out of the box and set about cleaning. When she went out to tighten the tent ropes, the brother grabbed her. "Who are you?" She said, "I'm a Muslim." Then she told her story. When the other brothers came home they heard her story and then asked her what she wanted to do—marry one of them, go back to her husband, or find her old family. She said she'd stay and marry one of them. They decided she should marry the eldest brother, so she did and she stayed with them.

And that's the end. They went away and I came back.

Sons

"Lila! Come on." The engine was running and we said our good nights. The stars, as always, were bright as we made our way back. Through the shutters we could see lights still on at home, but we had to bang hard on the door before one of the girls opened. The creases in her reddened cheek spoke of sleep.

"Put down a mat. And get a pillow for Lila's back," Sagr ordered his daughter. A barefoot toddler rounded the corner, followed by Gateefa. He was affectionate with the little girl. "Welcome, welcome, welcome. What's this? Haven't you fallen asleep yet?" He cuddled her, nibbling on her neck as he pretended to be a ghoul and remarking to me that the youngest child is always the dearest. Winking at his embarrassed wife he said, "That's why I want to keep having children." He was not one of those fathers who remained distant from his children, he insisted. He reminded me that I had seen him with his children crawling over him and riding him like a horse while he was trying to do business. I had also seen him clipping his young daughters' fingernails and even sometimes wiping their runny noses.

Everyone loves children, he added. All little creatures are cute, even puppies. You see how God created things! There is an old story, that they once asked an old man, "Who is your favorite?" He said:

> "The one who's absent, until he returns
> The one who's ill, until he recovers
> And the one who's small, until he gets big."

But a girl is not like a boy—he will become a man; the girl doesn't have as much strength of will. As long as her father is alive, a girl does not feel any pain. But when he dies, it is hard on her. Daughters, Sagr said, are dearer to him than sons. A father doesn't want anything from his daughter. He just wants to make sure she marries well and can take care of herself. But a son needs testing. He must make sure he has turned out well, has managed to make a living. If not, his father must yell at him. This is not because he doesn't love his son. That could never be. No matter what they do, a father can't stop loving his children. It is possible for a child to abandon his father or mother, but not the reverse. A proverb says, "The one who gives birth is not like the one born."

Sagr asked me what I'd done all day. I told him where I had been and mentioned that I had tape-recorded stories the women had been telling.

He objected. "These stories, Lila, they're not true. An old woman or old man will tell them to the grandchildren. We call them 'little somethings.' Children love this sort of talk."

A sleepy Gateefa added, "If a child is unhappy, he says, 'Please tell me a story.' We use stories to bribe them. 'If you do this—say, go take the goats out to graze—then I'll tell you some stories.' So the kid goes and does what you ask so he can get a story."

Sagr went on, "What is worth writing are tales of things that really happened. That's what should become known, the stories with real meaning. There was so much good poetry before. Not anymore. I used to know so much. You need to find someone who's relaxed and carefree enough to remember. When I'm busy and worried about things, I can't get it right. Yesterday, when I was alone and had no guests, I remembered a lot of poems. But now I've lost them again."

After a short silence, he began, "For example, there was once a rich important man. His brother had been killed by another tribe. His brother had been very dear to him, and so he went blind. He stopped seeing. He did nothing about it. His sons were young, so he waited until they grew up. When they had become young men, he gathered the three of them and said, 'Come here. Anyone who wants something should tell me and I'll get it for him.'

"The eldest son said to his father:

'I want a small herd of she-camels
and a prancing stallion
and to live with the daughter of a good man.'

"He turned to his second son. 'And you?'

'I want some milking camels
and a majestic horse to ride on
and to live with the daughter of a tribal leader.'

"The old man said fine. But this wasn't what he wanted to hear. He wanted something about avenging his brother. He turned to the youngest son, 'And you?' The young man said:

'I want to be up on a young mare
And for times to change
To pursue someone who owes me and who had hidden
But like a fool has now forgotten our debt.'

"The father said to him, 'You shall succeed me. You are going to be in charge.' And to those others he said, 'Okay, go. You'll get what you want.' Then he bought the young man his mare, and he bought him a gun. And his son set off. Day followed day followed day until the young man found the one who had killed his uncle. He killed him and returned home.

"It's a pity," Sagr added, "this was a long tale with lots in it, but I've forgotten how most of it goes."

We talked about having sons. It used to be, Sagr explained, that you needed sons. If you didn't have men, no one would respect you. They'd push you around. Gateefa protested. These days, she said, having many sons was a bad idea. You men all want to marry wives so you can have sons, she accused. But strength isn't in numbers. She gave the example of their grandfather. He was an only son, yet nothing could happen in his whole tribe without his being consulted first. And he was wealthy. The men, she complained, say that their bounty comes from God. But they forget how much they inherited. Their grandfather was wealthy, and his sons were only a few. Now if they were to divide the land, there would hardly be a square meter for each.

Yet, Sagr pointed out, women want sons as much as men do. Hadn't I noticed, he asked me, giving his wife a glance, that as women get older, they use their children to dominate their husband? They pay less and less attention to their husband. They tell him to go to hell. A woman raises her sons to displace him. Once she has grown sons, she doesn't need a husband at all.

But sons, at least according to folktales Gateefa had told, seemed only sometimes to be good to their mothers. One tale I had recorded about mothers and sons—and sisters—was an odd moral tale. This was how Gateefa told it:

There were two sisters. Each one married a man. One of them had children, and the other was barren. She didn't have children. So she started trying to have children, she went looking for children. She went to her sister and said to her,

"My sister, I haven't gotten pregnant, and now the man wants to take a second wife. What do you think?" Her sister said to her, "My dear, I'm pregnant. Why don't you come back the month I'm due? When I have the baby, you can take it."

Time passed, time passed. Finally the woman told her husband, "My sister is going to have her baby this month. I'll just go and bring back the baby." She went. She went and stayed with her sister until she gave birth. She washed her clothes for her, cooked for her, and cared for her. Eventually she said to her, "My sister, I want to go home now. What do you think? Will you give me your baby?"

But her sister said, "Oh! I just can't do that."

"What? How could you lie to me? I came here and spent a month with you and I told my husband you were giving me the baby. I told him to wait until you'd marked your fortieth day and then come for me."

Her husband came. He had brought her a camel, and he had brought her a blanket for the baby. So she bundled an extra dress, to make it look like a baby, and she wrapped this in another dress and carried it in the blanket. They traveled and traveled until they got close to the camp.

Then she said she had to stop. When they got close to the camp she got down and said she wanted to go over to a shrub. She told her husband he should go on ahead and she would follow. Her husband asked why. She said, "For the child. Go ahead, I'll catch up with you." (She was just lying. There was no child, but she didn't know what to do.) She began walking and walking. He went ahead on the camel, and she stayed behind.

Soon she saw a bird come down from the sky and peck at something. She went toward it. She walked and walked, and when she got close she saw that someone had left a baby there. It was still crying. She got a bit of broken glass and cut the umbilical cord, swaddled the baby, wiped him clean, and bundled him up. And she went home with him.

See? See what God sent down for her? So she walked and walked. Her neighbors greeted her ululating and announcing,

"She had a baby! She had a baby!" The women came to visit and bring gifts.

After about a year, she got pregnant. She got pregnant and had another boy. Time passed, and then her sister came to visit. She had sent for her to attend the circumcision celebration for the boys. Of course, the last time she had seen her, she had refused to give up her child.

Her sister was surprised. "What's this, my sister? When did you have a baby?"

The woman said, "My dear, God gave me of his bounty. I came and stayed with you, and when I went home I went blind crying. I got off the camel, afraid to come home and have the women laugh at us when the man came saying I was carrying my new baby. I didn't know how I would lie. I was embarrassed, so I said to myself, I'll stay here until God opens a way for me. I brought the bundle with me. Then I saw a bird pecking at something, wanting to eat it. I rescued the baby, wiped it off, and took it home. I raised him and cared for him, and a year after I weaned him God granted me my own child. And I had him and now I want to circumcise him." Then she gave her sister a dress and a scarf and some gifts for her boys.

Time passed, and the boys grew up. One would ask, "Mom, what can I get you?" The other would ask, "Mom, what can I do for you?"

But the other woman, the one with seven sons, got thrown out. The sister who had denied her a child was thrown out by her sons. One day she arrived carrying her bundle of clothes on her head. "Who's this? Who's this?" "It's your sister," she said. "My boys threw me out and I want to stay with you."

Her sister said, "Come in." And her sons said, "Here is a house for our mother and for our mother's sister. And here is our house. Whatever we bring for our mother, we'll bring for our aunt." If they brought clothing, they'd bring the same thing for both of them. And if they brought food, they'd bring equally for both of them.

Time passed and passed, but not a single one of the other woman's sons came to support her. Not a single one came looking for her. So she stayed with her sister until finally she died. She got old and died.

The boys said, "Should we bury her before even sending for her sons?" Their mother said, "Go tell them, 'Your mother has died.' " One of the young men went and told them, "Hey men, come. Your mother has died. Come attend." They said, "No, we won't attend. Bury her wherever you want to. We don't want to bury her. We don't want her."

So her sister held the funeral for her and buried her. And she told her sons, "This woman is like a holyperson. There's no one in the world like this dear one who died. Every year I want you to make a pilgrimage to her tomb."

When they did, the boys found some gold, a pot full of gold. They'd circle around the tomb and they'd find a little pot of gold by her head. They showed their mother. She said, "Don't tell anyone." Every day that they went to visit her tomb, they found gold. They kept making pilgrimages to her tomb until they became wealthy.

Good mothers, bad mothers. Good sons, bad sons. There is pain for mothers whose sons do not come to ask each day, "Mom, what can I get for you? Mom, what can I do for you?" In a poor family like Ngawa's, a son might leave to find work. In fact, Ngawa's husband's older brother had a son in Libya. After ten years, they had despaired of his return. His mother's song for him was a song about herself.

> My dear, have you forgotten my love?
> Oh how long I carried you around . . .

Chapter 4

PATRILATERAL
PARALLEL–COUSIN MARRIAGE

Prohibited to you are: your mothers, daughters, sisters, father's
sisters, mother's sisters, brother's daughters, sister's daughters,
foster-mothers (who gave you suck), foster-sisters, your wives'
mothers, your step-daughters under your guardianship, born of
your wives to whom you have gone in, — no prohibition if you
have not gone in; — wives of your sons proceeding from your
loins; and two sisters in wedlock at one and the same time,
except for what is past; for God is oft-forgiving, most merciful.
Also (prohibited are) women already married, except those
your right hands possess. Thus hath God ordained against you.
Except for these, all others are lawful, provided you seek them
with gifts from your property, desiring chastity, not fornication.

Qur'an 4:23–24

Sabra shyly pulled out from under the bed a bulging suitcase. As
she dusted it off and unbuckled the straps, she mumbled that her
mother had been saving up for her. One by one she began showing
me the swaths of dress fabric. This one, a patterned olive-green
silk, was a gift from a Saudi friend of her father's; that one, a
pink flowered polyester, came from her mother's aunt, who had
brought it back from the pilgrimage to Mecca. The solid-yellow

satin she had traded with a neighbor for a red that her mother's maternal uncle had brought for his niece. In the jumble I spotted something familiar: a beige nylon nightgown with a maroon ribbon I had brought from Boston many years earlier as a gift for Sabra's mother, Gateefa. In among the fabric were cheap perfume, bead necklaces, fringed scarves, and tiny glass bottles of musk.

"It's better to have this cloth ready," Sabra commented on the contents of the suitcase, "so you can put the whole brideprice into gold. Especially if you marry within the family, because then the brideprice is so much less."

Marriage was on her mind, just as it had been when I had first come to live with her family in 1978, seven years earlier. She was fourteen at that time, and, along with her other grown sisters, she had slept in the same room with me during that first winter. On those long dark evenings after the others had gone to bed we would chat about many things. The girls' favorite topic had been weddings.

One evening they drew pictures for me. Concentrating hard, Sabra, who had never been to school and had rarely held a pen, began to draw a line of trucks and cars. "A wedding procession," she explained. She showed me the bride, sitting in a Peugeot, the piles of stuff she was bringing along with her packed onto the roofs of the cars, and finally, in the rear, the truck carrying her bed and wooden wardrobe.

Long before I attended my first wedding in the community, I knew what to expect. The girls had been anxious to describe the events. They sang me wedding songs—softly, so no one could hear them—and they went over the whole procedure. Sabra introduced me to the terminology—for the marriage negotiations, the gifts brought for the bride, the wedding procession, the defloration. She described how families agreed to a marriage, and what the girl's parents and relatives bought with the brideprice: blankets, a bed, suitcases, a wardrobe, and the bride's gold—earrings, a necklace, a ring, bracelets. I had already seen this jewelry, identical except for weight, on all but the poorest of the married women in the community.

Sabra and her sisters were particularly animated when they described the wedding day. In the morning the bride would get dressed up and wait, surrounded by her women relatives and neighbors. Cars from the groom's family would come early to fetch her—lots of cars with lots of women. Young men, too. One car would come right up to the door so she could get in. They'd clap and sing and the drivers would toot their horns. On the way, the cars would circle around the local saint's tomb four times for blessings and then go on to the groom's father's house. The groom, Sabra explained, would not be there but at a neighbor's, because he was thought to be too embarrassed to be around his father. The older men and their guests would all be gathered in the men's guest room or a large tent. The bride, her face covered, would be brought into the room that would be hers and welcomed by women singing and drumming around her.

Then the young men would bring the groom. The women and girls would leave the room and wait outside the door when he entered, except one or two or three older women who would stay in the room to hold the bride. Then, Sabra whispered, the groom would wrap his finger in a white cloth and take her blood. The bride, she explained very matter-of-factly, would scream and struggle against him and sometimes there would be a fight—she'd hit the groom or he'd hit her or the women would hit her. Then the groom would throw to the gathered women the cloth with the blood on it, which they would carry off and hang on the guy ropes of a tent. The women and girls would begin to sing and clap and drum again. The bride would get bathed, changed, and perfumed.

The same narrative of the wedding included the bride's return visit to her parents' house a week or fifteen days later. Not her husband but his uncles or older brothers would accompany her, bringing two or three sheep for slaughter and lots of food: rice, tea, sugar, macaroni, candy. They would stay only for a meal and then take her back. The description ended here.

When I attended my first wedding a month after this conversation, I was disappointed. It was a small affair, even if it did follow the lines she had described. Later I would understand why: the groom was poor and from an undistinguished family and his wife a poor stranger; this was his fourth marriage, his previous wives having left him when they did not get pregnant; and it was bitter cold. I would have to wait for the summer and fall to begin to appreciate the girls' excitement and to sense the riot of feelings that weddings generated.

Arranging Marriages

I was surprised to find Sabra still unmarried when I came back again in 1987. She was now around twenty-three, although small and thin from a childhood illness and, with her long lashes, large brown eyes, and gentle smile, still quite young looking. I noticed her old suitcase piled on top of one of the wooden wardrobes, half buried by cases holding her father's winter clothes, flight bags stuffed with his important papers, and even a bag carefully packed with all the clothes I had left behind hoping they might find a use for them.

When I had first come to live with them, I had asked the girls anthropological questions like "How are marriages decided?" Sabra had given me the official answer: "It is the father who decides." Someone comes to ask for her and her father decides. A girl, she had told me, cannot say anything until after the marriage. If she does not like the groom, she can come home then; but she cannot say no before the marriage has taken place. But then Sabra had added, "Some girls do protest—those who have no modesty."

Why had Sabra's father not yet arranged a marriage for her? Various families had come to ask for her. Her father had refused to consider a request from his older sister's only son because, twenty-five years earlier, the boy's tribe had withheld from him a woman he had wanted to marry. Sabra's two sisters, Safiyya's daughters, who were among those who had spent those giggly evenings with me, were now married to two brothers, Sabra's first cousins. Why had they bypassed her?

Sabra's younger sister told me how it had happened. They had planned for years the marriage between Safiyya's eldest daughter and one of the cousins—they were only waiting for him to finish his military service. I knew that. But just a week before the wedding, Hamid, the boy's father, had come to ask for Sabra for his younger son, thinking to save money and trouble with a double wedding. Sabra's mother, however, had refused. (We all knew that Gateefa's relations with the family were strained.) Instead, Sagr offered his brother another of his daughters, from Safiyya. This left Sabra, though she was older, unmarried.

Gateefa told me about another family that had come asking for her daughter Sabra. As she told it, Sagr had run into some friends at the market. They had asked if he would be willing to let their two sons marry his daughter and a niece. He had tentatively agreed. When he came home and informed his wife, she was furious. She told him she would never make her daughter marry into that family. They lived in tents in the desert, and her daughter, who had grown up in a house and had few of the old Bedouin skills such as caring for tents or milking sheep, would find life too hard. Moreover, the family that had asked for her was in trouble. The reason they were living in a tent camp when everyone else was in houses was that two of their men had accidentally killed a man in a fight. As was customary, they were forced to seek refuge with another family, leaving behind their homes and land. They lived in fear, knowing that the victim's kinsmen would want revenge.

Sabra's mother did not want her daughter to be a widow. She said no. Her husband was angry, she told me. "What am I supposed to tell them? I already agreed," he had said. He then marched off on foot to talk to his niece's mother, to enlist her support. But she, too, refused to let Selima, her only daughter, marry into that family. The women suggested that he inform his friends that the girls' male cousins had asserted their right to claim them. He would save face, and Sabra and Selima would not have to go. And that is what happened.

Another request, from the family of Sabra's father's third wife, Azza, had been trickier to deal with. The accounts I heard conflicted, and, knowing Haj Sagr's deteriorating feelings toward his wife and her relatives, I believed none of them.

According to one sister's version, Sabra's father had set tough conditions for Azza's family, but these had been met: a high brideprice of five thousand Egyptian pounds (then worth about $2,500) and a separate house for Sabra to live in away from the man's parents. The house was built in Matruh, and they even, it is said, put in electricity. But then Sabra's cousin claimed her. He went, according to this version, and informed the prospective groom that unless he arranged to give his own cousin to the new claimant in exchange, the man could not have Sabra. The poor would-be groom protested. Had it been a sister he might have managed, but in his Egyptianized town family he had no say over his cousin.

Sabra's version was different. The man, she insisted, had not asked specifically for her: rather, he would take any of her father's daughters. Moreover, it was Azza who had approached Sagr, and he had told her he had no objections. They settled on a day when the family would come to make arrangements. In the meantime, though, Sabra's uncle Hamid had run into Azza's relatives at the market. When he had asked who the groom was to be, one of the men, joking, had pointed to an old lame man who was with them.

Her uncle was furious: no way would his family give one of their girls to that old cripple. The men had just been joking, but Sabra's uncle had made up his mind. The next thing they knew, he had sent his son to demand an exchange. In this version, too, the prospective groom had said, "We're not like you. We don't have any say over our cousins. Everyone is responsible only for himself." Sabra's cousin had said then that the man could not have her, so the groom and his family got angry and did not come on the appointed day.

Was she hurt when she heard that her cousin had gone to claim her, knowing it was a bluff?

"No," she had said. "Why should I be upset? A Bedouin girl has no say, they don't care what she thinks."

I persisted. "But inside, even if you don't say anything, do you get upset?"

Her answer added a crucial new bit of information. "No, I don't ever want to have to marry a man who already has one wife. I was glad my cousin did it. I want to marry someone young, someone who is not yet married."

"And what if he hadn't been married?"

"Then I would have gone to my cousin and said, 'Isn't it wrong, cousin, to do that?' "

I tried to probe her feelings about being still unmarried. As we sat with a neighbor of about Sabra's age I asked, "Do girls like yourselves get bored sitting at home? I mean, if it takes a long time before you get married?"

"Does anyone get tired of her own family?" Sabra's friend had replied. Then invoking the special strength of Bedouin family bonds she explained, "Among the Arabs, girls don't get bored. It is only among the peasants that people gossip. They say, 'No one has come for her and she's gotten old . . .' But the Arabs want their daughters to stay with them, they prefer it. They don't marry them off so young because they think it's hard if they have children when they're too young. No one says, 'She's gotten old.' "

Sabra just listened quietly. Not long after the last rejected marriage request—the joint request for her and her cousin Selima—it had been arranged that Selima would marry another first cousin from the camp. This made it easier for Sabra's father to face his friends in the market, and everyone was pleased with the match. But everyone also knew that no more male cousins remained in the camp the right age for Sabra.

Night of Henna

There was much running back and forth as Selima's wedding day drew near. Everywhere clusters of little girls, some no more than three years old, giggled and sang wedding songs. I asked Sabra and her sisters why they liked weddings so much.

"Who doesn't like weddings? Don't you like weddings?" They were puzzled.

When I said I liked other things just as well, they pointed out that they never got to do anything except run around and work all day. "It's nice to be able to get away from that. You do other things you enjoy. We don't."

The evening before the wedding, Sabra hurried to get supper ready early so she could put on her new yellow dress and fringed scarf and take off, in the dark, to her uncle's. Her younger sisters had already slipped away during the day, escaping their chores. They had wanted to help prepare their cousin for the wedding. I had seen them earlier in the day combing and oiling Selima's hair, plucking her eyebrows, and dressing her, this time in a red-and-gold brocade dress. They had sung songs of compliment, clapping to keep the rhythms. I had dutifully admired the bride's wide gold bracelets, her new earrings, her dresses, and rummaged through the straw basket piled with the shawls, scarves, slips, and negligees of her trousseau. It was whispered that the necklace she wore was really her mother's: the brideprice had been too low to allow for much gold.

Because the bride and groom were close cousins, their fathers being brothers and their mothers sisters, we would be busy that evening: we had to celebrate at both households, beginning at the groom's, where the wedding would take place the next day. Guests, male and female, had been gathering. It was still mostly family, swelled by the happy presence of Sabra's great-aunts, aunts, and cousins—women who had married men from other families and visited only a few times each year.

When Sabra and I approached the camp, we heard drumming and saw faint lights shining through the threadbare tent where the women sat. Made of burlap sacks, the tent had been pitched for cooking. Inside, lit by kerosene lanterns suspended from the two center poles, the flushed girls were on the ground, crowded together in a circle. Sabra squeezed in next to the girl drumming on a round aluminum tray. The beat was strong, and the girls sang song after song. These were short rhyming two-part songs appropriate to the "night of henna"—the evening before the wedding when women decorate their hands and feet with henna paste.

The girls took turns shouting out the first lines of new songs, some of which welcomed the guests, while others referred to the festivities themselves:

> We're playing at a wedding of ours
> And damn anyone who tries to stop us
>
> Those who came to our wedding we'll go to
> We won't bother with those who didn't
>
> Those who come to congratulate you, my dear
> May they be next so I can go to them
>
> You who've come to keep me company
> Make your night last until morning
>
> If you'd not been very dear
> Late at night we'd not be here
>
> My brothers and my uncles' sons
> I'm happy when they come before me

> Go tell her aunt who's far away
> To attend this happy evening
>
> Uncle, those who've come to congratulate
> That's a favor I'll not forget
>
> A hundred blessings on our aunt
> Who held a wedding and gathered us all
>
> You who've come here from out west
> Welcome, welcome, you've honored us

The older married women ringed the circle of enthusiastic girls. They sat back to listen and chat quietly. Every so often one of them—the groom's mother, his aunt, his grandmother, his father's wife—broke in with a melodic song of a different sort.

> The maternal and paternal aunts
> are happy at your marriage, O beloved . . .
>
> He wore himself out to set you up
> Bravo for your father, son . . .

At the end of each song, other women ululated and the girls resumed their drumming and rhymes.

Suddenly, laughing as she protested, a girl would be dragged into the middle to dance. A shawl would appear and someone would knot it around her hips. Of the women in the outer ring, only one or two would take special notice—usually her mother, perhaps an aunt. To get the older women involved, it was necessary to inspire someone from their midst. Then, to wild shouts of encouragement and wide smiles, this older and more robust woman would begin a shimmy of the hips that no younger girl could imitate. The girls would sing to these serious dancers:

> If you dance, those here will come
> To repay you at the wedding of your son

Even if her topknot is grey
[Dancing] on Little Ali's wedding day is no shame

Even if she's gotten old
To sing and do it, she knows how

Out little boy, she's not for you
This lesson's from an old lady, an old man's thing

Gateefa was moved to break into a song as her older cousin got up to dance, playing with a cane as women had in the past.

Gold dipped in gold
the beloved is the pure coin of old . . .

I had heard that many years ago, when it was still acceptable and expected, many of Sabra's aunts had danced at their brothers' or cousins' weddings—not just, as now, among the women and girls, but in front of all the young men. The men had serenaded them with the sort of song one heard now only on cassettes, mostly smuggled in from Libya.

When Sabra's aunts and great-aunts had been young, they had also danced in the wedding parties that accompanied the bride to her new home. As Migdim had been, these brides were carried inside a litter on the back of a camel. Dodging celebratory gunfire, the women had danced completely veiled, their waists girded thickly with the same white men's cloak that brides come covered in today. This had not stopped men from singing to them in praise of their beauty.

In the market today one can buy the cassettes of 'Awadh al-Maalky, the most popular of the new local singing stars, who still composes lines that follow the old form. On one tape he welcomes and then describes minutely the totally veiled dancer.

Welcome, welcome to the one who's come.
Welcome, welcome to the one who's come.

Welcome, you with the trailing bangs,
Welcome, you with the eyes so black,
Welcome, you with the eyes rimmed with kohl,
Welcome, you, the best of your age.
So now, it will make me very happy
to describe you exactly right;
to say in front of all those present,
to say in front of all those sitting here:
Your hair is thick
and your braids swing to the left . . .

After more on the dancer's braids, the poet begins a new conceit—
drunkenness—that marks it as a song of the present.

Like a man coming out of a bar,
like a man who's drunk—
who has drunk every variety there is,
who careens from wall to wall,
I'm dizzy, caught in the current,
I'm dizzy, caught in a whirlpool . . .

With the lines "We've talked enough about the drunk, and still
there is more of you to describe," he goes on to describe her
glowing cheeks, her eyes, her smile, and the blush in her lips that
has set his heart on fire. No sooner do the words become less
innocent than he checks them with pious expressions, in line with
the new seriousness people show toward religion.

Praise be to God who created in you
your neck and shoulders and arms,
small hennaed hands.
And under your necklace I saw in you—
now I'll talk about them and show you
forgive me since I'm a poet
you'll permit me and oblige—
You, about your breasts, what can I say? Wow!
He whose heart is patient loses it,

> He who recites the Qur'an loses it.
> May God protect me from the Devil!
> I worship God the Glorious
> and I pray, and the neighbors know it,
> but you made me possessed by spirits;
> the Lord created for you breasts,
> standing firmly like pomegranates,
> that would warm someone shivering in the cold . . .

Like all such songs, this one goes into many verses. Girls of Sabra's age have never heard men sing them for female dancers, just as they have never seen a woman dancing in front of young men. They have heard, as I had, about things that are hard to imagine now: male singers vying for the attention of dancers who defiantly jump out of their reach or walk away in anger if the men's songs don't please them.

For the girls, weddings have always been—as Selima's was—divided into women's and men's activities. Only girls sing about the dancer—a recent practice, says Sabra's mother, that began a mere fifteen years ago. Many of their songs are compliments—the risqué ones they learned from wedding guests from areas near Alexandria with peasant influence. To encourage their sisters and cousins as they danced, then, Sabra and the girls sang:

> Take the sash and tie it around me
> Drum a lively beat, then teach me
>
> Your mom's bloomers are made of satin
> Shake 'em or get out of here
>
> Hey beautiful, may God protect her
> She's dancing, her hands held up there

At times like this of great happiness and display, people feel vulnerable. They dance with their hands held up against the evil eye. A tale Sabra heard from her uncle's wife shows why. A woman, the story goes, was heading off to a wedding. Her father stopped her and made her fill her mouth with water so she wouldn't join in when the other women said of the bride, "She's ugly," "Her nose is too long," or "Her legs are too short." At the wedding this woman said nothing, but she did notice some small flaw in the bride. When she got home, her father told her to spit out the water in her mouth. They found it had turned to blood— just from this bad thought. Thus the girls sang that evening about warding off people's envy:

> Our bride is fair and beautiful
> In the envying eye put a burning ember
>
> Into the eye that envies people
> We'll stick a brass comb
>
> If you fear the eye
> Wear amulets of a hand and a red pepper

The girls know special songs for celebrating marriages between cousins. Although under normal circumstances Sabra's sisters, away from the camp, as they rode their donkeys to the public water tap, would sometimes sing rude ditties about the boys living on their hill—

> I don't want the old cap on the hill
> What I want is a new Peugeot
>
> Mom, get me off this hill
> No firewood and no sweet water
>
> God damn the uncle's son
> Lord don't lead me near no blood relative

—tonight they had only praise for marriages within the family:

> O Lord, let them be many
> The weddings between cousins

> The bride belongs to us
> And the groom is our aunt's son
>
> O Grandma, bless our joy
> She's our little girl and she's at our son's

As the girls sang, older women like Selima's aunt Ngawa, with her raspy voice, and Gateefa, her voice strong and clear, interrupted the drumming to sing their slow songs about the virtues of this kind of marriage:

> Even on the scales
> her splendor is like his . . .
>
> Silk on silk is beautiful
> better than gathering at strangers' . . .
>
> Some people travel to strangers
> but we take from our own . . .

The muttering began after this song. A neighbor had taken offense because her daughter, who had recently married Hamid, Selima's father, was a "stranger," not a relative. Women tried to calm her by pointing out how many of them were outsiders. Her daughter, they reminded her, was hardly the only one.

But as in their parents' generation, in Sabra's and Selima's there had already been matches between cousins. All these marriages within the camp appeared happy; all had produced sons. Girls who listen to traditional romances get mixed messages about marrying cousins. Some stories expose the tyranny of a young man's right to marry his first cousin; equally as many glorify cousin marriage.

Even in Sabra's family a story was told about grandparents who were related. Sabra's great-great-grandfather, it was said, had been an only son. Because his father had died young, his mother took him home with her to Fayoum, but early on she had arranged with her husband's relatives that he would one day marry his cousin

Aziza. While he was away she grew up to be a beautiful woman much desired. Her family finally agreed to give her in marriage to some people living far to the west.

A cousin heard about the match and set off by camel on the five-day journey to Fayoum to inform the young man. When he arrived at the tent he found the young man's mother and gave her the news. Her wailing brought her son, who came running to ask what the matter was. "Nothing," she said. "It's just that when I asked about your cousin Aziza he told me she was about to be given to some people out west!" The two had loved each other when small. So the young man traded his horse for a camel and rode with his cousin for five days until he got to Aziza's camp. He found that the wedding had already taken place.

Without even spending the night the two men set off again, riding west for several more days. When they reached the camp the young man insisted on going in alone. He saw a tent set apart in front of the camp—the bridal tent. As he approached, the men of the camp came out. They had heard of him and knew that their bride was his, but her relatives had thought he was so far away that he would never hear about it. They came out to greet him and invite him to rest, but he refused to dismount. Since he refused to go to the tent, they picked it up whole and brought it to him. Then Aziza came out to greet him, hugging him and kissing his cheek. The men admitted they had been wrong to take his bride and offered her back.

After accepting their hospitality, he said he would not insist on taking her. She chased after him, and his companion argued with him: "After all this, you won't take her? You'd better bring her." The men of the camp gave the bride a riding camel and loaded up seven more with provisions, which they said were the young man's to keep. He proudly refused them and agreed to keep only the one camel for his bride. They rode back to his father's territory, then married there and planted barley. That year the rain fell only on his land. Year after year, it rained only on his land, and soon he became one of the wealthiest men in the region.

The happy ending of this "true" story of the cousins who founded Sabra's line is like the ending of many romantic tales full of poetry about cousins who love each other. Trouble begins when the girl's father, for one reason or another—often because his nephew is poor—violates the young man's rights by promising his daughter to someone else. These stories are about longing and cleverness, about cousins who outwit their parents by feigning illnesses, playing tricks or reversing roles so that girls pursue their male cousins, or simply eloping. Many of the Bedouin stories of the past, mythical and true, are about marriage between cousins. As Sabra's old aunt Dhahab says, "If you don't tell the stories you forget them. Now that there are radios, we don't tell stories anymore."

The Bride

The girls' drumming suddenly stopped. The groom's father was causing a commotion after having made his way in the dark from the ceremonial white tent where the men were sitting. Although the tent had been pitched far from the house and the women's cooking tent, he complained that the sound was carrying in the still night air. There were men there, outsiders who had come as guests, and the women would have to stop.

The old women protested. They often spoke about how weddings had changed. Migdim had said once, "No, the things they did before you can't do anymore. Nowadays weddings are small, like a shrunken old man. People used to really celebrate, staying up all night, for days! But they have become like the Muslim Brothers now."

The younger woman she was talking to had explained for me. "They say it is wrong. Now everything is forbidden. People before didn't know. They were ignorant. Now they say it is wrong for women to dance in front of men."

Migdim held her head and sighed. "Everything passes. Now they don't sing or ululate. They just bring the bride and that's that."

"The men say no," her daughter-in-law added. "Like at the last wedding we had. They sang and clapped only the day before the wedding. The day of the wedding itself the men said not to sing because there were people from all over visiting."

In the name of religious propriety older men had begun to interfere, like tonight, in the women's celebrations. I had heard a couple of times the favorite story about the last wedding in the camp. The girls and women had been celebrating for many evenings with drumming and singing. The older men kept trying to stop them. On the night of henna, when they had assembled again and begun the fun, the groom's father came in to welcome his aunts and cousins. He also hoped to quiet the group of women. When he walked into the women's tent, he saw his own older sister, a dignified woman in her sixties, dancing.

"Hey, what's this!" he had said. "Rottenest of days! Even you, Hajja?" He called her by the respectful title reserved for those who have performed the pilgrimage to Mecca.

"That's right," she had answered defiantly, "even me!" Everyone thought it exceedingly funny.

The old women contrast this situation with a time when girls danced veiled in front of the young men and women and men exchanged love songs. Some songs, like those exchanged as the young woman danced, were challenges. Migdim remembers one exchange between Sabra's other grandmother and a shepherd attached to the family at the time. As her sister danced, the woman had sung:

> A bird in the hot winds glides
> and no rifle scope can capture it . . .

The man had responded:

> The heart would be no hunter
> if it didn't play in their feathers . . .

None of this could go on now. The same men who when younger had sung such songs to women had now become elders.

Unlike their fathers, these men felt they had to keep the women quiet when outsiders were there. That evening, we had no choice but to give in to the men's wishes and stop singing.

Anyhow, the girls decided, it was about time they went to celebrate at the bride's place—she had been sitting alone all evening, with only a few girls and a couple of the young married women to keep her company. Two brave girls led the way with lanterns as we trailed off across the camp under the starlight. Since all the men were at the groom's household, we spilled noisily into the girl's courtyard and sat on the ground. Selima, the bride, was brought out and put on a chair in front of us. She looked happy as another old aluminum tray was brought out for the drumming. "Come on girls, liven up!" shouted one old neighbor, getting up to dance. "Come on, faster!"

> Fair and her bangs hanging down
> A girl you'd say was a lowland gazelle
>
> Fair, unblemished with not a mark on her
> Like the moon when it first appears
>
> She takes after her maternal and paternal aunts
> Gold threaded with pearls
>
> If you want love from a girl of our tribe
> Put down nineteen hundred pounds
>
> Her father doesn't care about money
> What he wants [in a man] is importance and honor

Encouraging Selima to feel good about the match, the girls sang songs that praised their cousin, the groom:

> The one you took is the son of a Bedouin
> Not a good-for-nothing who hangs out in cafés
>
> The boy you got is from a good family
> So don't cry and don't say "O Mommy"

One by one, the older women broke into this wildness with their slow songs, many conveying the same sentiments about marriage to cousins.

> Pastures where your family put down
> set up your tent there, dear, blessed . . .

> The dear one, may her steps be blessed
> she sowed her seeds in her homeland . . .

> The dear one, may her steps be blessed
> she planted high in her homeland . . .

We had found the sisters of Selima's father's new wife at the household. They hated dwelling on this insider aspect of the marriage but wanted to show that they wished Selima well. Only one of them offered a song about marrying a relative. The others' songs had different themes:

> Apples from the gardens of the pious
> No one eats but the pure . . .

> May God's mercies on you, daughter
> be as numerous as the waves of the sea . . .

Many songs for the bride are, like this last one, tinged with sadness. But Selima was lucky not to be going far, or to an unknown life, so there were few such sad ones sung that evening.

Singing for hours on end, the girls are not always able to tie their rhymes to the specific wedding; they grab for any songs they know. A girl, though, will know many. One day Sabra's young sisters, aged eleven and twelve, had recited with barely a pause forty-six songs for my notebook. Their all-purpose songs might compliment the bride, groom, or their families:

> God protect the father who raised her
> Then to good people gave her

Their mothers reproach the girls for songs that are little more than nonsense syllables. Unlike the songs of older women with their images of spring pastures, sown barley, princes' steeds, and woven tents, the girls' songs appropriate whatever is new.

> If he doesn't bring a refrigerator
> I swear he won't have a taste of dinner

> If he doesn't get a television
> I swear I won't make up my eyes

> Anyone who tells me my sweetheart's in jail
> May he find himself hooked up to a glucose IV

> Hey you with the silver car
> Turn off the headlights, you're blinding me

> The one who owns the big truck
> Doesn't get drunk and doesn't touch beer

> Swing by, swing by in your Toyota
> To toss me the price of some cookies

> Put the bridal veil on her hair
> And let the photographer take her picture

The women disapprove because so many songs are indecent. The girls who helped me write down one sequence suddenly warned, "Don't ever show these to our father!"

> Hey woman, explain to your daughter
> Or she'll go to bed with her clothes still on

> Him with the patterned red headdress
> If God wills, I'll soon be counting his money

> Let's go, you and me, my sweetheart
> And the money we need will come from God

> You and I are the sweetest candy
> Let's go play up on the hillside

These are cruder than the older rhymes that get mixed in, though the old ones are also about love—like one that refers to the drops of water given to a person who has died:

> My eyes will never forget their sweetheart
> Not until they get the droplets at death

and a second about a dancer:

> A girl you'd say was a year-old calf
> When I come near her she jumps back

Other songs from an earlier generation reveal the intensity of love:

> Don't forget the one who's far away
> When the plant shoots come up he'll return

> No one has yet forgotten them
> They're still precious to the eye

> The tears of the eye at losing them
> Filled seven wells around them

On and on, late into the night, girls sang and women danced. As the guests drifted home, a dancer brought out the henna paste in a pot balanced on her head, a song about henna announcing its arrival. Those who wanted to smeared the paste on their palms; in the morning their brightly stained orange hands would mark their joy at the celebration. They sang to the bride one last time:

> Tonight's the night of henna
> And tomorrow at your sweetheart's you'll sleep.

The Blood of Honor

Sabra stayed overnight at her grandmother's. Like the young women her age who could cook, bake, and wash pots and pans, she rose at dawn and went to the groom's household to help her aunt with the work. Hundreds of guests had to be cooked for; each would eat two meals. Men were butchering lambs and goats. Bread needed baking, vegetables chopping, rice cleaning. The wedding had mobilized the whole camp.

Sabra wanted to be there not just to help with the work—after all, she had plenty of the same at home—but also to be there when the cars headed off toward the bride's, no matter how early. Everyone was waiting for this moment. As a rule, the older women angled most actively for places in the cars going to fetch the bride. They liked to see the houses and relatives of the bride, and they liked to sing songs that the bride's family would hear and perhaps respond to with their own songs. Contacts between the two families were usually competitive. Today, though, because the wedding was within the family, the number of cars and trucks the groom's family could muster, the number of women who could go, and the status of the men who would drive mattered little. The display was only for the guests, who would watch the cars cross the camp and return the long way around, detouring to circle a local saint's tomb.

When the time came, Sabra, like the rest of us, was ready and watching. Things began to happen quickly, though the morning had been slow. Tension was high as the convoy returned. We could hear the honking horns of cars and trucks that raised clouds of dust as they approached. Young men lined the entry to the courtyard, greeting the arrivals with volleys of celebratory gunfire. Selima, swathed in her father's white cloak, was rushed into her new room, followed by women and girls singing and dancing in welcome.

The bride is welcomed with song:

> The corners of the tent lit up
> happy that the desert gazelle has arrived . . .

The girls sang the same sorts of songs as the night before, but now with wishes as well that she would do well in her new family.

> May she be good
> And bless us with children and wealth

> May she be a real Arab
> To enter the community and not make trouble

During a lull, food was brought for the women who had come with the bride. Then more car horns, more gunshots. The groom was coming! Flanked by his friends, he was rushed through the crowd of women and children into the room where his bride sat. The door, newly painted blue and red, shut tightly behind him. All eyes were on it. The women and girls outside sang wildly, this time about what was going on inside. The songs told of how many people had stakes in the appearance of the "blood of her honor."

> Make her dear mother happy, Lord
> Hanging up her cloth on the tent ropes

> O Saint 'Awwaam on high
> Don't let anyone among us be shamed

The more serious songs of the older women had the same themes.

> When the people have gathered
> O Generous One favor us with a happy ending . . .

> Behind us are important men
> who ask about what we are doing . . .

Selima's aunt expressed faith in her niece's chastity.

> I'm confident in the loved one
> you'll find it there intact . . .

Not just the bride but the groom was on their minds.

> Khwayyir doesn't tremble or fear
> He brings forth her honor in a flash

It seemed like forever (though later they said two minutes, stopwatch timed). My heart was beating and my camera trained on the door when it was finally flung open. I jumped as the guns went off and the men rushed away. The women streamed in to surround Selima, dazed and limp in the arms of a relative, singing and dancing with relief. The cloth with its red spot of blood, a faint mark, was waved above our heads. Selima's maternal aunt exclaimed, "Praise God! Blessings on the Prophet! How beautiful! Blessings on the Prophet!"

The Most Important Moment

It was over now. People began saying their goodbyes. We were tired, especially the relatives who had been there for days, worrying about their girl. I took my bundle of clothes and walked with Selima's aunt Lawz. She knew her husband would come soon to pick her up and take her back home, and she wanted to spend her last hours with her mother. Other women came to join us at Migdim's. They began to go over what had happened: who had come, what these guests had brought with them, how well organized the cooking had been, whether there was enough food, who went in the cars to get the bride, who stayed in the room with her.

I had managed this time, juggling camera and tape recorder, to tape the singing outside the door after the defloration. I played back the tape for them. Amid the sound of wind and guns were enthusiastic voices. The women could make out the songs — or did they already know them all by heart? One was sung for the benefit of a nephew nearby:

> Go tell your father, O Sultan
> the banner of her honor is flying high . . .

Most of the songs were about our bride and the pride she brought to her family:

> They lived like falcons
> the hunters of the wild couldn't touch them . . .

> Bravo! She was excellent
> she who didn't force down her father's eyelashes . . .

> Look at her cloth, girls
> You'd say it was burst pomegranates

> Little Selima, blessings on your marriage
> You're lit up by the faces of your kin

> Little Selima, bless you for hiding it
> Your brother came back proud as a pasha

> Go tell her father to be happy
> The girl's blood came down on her hennaed feet

> The cloak I covered you with
> May God shine on your face, you filled it with light

The voices were hard to hear, and the women began to lose interest. These were only girls' songs anyway, not women's.

Suddenly one old aunt turned to me. "Hey Lila," she asked, "where you are, do they do it with the finger or with 'it'?"

I'd had this question many times, from my earliest days with them, and I laughed. Unlike the first time, I knew perfectly well what they meant by "it."

Gateefa, who had been with me on these previous occasions, answered for me. "No, they're like the people out west in Libya."

Before I had married, the women had often teased me about my fiancé. They had warned me not to let him enter with "it" on the wedding night. It was painful enough with the finger, which was, they pointed out, much smaller. They had also advised me not to permit my husband to sleep with me the first few nights after the wedding—to give the wound time to heal. Sabra's mother, Gateefa, always winced and commented after weddings, "Poor things," even though her own daughters were not involved.

But these other women were not like Sabra's mother. They were blunt and no-nonsense. One asked me a second question, "Hey Lila, did your man use a piece of cloth or a cloak?"

"We don't have cloaks," I answered. But to make it seem less strange, I added, "In the past they used to inspect the sheet the couple slept on."

But then they wanted to know, "Does the bride take it home to her family?"

Sabra's mother again explained for me. "It's considered shameful. The man just knows, and that's that."

"Doesn't her mother hang up the sheet or slip?"

"No," again I explained. "People would say it was embarrassing. It's something between the two of them."

Outraged, an old woman laughed. "Between who and who? They say it's between the two of them?!"

I had been through this just a few days earlier in a conversation with another woman. I had found myself feeling embarrassed to be from the West. She had begun by asking me a simple question. "In your country, do they marry their paternal cousins?" I'd had to say they didn't and that it was even forbidden, although I knew this was for them the best kind of marriage, sanctioned, so they told me, by the Qur'an. Next she had asked how much a family paid for a wife.

Gateefa, sitting with us then too, had laughed and said, "Without dowry. There's no brideprice. You like her, she likes you, and you marry her. That's that."

The woman thought we were kidding. "Do you swear by your father?"

Sabra's mother swore it was true. Sabra and her sisters had laughed at the incredulity of this old woman. Sabra had repeated her mother's words, "I swear by my father they don't pay."

To save face, I offered, "They'll get a wedding ring, and a diamond ring worth at least two thousand Egyptian pounds."

"That's the brideprice?"

Gateefa would not let me get away with this. "But they don't set conditions the way we do, or have a feast and slaughter sheep, or pay the brideprice, or get a trousseau for the girl."

The next familiar question came quickly. "Hey Lila, do they go in during the day or at night?"

"At night."

"Really? That's like the Egyptians. And do they do it with the finger or the other?"

"With the other."

"And Lila, do they get out the blood, like Arabs, the girl's blood? Do they get it out and show it, or don't they bother?"

I had to confess. "They don't show it."

Sabra's mother explained, "It's just between the two of them."

As the old woman turned this phrase over I added lamely, "There's no one there to show it to. It is nighttime and they've gone somewhere, like to a nice hotel. Or they've traveled far away, on a honeymoon."

She repeated, "So there's no one. He'll know and that's all, the groom."

Tired, after all these years, of their horror at the immorality of Europeans, I decided to try to explain a different way of thinking. "They say," I continued, "that it's just between the two of them — that it's shameful for others to enter into it. What business is it of theirs?"

The old woman repeated the phrase. "Right, what business is it of theirs?" Then she lowered her voice. "And what if, for example, what if the blood doesn't come out? What do they do?"

I said I didn't know.

"Maybe it doesn't matter to them," she suggested.

"It doesn't matter to them," confirmed Gateefa.

Suddenly Sabra's younger sister, quiet until then, had said something. "They don't care about it, Grandma. You know Ramadan's wife, the one in England? She said there was no difference in England between unmarried girls and divorcées."

This had set them talking all at once. I broke into their excited laughter to ask what she meant. Azza had piped in, "She said there were no virgins at all!"

The old aunt was puzzled. "What do you mean, there aren't virgins?"

"It's total chaos there," was the answer.

Perhaps sensing my discomfort, the old aunt tried to be reassuring. She said, "But Lila's not like that. She's proper."

Of an older generation, this woman had lived all her married life in an isolated desert area. She had had little contact with Egyptians from the Nile Valley, and she knew even less about Europeans. Here, closer to Alexandria, with marriages taking place between desert families and families from the agricultural province nearby, with schools and television and radio, people knew more about differences in the ways things are done. A few men I had talked with might even have been a little defensive about their wedding practices.

I had two interesting conversations of this sort during my first stay in the late 1970s, both with respected men in the Bedouin community. One, the sophisticated regional representative to Parliament, lectured me on a few Bedouin practices that were wrong: the first was that cousins had the right to block marriages and that girls could be forced to marry against their will; the second was that they "used the finger" and insisted on daytime deflowerings. Still, he had said, sitting by his Mercedes and wiping his sunglasses with his handkerchief, this taught girls to be careful—to act with thoughts of that future day.

The other man, a worldly businessman, had explained to me that "entering with the finger" was wrong. "We're the only ones who do it this way. Nothing in our religion says you should." He had added, by way of excuse, "But the faster the groom does it, the better—the more he is admired because it means he was not shy or afraid." I had heard women sometimes complain that it was stupid the way wedding guests waited and waited just to see that drop of blood. No one criticized the daytime ceremony, though. It allowed all the people to see, "So there would be no doubts."

Knowing how they felt, and sensing how badly Western practices could reflect on me, I was generally evasive on the subject. The afternoon of Selima's wedding I therefore found myself again trying to shift the conversation away from myself. Instead I saw a chance to find out what really happens in the room when the bride's virginity is taken, because here with me were the women who had been with Selima.

I took the offensive. "You didn't finish what you were saying. Did you say that people out west, in Libya, don't use a cloth or a cloak? Do *you* use a cloak? Does he wrap his finger in it?"

"No, no," said one aunt impatiently. "He wraps his finger in a piece of cloth. The blood comes out on the cloak she's sitting on. The bride sits on the man's cloak—they've laid it on the ground. And then they hang it up."

I was confused now. "They hang up the cloak but not the cloth?"

"They hang up the cloth too. The cloak she takes home to her family."

"When she goes for her visit?"

"Yes, after seven days she visits and they hang it out on the line."

Gateefa was used to explaining things to me. "They hang it at her family's so people can see . . ."

"So first they hang it at her husband's family's, then at her family's?"

Migdim interrupted to remind them about the first of her granddaughters to marry outside the community. "When she came home she brought her slip. Remember, I hung it here on my door. It was a half-slip."

This started them talking about recent weddings and comparing the sizes of blood stains. They discussed Lawz's daughter, a girl they had not had the strength to hold.

I worried it might be a delicate subject, but was too curious not to jump in: "Do the women have to hold her well? How do they hold her?"

They laughed when Lawz grabbed me and held me from behind. "Like this—we hold the bride like this," she mocked.

I struggled to get free and asked, "Does the bride scream?" I had heard that she did but that the screams were drowned by the singing. Sabra and the girls had told me a girl struggled "to show that her father had raised her well." Was there also fear?

Lawz, it turned out, had been one of the women in the room with her niece Selima. Hoarsely, she began telling us about the encounter. "Does the bride scream?" she repeated. "Why, the moment Selima saw him at the door, inside, she moaned, 'O my father! O my father!' "

"When she saw him?" I asked.

The bride's maternal aunt added, "She turned her head like this—and looked." She had been there too. "I guess she saw him—they were face to face, and he was inside the room. She turned her face away and went 'O father! O father!' I stood blocking her view of the door. I stood there so she wouldn't see his robe."

Gateefa wanted to get things clear. "Who was holding her?"

Lawz interrupted, "*I* was holding her." Half laughing at the memory, she described what happened: "I was holding her by the legs. Her other aunt was there too. She had sat her in her lap and put the cloak on the pillow under her. She had her arms around her and held her."

Migdim addressed her daughter, "Hey, woman, that reminds me. Did I hear that our neighbor went in there with you?"

Gateefa was surprised. "What? She was in the room with you? Why?" They discussed this angrily. Why was someone who was not a relative in the room, especially when relations between the bride's mother and this neighbor were not particularly good?

Lawz wanted to continue the story. "The moment she saw him, she said, 'Woe is me, my father! Woe is me!' She turned her face away and I told her, 'Stay quiet, don't you dare say a word! Be quiet.' And then, what happened? The woman met him at the door. I'd given her the cloth and told her, 'When he comes in, hand him the cloth and tell him to go ahead.' Well, he took the piece of cloth and put it around his finger. The boy approached Selima, still putting it on. He came near and what did I do? I opened her legs. I opened her legs and told him, 'Go ahead, extend your hand.' He reached out and I said to him, 'Twist your finger. Hard.' As soon as he pressed he got some blood. On the first twist. He said to me, 'Here it is.' Just after he said, 'Here it is,' though, that other woman pounced on the cloth. I told her, 'Give it back to him! Don't bother the boy. There's still plenty of time. Give the boy the cloth. Don't take it yet!' We said to my nephew, 'You'd better try one more twist like the one you just did.' "

Migdim was curious. "And so did he change the cloth?"

"Yes, he changed the cloth. He wrapped his finger again. He left the other spot and covered his finger again and did it again. It had been like a wipe—he just wiped it. When he wiped it, we said to him, 'Change the cloth, change it and put your finger *inside*.' As he was moving the cloth that other woman started yelling at him, 'You don't know how, boy. You didn't do it right!' "

"Bitch!" Migdim muttered.

"So we said, 'Give the boy the cloth! Here, son, take the cloth.' Then he gave one last rub. The last one got the blood."

The bride's maternal aunt added, "They told the woman to leave him alone."

"So why did he give this woman the cloth? What a scandal!" Migdim was indignant.

"She'd said, 'You didn't know how!' Didn't know how? How *should* he know? What's her problem?"

"What business is it of hers," asked the grandmother. "What did she want, that bitch, staying in the room?"

"How would *I* know?"

"Who let her in, anyway? You shouldn't have let her in," Gateefa insisted. "I'd refused to go in because I saw that Selima already had her aunt with her and there were three women there."

Lawz agreed. "Yes, she really was trouble. I told her to leave the boy alone. 'Don't interfere with the boy. Get away from him,' I said. 'He knows everything. He knows what to do.' "

I was trying to figure out why the women were so furious. I asked, "Did she want to do it for him? Was she afraid there wasn't blood?"

Migdim's daughter answered gruffly. "That is really wrong. You must never come near the bride. It's a great sin for a woman to go in and take the blood of a woman."

Another woman added, "Only if people are cheating do they do that!"

Lawz insisted, "But this wasn't a time when things weren't clear. From the first twist, he'd got it."

"So why was she interfering?"

Lawz continued, "She's the one who got people worried. She's the one who slowed us down. You know, if it hadn't been for her, he would have done it again and gone out right away! Don't you ever let her in again. She tied up the boy. 'Give it to me, give it to me,' she said. 'You didn't know how. Hand it over, you didn't do it right, boy!' And she took the cloth and wanted to put it on her finger."

This caused a furor, everyone talking at once. They wanted to know what happened next. They turned expectantly to Lawz. "So what did you say to the woman?"

She picked up the thread of her story. "I said to her, 'Stay away from the boy. Leave him alone! Let him be the one to get it.' I said to her, 'He got the blood already. Just let him get a little more. Let him be.' The woman said to him, 'Take this piece of cloth, take the cloth!' I was holding it, and holding the girl's arm. I held her this way, and our other friend was holding her too. We wanted him to do a second twist."

Migdim leaned closer to her daughter. "Did everyone see the blood?"

Lawz was firm. "No. But I saw. I looked and I saw. I've never been shy. I said to my nephew, 'Go ahead, son—you must not be shy about it. There should be no embarrassment, for you or her!' "

Her voice dropped to a whisper. "And then when he put his finger in the cloth, I lifted her up. Gave her a real lift, from below. With two hands. When he gave his finger a good twist, he brought out blood." With an expressive gesture, she added, "The spot on the cloth was *this* big. But then what did he do? He moved his finger and wiped, this way and that. He had just got a little. That was when the woman came after the cloth saying, 'You don't know how, boy. You don't know how.' But I'd seen the blood, from when he'd first put it in."

Again the women complained. "That bitch, that whore. What's the matter with her? God protect us."

Lawz was animated. "She'd said, 'I'm staying in the room with you. Are you staying, Lawz?' I'd asked her, 'Are you going to stay? Maybe you'll be needed out there. Your little girl has only just been weaned.' That's what I said to her. I wanted her to leave—the truth is, I didn't want her to stay. I said to Selima's aunt here, 'Stay standing just inside the door and when the boy comes in, give him the cloth right away so he can put it around his finger. That way when he comes to squat in front of her he'll be all ready.' But then the other one wanted to stay. So I said to her, 'Go hold her from there—hold her shoulder.' I didn't want her near the boy. But she started guiding the boy, guiding his hand."

The women exclaimed, "What? she started guiding him? She's the one that made him take so long!"

"And she tried to pull at the cloth, to blotch it. I said, 'Don't touch the cloth. Keep away from it.' "

"How shameless. Really shameless," said one listener. "What a disgrace," said another.

Lawz reassured them. "But she didn't touch the blood or anything. We gave the cloths to the boy—we gave him one first of all and then followed with the second right after. And the women came and took them, both of them. We didn't take off the girl's slip until later. As soon as I'd seen the blood come, I wiped her with her slip. I pressed it against her."

I wondered why.

The answer was obvious, "A woman, when she's wounded like that, her blood flows." Lawz went back to the narrative. "He'd come back toward us, wanting to take the cloth from that woman. We told him, 'That's enough. It's done! Get going!' I'll tell you, it's no good having too many women in the room with the bride. You need two to hold her, and then one standing near the door with the cloth ready for him. Good women. The third, she can come if she sees that the other two are having a hard time. If they don't have a hard time, even one's enough."

I was obtuse. "What do you mean, a hard time?"

"The bride, of course," Lawz said, "she struggles."

Gateefa laughed. She didn't have the courage to stay in the room with a bride. When she saw the groom coming, she told them, she started trembling and fled. "I don't have the strength for it," she said as the women teased her. "Some women do."

Outside Migdim's room the wide plateau was strangely graceful in the sun's glow, shadows touching the young fig saplings and gnarled olive trees. We thought we should start for home. Sabra and the girls had long since gone back. They had work to do: dinner to prepare, little ones to look after, bread to bake. Their mother only supervised.

As Gateefa and I made our way home, taking turns carrying her youngest daughter piggyback, again she sighed, "Poor things." She started recalling a nightmare she'd had the other day. She had dreamt that Sabra had gotten married and there was no blood. She had woken up sweating, her stomach knotted. She repeated what I had often heard her say: "Daughters are hard. Having daughters is so hard." And we walked.

The next day, when Sabra was resting, I brought out my tape recorder to entertain her. What a good wedding it had been, she said, as she and her sisters listened closely to the new wedding tape. I wanted to get the exact words of those defloration songs because no one had ever told me about them.

As we listened and I wrote, Sabra tried to make me understand. "For us Bedouins," she said, "this is the most important moment in a girl's life. No matter what anyone says afterward, no one will pay attention as long as there was blood on the cloth. They are suspicious of her before. People talk. 'She went here, she went there.' 'She looked at So-and-so.' 'She said hello to So-and-so.' 'She went to the orchard.' But when they see this blood the talk is cut off. This is one of the things wrong with the Arabs—they don't like their girls to go out. But once they've seen the cloth, she can come and go as she pleases. They love her and everything is fine."

I wondered how long she would have to wait for that day when her aunts would sing about her piece of cloth,

> Like a crescent moon on a cloudless night
> the honor of our loved one appears . . .

Chapter 5

HONOR AND SHAME

Say to the believing men that they should lower their gaze and guard their modesty; that will make for greater purity for them. And God is well acquainted with all that they do.

And say to the believing women that they should lower their gaze and guard their modesty; that they should not display their beauty and ornaments except what (ordinarily) appear thereof; that they should draw their veils over their bosoms and not display their beauty except to their husbands, their fathers, their husbands' fathers, their sons, their husband's sons, their brothers or their brothers' sons, or their sisters' sons, or their women, or the slaves their right hands possess, or male attendants free of sexual desires, or small children who have no carnal knowledge of women.

Qur'an 24:30–31

In a letter dated July 30, 1989, Kamla, another daughter of Gateefa and Sagr, wrote to tell me her good news.

In the Name of God the All-Merciful and Compassionate. It gives me pleasure to send this letter to my dear sister, Dr. Lila, hoping from God on high, the All-Powerful, that it reaches you carrying love and greetings to you and your family while you are all in the best of health and in perfect happiness.

By name she mentioned my brother and sisters (none of whom she has met) and asked me to convey her greetings and those of her family to them and to my parents, as well as to the one American friend of mine they had met ten years ago—in short, to everyone they knew about in my life in America. I had confided during my last visit that I would be getting married soon. She asked if I had; if so, she wrote, she sent a thousand congratulations and hoped, God willing, that he was a good man who would understand me. She hoped also that their new in-law was a noble man, the best in all of America, and that they would meet him soon. After wishing me many children (six boys and six girls) and more greetings, she squeezed her piece of news onto the bottom of the page.

Your sister Kamla has become engaged to Engineer Ibrahim Saleem, Aisha's brother.

I could hardly believe it. We had teased Kamla about him ever since his name had been floated four years before as a prospect. This was the match she scarcely dared hope her father would arrange. Not that she had ever met the young man. What mattered was that he was educated, came from a family that believed in educating girls, and lived in a town. She would be able to escape the kind of life her family lived, a life that annoyed her—the only one in her family, male or female, to have made it through high school— more and more.

Because she complained so much, I had asked her in the summer after she graduated to write me an essay on how young Bedouin women's lives were changing and what of the past she hoped the Awlad 'Ali would retain and what she wished they would abandon. She had proudly told me that her teacher had sent off for publication an essay on Awlad 'Ali weddings she had written in school. You can trace, in the stilted words of her essay and the candid comments (in parentheses) she made as she read it aloud to me, the outlines of the new world she hoped to gain by marrying the likes of Engineer Ibrahim Saleem.

The Education of Girls

*An Essay on the Young Bedouin Woman of Egypt
and the Changes in Her Life over 40 Years*

*If we are to speak of the Bedouin girl in Egypt we find that her life
differs from one era to another. The circumstances of the home and
family relations change from one age to another. If we go back to
discuss the way she was around forty years ago, we find that the
Bedouin girl was living a life in which she was of no value. When
she came of age, or maturity* (as the Egyptians say—I mean the
years when she is ready for marriage), *she had to do housework
at her family's home—for example, cooking, washing clothes, and
preparing firewood.* (Her only value was in the housework she
did—the sweeping and washing—and if she didn't do it
they'd laugh at her and gossip about her laziness. She was
forced to do it, even if she weren't capable. No matter what
her health was like. I'm talking about those who were my
age, from around the age of twelve on.)

*Also, she used to spin and weave, even though it is very difficult,
painful, and strenuous.* (When she was around fifteen, her
mother or any woman in the household, an aunt for instance,
would teach her. It's supposed to be the mother, though. Her
goal was to teach her daughter to spin and to make something, anything. The important thing was for her to weave
something, if only a border for the tent.) *She had to learn this
skill.* (This is what is important for the Bedouins, housework,
weaving, and such things. Forty years ago this was what a
girl had to put up with.)

Kamla had been resenting housework. Now that she had finished school she rarely left the house. With two sisters, she was
responsible for the cooking and cleaning one day out of three. On
another of those days she was in charge of baking bread with them.
She was on call much of the rest of the time, seeing to it that her
little brothers and sisters were bathed, dressed, and staying out of

mischief. Piles of laundry collected in the back room to be done when there was time.

Where before she had worn clean clothes for school, studied with her brothers in a quiet room of her own, and been given few household duties, now she had no privileges. Her clothes were as caked with dough and soot as her sisters'. Kamla's only escape was listening to the radio. She carried my transistor with her wherever in the house or courtyard she was working. She kept an eye on the time so as not to miss the radio soap operas. When she was free, she stared into space as she listened to Egyptian music, talk shows, and the news. So attached was she to the radio that I called it her sweetheart. Her mother, irritable from fatigue herself, scolded her and threatened to lock up the radio. When Gateefa complained, "My daughters are becoming lazy sluts," Kamla, like her sisters, simply ignored her.

Kamla had scored high enough on her final exams to secure a place in the agricultural college for which her high school had prepared her. She had no special interest in agriculture and had gone to this secondary school only because the regular high school was on the far side of town. Her uncles had given her a choice: quit school or go to the nearby agriculture school. School was still much on her mind. Her essay continued:

Education for the Bedouin girl used not to exist. It was impossible for her to study. (Forty years ago she lived a life, as I said earlier, that had no value at all.) *She was governed by the customs and traditions that the Bedouin families followed. These customs and traditions forbade a girl to leave the house under any circumstances. So going to school* (this is an example) *would be the greatest shame. She couldn't say that she wished to study, no matter what. Even if, as they say, she was the daughter of a tribal leader.* (So for example, a girl's father would be a tribal leader and she'd want to study, but her relatives would say no you can't. She'd say, but I'm the daughter of the head of a lineage. I must learn. They'd forbid her.)

This hypothetical example was, of course, from her own experience. She had been allowed to continue her schooling against the wishes of her uncles. They wanted to pull her out when she was no longer little. Because she was so determined, she and her parents had put up with the uncles' general suspicion and occasional accusations. She was a fierce child who had early on decided she wanted to go to school. She was not allowed to enroll in the public school, though, because, as is often the case, her father had never registered her birth. Yet still she went each day, as a visitor, borrowing her brothers' books. After three years of this her teacher finally required her to register officially. Haj Sagr went and had her papers drawn up. From then on she came in at the top of her class, while her brothers and male cousins flunked out. I had recorded in my notes from 1979 her bashful reaction when her brother told their father she had been appointed school monitor. Sagr had been hugging his youngest son, then in his first year of school, proudly predicting that his son would come out above the rest.

The primary school had been within sight of the camp, and its students were mostly relatives and neighbors. The secondary school, though, was about three kilometers away. Kamla's class had only four Bedouin girls; the rest of the girls were Egyptians from town. To get to this school she had to walk along the road past houses of people who did not know her. She said she walked with her head down, looking neither right nor left, but she still had to endure catcalls from men driving by.

Her relatives' suspicions were harder to cope with. One aunt had come twice to Gateefa to accuse Kamla of taking her son's schoolbook to give to a boy from a neighboring tribe. Kamla's mother had defended her. True, she had given the boy a schoolbook, but it was in exchange for a book that he had given her the previous year. And the book was one that her father had bought her, not one she had taken from her cousin. Fortunately, when they questioned the aunt's son, he backed Gateefa.

Kamla and her mother were angrier when Kamla's uncle told Haj Sagr that he had seen his niece Kamla walking home with a boy. Gateefa felt she'd been hit in the stomach with a rock. She argued, to me, "If it were true, why didn't he stop for her and put her in the car? Why didn't he get out and beat her right there, if he really saw her? If he's so afraid for her, why doesn't he ever offer to drive her to school?"

Kamla told the story as she knew it. She believed the problem began during her second year of high school. Her uncle had not wanted her to continue, but Sagr had defended his daughter's right to stay in school. Furious, her uncle did everything he could to prevent her from studying. If, for example, guests came to the house, he would knock on her door to ask her to make the tea. She'd try to escape, sneaking off to study outdoors under the trees. Two days before her final exams (when, as we all know, she added, nerves are on edge), she was walking home from school. Across the road a boy she had known since she was small was going the same direction. Because she always walked with her head down, she noticed her uncle drive by only after he had passed. He went straight to her father and told him, "Your daughter was walking hand in hand with a boy." Her father had questioned him carefully, then called in Kamla's mother. Gateefa in turn had come to her ("And you know how upset she gets!" she said to me) to ask her about it. Kamla refused to say "yes, no, or maybe" unless her uncle came and accused her to her face.

Her father, she said lovingly, believed in her. He asked her why she didn't walk home from school with her cousin, and she explained that she was not about to go out of her way just to walk with him. If he wished to walk with her along her route before cutting off to his house, he was welcome to. Kamla's uncle had also told her father that this cousin had informed him that the boy waited for Kamla at the school gates to walk home with her every day. Fortunately for Kamla, her cousin happened to pass by the house that afternoon. Sagr called him over to question him—right in front of her uncle. The boy swore that he had never said such a thing. That ended it.

Arranged Marriage

The next paragraph of Kamla's essay took up the matter of marriage. Commenting on it, Kamla said, "This was a topic the Bedouin girl would hear nothing about and wasn't supposed to have anything to do with."

> *She had no right to an opinion in any matter, however much the matter might concern her personally. She had no say even in the choice of a husband. She had absolutely no say in this matter.* (And to this day, no matter how educated she's become, very seldom does she have any opinion. The Bedouin girl has no say.) *In this matter what she had to do was carry out her family's orders even if she didn't want to. It was not right for her to refuse.* (Even if she didn't want him, she had to agree to it against her will. Even if he was older than she was, for example, or very different from her, she had to agree to what the family wanted. For example, if they said I had to marry someone and I didn't want him—I hated him—but if my kinsmen had agreed to the match and told me I had to marry him, what I would have to do, despite my wishes, was marry him.)

I was surprised that Kamla depicted women as powerless in decisions about marriage. She had heard the same stories I had—stories, like her grandmother Migdim's, of resistance to marriages arranged for them by their kinsmen. She knew plenty of young women like one who, in love with someone else, had married Kamla's cousin but then had gone home to her father's household at the slightest provocation, eventually forcing her husband to divorce her. The specter of forced marriage, especially to paternal cousins, may have loomed large for Kamla because she, like her sister Sabra, was waiting. As her mother joked with a friend, "Kamla's got her diploma. Now we're going to give her the other diploma!"

Her religious training at school had given Kamla moral ammunition against arranged marriage. The Prophet, she would explain, says that it is wrong to marry someone you have never seen. Moreover, the girl must give her consent: the bride's relatives are supposed to ask her opinion. Kamla is not sure her opinion will be sought. Already she has made it known throughout the women's community that she does not want to marry her cousin Salih, the young man closest to her in age who has been lined up with her, at least according to the calculations of his father and uncles about marriages between their children.

Kamla is fond of Salih, but he is "like a brother." She and her sisters boldly ask him to get them things they want from town; they reach into his pockets to grab the latest cassettes he has brought for himself. Kamla sometimes teases him, threatening to make him wash the dishes and sweep the floor if he marries her. Kamla even jokes with his mother. I had seen the woman grab Kamla and warn her to be good or else she'd exercise her prospective rights as a mother-in-law and make her quit school. Kamla broke free easily, laughing as she shouted defiantly, "Not until I come to live with you!"

Women in the camp mutter that Salih is not right for Kamla. Even her grandmother half supports her. Although Migdim tries to persuade her granddaughters of the virtues of marrying cousins, she is angry with her sons for wanting "what nothing good will come of"—this set of matches within the family between children who have grown up together and say they feel like siblings. She fumed, "Her father wants Kamla for Salih, and Kamla says she won't marry him. And Salih says he won't marry Kamla. She's older than he is!"

Her unmarried granddaughters enjoy provoking Migdim by maligning cousin marriage. They say they want out: they want to marry men who live far away so they can have new lives.

"They're good for nothing!" insisted one of Kamla's cousins once about her male cousins.

Migdim scolded her, "You slut! What is this outrage? You gypsy!"

She and her sister laughed wildly, "Damn them, our cousins! What do you see in them?"

A cousin agreed, "They're all ugly. Not a handsome one among them. No, we'll marry outsiders, Grandma, ugly or handsome."

Kamla shook her head. "I'm marrying an Egyptian! Someone educated."

Her grandmother retorted, "Your father won't agree to it!"

Kamla hugged her grandmother. "We're just talking with you to see what you'll say. Is there anything in our hands, Grandma? Or in my father's? Only God knows what will happen."

Generations

In the past, according to Kamla, a girl had no say in the matter of marriage because, as her essay continued,

> *They thought that girls shouldn't be concerned with anything but clothing and food and drink. In her kinsmen's eyes a girl had no value.* (Even now it's true. You might think conditions had changed and advanced a bit, but it's still true.) *They did not know that a girl had something she valued more than food and such things—and that was feelings.* (Feelings were forbidden to the girl.) *But she had feelings and sensitivity and affections just like any other person on this earth.* (This is true. There is no person God has created without feelings or sensitivity.) *Her kinsmen had feelings and sensitivities and affections.* (Take my father, for example. My father loved in the days of his youth; but then he thinks a girl doesn't have any such feelings.) *But they did not care if the girl had feelings. Her feelings and desires were not important.*

Kamla laughed conspiratorially as she read the next section.

> *So, for example, if she loved a person, she could not show this love, however precious and strong her love was. She would be very afraid that her relatives would hear about it, because they considered it a*

big scandal for a girl to love, even though they had. They say that only men have the right—a young woman does not have the right to know or speak with any man except her brothers and their relatives. All of this has governed the Bedouin girl for as long as she has lived on this earth. (This is true. For example, if a boy meets a girl and talks with her, they say it doesn't matter—"He's a man." But you, the girl, if you do this? They don't say anything to him. If my father heard that my brother was in love with someone and talked with her, he wouldn't say anything. But if it was me? That would be dealt with very differently.)

This talk of love and vocabulary of feelings was new. Ever since I had known Kamla, from the age of twelve or so, she had been a tough little girl, the kind who would say to her uncle's new wife, "I don't even know what this 'love' is. I hear about it in songs and hear about this one giving her necklace and that one her ring, but I don't know what they are feeling." She used to amuse her great-aunts when they hugged her and teased her about which of her young cousins she would grow up to marry by proudly shouting, "I'm never going to marry."

Just a year before she wrote this essay she had demanded of her mother, "Does a woman have to marry? Does she have to have someone to tell her what to do, to boss her around?"

"Yes, a woman has to marry," Gateefa had answered. "If she doesn't, people will say, 'The poor thing!' "

But things had changed. Kamla now quoted from a book she had read at school: it was natural as one entered adolescence to begin thinking about members of the opposite sex. She admitted that such things had never even crossed her mind before. But then it had happened. It was at her cousin Selima's wedding that she had first revealed to me the new experiences she had begun to have at school. During a quiet period of the day before the wedding we had gone for a stroll on the hillside. Scattered on the ridge were groups of women in twos and threes, sisters who rarely saw each other, aunts and their nieces, old friends, also talking privately.

Looking into the distance—and, as it turned out, toward a certain house—Kamla had asked me, "What do you think, Lila? Is it wrong for two people to think about each other all the time?" I was puzzled. She told me about a young man at school—a well-behaved and good person, she added quickly—who had taken notice of her. He had asked her friends whether they could persuade her to agree to talk to him. She had refused at first. Finally she agreed to a brief meeting, with friends present. He wanted to know if she would be willing to marry him if he got his father to request her from Haj Sagr. She wondered if there was any hope that her father would accept. Knowing the family, I said I doubted it.

Usually she was more realistic. When I would ask whom she wanted to marry she would give various answers. She was adamant about her cousins: "If they think I'm going to take any of these, my cousins, or anyone from the camp, they're wrong." Then she would deny that she cared whether or not it was the boy she knew from school. The brother of their family friend Aisha would be just fine. As long as the man was educated. Backtracking she would say, "It's not even important that he's well educated. But he must be knowledgeable." The boys in her camp didn't know anything; they would not know how to get on in the world. Dependent on their fathers to feed, dress, and marry them off, they were incapable of taking care of themselves. "They're men in name only," she scoffed.

She blamed her elder kinsmen, especially her father, for her cousins' failures. Despite the double standard in matters of the heart, she acknowledged that her cousins and her brothers were having almost as hard a time dealing with their old-fashioned elders as she was. One time when I returned from a short trip to Cairo, Kamla greeted me with the news that her grandmother was distraught because her cousin Salih, the woman's favorite grandson, had run away from home after his father had hit him. No one knew where he had gone.

I would hear the story several times from Migdim, once as she told it to a visiting niece who began by asking, "Who hit Salih?"

"His father hit him."

"And why?"

"He went to a wedding at So-and-so's and they say he drank liquor."

"Liquor? What kind of liquor?"

Migdim didn't know much about it. "The stuff you drink that makes them drunk. They said he drank. Each of the men came and asked him. They'd told his father on him."

"Beer, must have been beer." Migdim's niece knew things. Her husband, now dead, was rumored to have been a womanizer and an alcoholic.

Migdim did not want her story interrupted. "His father came here and hit him."

"Beer. Liquor?—why a bottle costs twenty-five pounds! There is beer and white water. The beer costs two pounds fifty a bottle."

Migdim went on. "I said, 'Son, listen, sometimes he hits his sisters just to get half a pound from them. Another time he'll need a pound. By God, he doesn't have a piaster.' I said, 'Son, your boy didn't drink. He doesn't have any money.' Salih told him, 'Father, I didn't buy any. Dad, I didn't taste it. Dad, I didn't drink.' Every time he said something, his father would give him a slap. And in the end he looked for something big to hit him with, but we grabbed it away."

Her niece was shocked.

"The women stopped him. The boy cried and cried—and I was crying too—until his eyes were red. And he said, 'Swear to God, I'll go to Libya. I'm leaving.' I thought maybe he'd go stay with his maternal uncle. That would have been fine. In the end, though, they said he headed east."

Migdim went on about her own feelings. The night Salih left, she says, her head never touched the pillow. She and his sisters sat up crying all night. "It was hard on me. He really was so generous, he was generous. I swear to God, that time he got a job with his uncle out west and had some money, he'd give me five pounds, his sister five pounds, his aunt five pounds, and his nephews one pound each. So generous. And in the morning, he never left without coming to say, 'Good morning, Grandmother. How are you, Grandma?' And he'd kiss me from this side and that. He was always there around me."

Although they thought Salih was wrong to run away, the other women in the community were angrier with his father. One of them had tried to calm the man, saying, "It's something that's already happened. If the boy went astray it has passed, and if it didn't really happen, then people lied. He's your son." The man had refused to be calmed.

Migdim was upset that her son was now threatening to pursue the boy. She says she cursed him, "You've gone crazy, my son, and you've made him go crazy. If you got him angry, may God bring you no success! May God not grant you success!"

Her niece commiserated.

Migdim continued, "I told him, 'If you hit him, may God not favor you! You should just talk to him. How can you say you're going to make him go out to herd the camels, living for three or four months on unleavened bread? You drove him crazy! Why didn't you scold him gently and say, 'Son, this is wrong, this is shameful?' "

Migdim's niece gave an alternative. The man should have said to his son, "Okay, it was the first time. Now say it will be the last time." She added, "After all, someone invited him, rottenest of invitations. The boys figured it would pass, but they caught it."

Had Salih really bought the liquor? Who was with him? The women of the family disagreed. Migdim cursed the family that held the wedding. "May God ruin their houses, those who had a wedding and brought—I don't know what dog it was who brought a box and sold bottles from it—who was it?" Others knew that beer was often sold at these kinds of weddings, where professional performers entertained. They suspected that the drinking had gone on. All the women agreed that the boys were just kids who didn't know better; his father should have reprimanded the boy, "My son, this is wrong. This is the Devil's work."

Kamla, too, criticized her father and her uncles, but not just for the way they had reacted to this rumor of alcohol. She thought they were mistaken to be so strict with the boys. They wanted the boys to be straight, but all they would get from applying this pressure was stubbornness. The pressure, she warned, would produce the opposite of what they wanted. She gave examples. The men wouldn't let the boys play soccer. "What's wrong with soccer? It's exercise." They wouldn't let them have a television, go to cafés, or visit the local cafeteria where videos are shown. Needless to say, they wouldn't permit them to grow their hair long. The men wouldn't even let the boys get jobs, making them stay on the land and tend the new fig trees. Noting that her brothers and cousins had no money, Kamla added, "They treat them like girls. If only they would give them a bit of freedom."

The freedom she wants for them, and perhaps for herself, is the subject of a popular song, an early recording by ʿAwadh al-Maalky, that includes a comical tale of woe. The singer is moved, he begins, by the suffering that customs of the past have caused a young man. Hundreds of others have come to him to complain. Assuming the voice of the aggrieved young man, the poet describes what happened in the three marriages his kin arranged for him: when he reached out on the wedding night to touch his first bride, he discovered she was completely bald; the second bride, though beautiful with long thick braids, could not speak; the third tried to strangle him in his sleep—she was insane. The young man declares he won't marry again unless he is allowed to choose his own bride. Resuming his own voice, the singer comments on the young man's predicament with some advice to the elders:

> My warnings are to the old man
> who imprisons the freedom of the young,
> who has forgotten a thing called love,
> affection, desire, burning flames,
> forgotten the strength of lovers' fire,
> the fire of lovers who long for one another.
> What's exquisite is that they're afraid,

they say, any minute my prying guard will turn up:
my father's about to catch us.

The Dangers of Schooling

Kamla thinks her elders are wrong to fear an abuse of freedom. Her
essay described what happened when her generation began to go to
school.

> *Life began to change for the Bedouins, a change of conditions and
> location. Those Bedouins who began living in town started sending
> their sons and also their daughters to school to learn right from
> wrong, prayer, and writing.* (That was my father's single goal
> in educating us. He wanted us to know this. They don't put
> us in school to learn—who cared if I got educated? My own
> reason for being there was to learn right from wrong and the
> Qur'an. That's all.) *After that they would pull them out of school.*
> (Even if a girl was clever and came out first in her class, once
> she had learned right from wrong and had come to under-
> stand, they would say to her, "Come on, that's enough.")
> *Some might let her stay through secondary school.* (Like me. After
> I finished secondary school, that was it.) *The Bedouin girl could
> even gain such a mastery of learning and knowledge* (it would be
> great if every girl could go to high school) *that she could enter
> university.* (In Alexandria you'll find Bedouin girls who've
> gone to university.)

Kamla was grateful to have been allowed to continue so long in
school. She had dreamt, when still in primary school, of going to
college to study politics and economics. At the time, she says with
amazement, she didn't understand the problem of being a girl. She
had hope. Now they tease her younger sister for similar ambitions.
Her father had proudly congratulated the younger girl for a good
report card and said it was a pity her brothers had given her such
a hard time when she announced that she wanted to be a doctor.
Kamla was scornful. "They'll make her quit long before she becomes a doctor."

The problem with being a girl, as Kamla explained in her essay, was what other people would say and think about her family if they let her go to school.

What happened was that people began competing over the schooling of girls. (For example, my father sees Aisha's father, who has educated all his daughters; so my father looks at him and says, "Why should he educate his daughters and not me? I have to educate my daughters." One looked at the next until all of them started educating their daughters. . . . But around here, they see that others' daughters aren't in school. No one here has daughters in university. In Marsa Matruh they all sent their girls to school, each imitating the other. My father looks over at Aisha's father and his daughters. If one of them did anything wrong—may God protect us!—*anything* wrong, my father and all of them would decide not to follow. But when I look, I see that the Bedouin girl does not give up her Bedouin values. The girls went to school and nothing bad happened.) *They put them in school, and the girls repaid their precious trust. The Bedouin girl made them see clearly that their daughter was as good as any girl from the biggest city—in intelligence and level of learning. She would get the highest grades in all fields of learning.* (This is true. If, for example, you compare someone from Marsa Matruh and someone from Cairo who've both graduated from the same school, you'll find them equally good. You'll even find that the Bedouin girl is better because she is also modest, pious, and respectful of her traditions and customs—better than the Egyptian girl who may have graduated from medical school but does not dress properly. Everything in her lifestyle is not right. Even if she gets educated, the Bedouin girl is better. You know, the Bedouins used to think that girls were a scandal. They used to think that if a Bedouin girl left the house she would have to do something wrong. They were sure of it. They'd say she can't go out—she's an idiot, she can't think. Like a beast of burden, she wouldn't know right from wrong. But when she got educated she showed them that what they had thought was wrong.)

Kamla still struggled against community opinion. Her relatives opposed sending her to college. An aunt put it bluntly: "What? Let her study in Alexandria? She's a kid. What does she know? Someone might take advantage of her. If it were here in our territory, it would be fine. But it's in Alexandria. She's gotten enough schooling."

Her father was more honest about their concerns. He had defied his brothers (with Aisha and perhaps even me in mind) to let her complete high school. The summer she graduated a school friend of Kamla's came to visit. She was dressed differently from the girls in our camp, having adopted the modern Islamic modest dress that included a severe headcovering. Haj Sagr knew her family; she spoke freely to Kamla's father, while his own daughter sat silent. The young woman told him how they wished they could go on to college. At first he tried to dismiss the idea by asking what use agricultural college (the only kind they were qualified to enter) would be for a girl. Then he got to the heart of the problem: "What would people say? 'His daughter's in college. I wonder if she's really studying or just going out a lot.' " Even if she were truly doing nothing wrong, he said, people would talk. The young woman argued with him, but he ended, as Kamla had predicted, by saying, "Listen, if your father agrees to it, tell him I'll agree too."

He inquired about her family situation, and she told him her father was refusing to marry any of his daughters to cousins. His excuse was that blindness ran in the family. Kamla was encouraged, momentarily, when her father agreed that a girl who is educated should be married to an educated man so there could be mutual understanding. But then Haj Sagr suddenly reversed his argument. He told Kamla's friend that he had been willing to send his daughters to school because he wanted them to know how to organize their lives, their home, and their children. An educated mother could help her children with their schoolwork. Therefore, he said, he would prefer to keep these girls in the family: even if their husbands were not educated, the next generation of the family would benefit. If you give women to outsiders, he noted, the benefits go to the other tribe.

His model was Aisha, the woman whose father had been an old friend, whose husband was Sagr's business partner, and whose brother he was eventually to accept as a son-in-law. Aisha was the only college-educated Bedouin woman they knew. Whenever she and her children accompanied her husband on a visit, Kamla assumed special charge. Although all the women were warm, it was Kamla who saw to it that Aisha got water for ablutions, a prayer mat when she wanted, and who kept the conversation going.

Aisha was tall, slender, and elegant. She wore nicely styled full-length, long-sleeved dresses. Instead of the usual black head-cloth, she wore the fashionable modern headcovering that now marks Muslim modesty and piety. Unlike the Egyptian women who sometimes visited, she did not turn up her nose at the food that was offered her, and she was relaxed with the women of the household. She'd just laugh when old Migdim teased her about her husband. "After He created your husband's tribe, God created the donkey." Insults were expected between people from Aisha's tribe and that of her husband.

Aisha was and was not part of their world. A distant relative, she had people and interests in common with Migdim, Gateefa, and the others, but she was defensive about her family. Although they lived in the city, she was quick to tell stories that showed her brothers to be proper Bedouins. Describing her own wedding, she recalled how her husband—whose family were real desert Bedouins—came to her house the evening before the ceremony. He had brought along a Western-style suit, intending to have his photograph taken with her. Her brothers, she reported, had said, "If you're coming to have dinner with us, that's fine, you are very welcome. But if you're coming for anything else, don't bother."

Later she would try to cover for her sister, who made an unconventional marriage. We had met this young woman once, a student of pharmacology at Alexandria University who came to visit dressed in a long woolen suit, her hair covered with a turban and scarf, an alternative "Islamic" style. We heard later that her brothers had agreed to a marriage offer from an Egyptian doctor living in Marsa Matruh. Aisha insisted that even though the groom was Egyptian, her brothers had required a Bedouin engagement ceremony, where sheep are brought and eaten, first, before the Egyptian-style engagement party the groom's family wanted. She also claimed that they held a traditional henna party on the eve of the wedding—before the Egyptian-style wedding in a club. She denied that anyone except one brother had attended the wedding itself, but I didn't believe her: I knew she knew how scandalous it would be to admit that the bride's relatives had attended such a wedding.

Aisha switched easily between the Bedouin and Egyptian dialects. When she and her husband entertained Bedouins in their home, she served the men the customary lamb and rice but otherwise remained in a separate room from them. When they were with Egyptian friends, she served different foods and they all ate together. They even got different videos to entertain their guests. For Bedouins they always rented the same film about the Libyans' struggle against the Italian colonists. Their guests, Aisha explained, loved the early scenes showing a traditional Libyan Bedouin wedding and the scenes of men fighting on horseback. Egyptian films, she said, contained risqué scenes, so these were never shown to Bedouin guests. Aisha also owned two photo albums: one she showed to their more traditional Bedouin friends and family; the other one she kept hidden because it contained photographs, taken with a self-timer, of herself holding hands with her husband. Yet Aisha worried about trying to raise her two small children in an apartment on the outskirts of Alexandria. She did not want them to play with the neighbors. She feared they were learning bad language, and she apologized for their having picked up the Egyptian dialect. Her five-year-old daughter had just begun school and had started to deny that she was an Arab. "She says she's Egyptian," her mother reported. "You know," Aisha said earnestly to Kamla, "Egyptians aren't like us."

Egyptians

Could Bedouin identity be maintained after schooling? Kamla's essay took up this question.

The Bedouin girl preserves the traditions and customs she was raised by. (People stay with what they have grown up with because they came of age with it. Me, for example, I grew up knowing this was shameful and that was not right, there are customs, there's respect and modesty. Even when I'm old and my hair is grey, I'll have to follow these.) *She has sense and preserves her family's reputation.* (Of course, she'd be afraid that if she did something wrong they'd pull her out of school.) *The Bedouin girl tries to overcome the special obstacles she must confront.* (For example, she doesn't let her customs and traditions, or people's talk—saying this is wrong and that is shameful—make her fall behind other girls. The Bedouin girl follows her customs but in a way that doesn't tie her up or block the path before her.) *She attempts to live a life enlightened by learning, happiness, and contributions to her country and family.* (She gives to her country. The Bedouin girl feels for her country and understands the meaning of Egypt as much as any girl from Cairo. The girl living in the Western Desert has feelings for Egypt that may be even stronger than the Egyptian girl's. The educated Bedouin girl knows the meaning of her country. . . . Boy, if my father heard this!)

Kamla's comment about her father gives a clue as to the obstacles she faces as she moves between home and her state school run by Egyptian teachers. While Haj Sagr bemoans the Awlad 'Ali's lack of foresight in failing to request an independent state from the British and chafes against every government restriction on his activities, Kamla patriotically defends Egypt and speaks proudly of President Mubarak. Once, when her father confronted her for being a few hours late from a school trip, she argued back. He then scolded her for raising her voice and waving her hands as she spoke. "This is the work of Egyptians!" he yelled. Anger fighting fear, she answered, "I *am* an Egyptian. And they are the best people, and this is the best country!"

Kamla listened closely to the detailed reports of city life that Safiyya, her father's second wife, gave each time she returned from visits to her brothers' homes. These were brothers whose sons were becoming lawyers. Kamla was also riveted to broadcasts of Egyptian radio melodramas, with plots like that of "Bride by Computer," about a young man whose life is nearly ruined by computer matchmaking. Kamla can envision this world better than her sisters can, although she was as puzzled as they were about what a computer might be, and just as disapproving of the female characters in this conservative moral tale.

The plot of this serial, as the girls explained, followed the usual formula: A man loves someone but cannot marry her; in the end, though, he succeeds in getting her. The main character was a young Egyptian who worked in a company. When his mother objected to him marrying a co-worker whom he loved, a friend suggested he "talk to the computer to find a bride." The results, predictably, were disastrous. The first bride was a doctor. "She worked day and night," Kamla recalled. "Even the night of the wedding she was busy."

"You know what she was doing?" Kamla's neighbor intervened. "She was doing experiments with mosquitoes and rats."

"So he divorced her," Kamla went on. "He got engaged to another girl but didn't marry her. After he got engaged to her, she wanted him to go swimming with her and to dance with her, to act like foreigners."

The neighbor was excited. "The day he wanted to marry her she told him she wanted him to come over. He went there and found it wild. There was loud music."

Sabra explained. "She was at a nightclub. When he got there she said, 'Play that music,' and people started dancing. She asked him if he knew how to dance. He said no. She said, 'Look, see that man who's moving wildly on the floor?' The girl moved wildly as well, asking them to play a foreign tape."

The young women laughed as they described her. "She said to him, 'Get up, get up.' But he wouldn't go with her. He wouldn't dance with her."

When they paused I asked, "What was the problem with the third bride?"

The girls were confused. Sabra ventured, "I don't know, she had put . . . she had made a workshop in the house. They had a guest room, and she put her workshop in that room."

"No, she turned the bedroom into a factory."

"And she started fighting with her in-laws. She experimented on the old woman. She gave her something to try that made her almost die. When the man came home from work he asked his wife, 'Where is my mother?' She told him, 'I took her to the hospital.' He asked, 'Why, what's the matter?' He couldn't bear that any harm would come to his mother. When he went to see her she talked to him. She said, 'She was doing an experiment and I'm the one who drank the medicine.' "

They giggled as Kamla repeated, "The old woman almost died. He said, 'No, if she wants to kill my mother, I don't want her.' "

"He loved his mother," Sabra noted.

"And the fourth one, he brought her and then couldn't get any peace. She gave him a headache. She'd bring the onions and potatoes to peel. The man would be resting on the bed and she'd climb up next to him at night to peel potatoes. She'd say, 'Put down that newspaper and let's talk, me and you.' "

The girls found it hilarious to think of the woman peeling potatoes in bed. One of them explained, "She was a real peasant."

Kamla argued, "It's just lies. A peasant woman wouldn't do that."

Her neighbor was emphatic. "She was a peasant from Upper Egypt. They are like that."

Kamla will only go so far in her defense of Egyptians. She often criticized their neighbors, a poor family who had lived among Egyptians and had picked up different ways. As evidence of their immorality she disclosed that the men and women ate together.

Another nearby household fared little better. They knew no modesty, she said: the son listened to cassettes in front of his father, and the young daughter-in-law neither covered her hair with a black headcloth nor avoided her father-in-law.

In her essay, and even more clearly in her commentary, Kamla underlined this distinction between Bedouin morality and Egyptian immorality. Still writing about the young Bedouin woman who had become educated, she said:

She doesn't forget her origins or her customs and traditions. She raises her children as well as the people of the city do. (Now we're talking about what the Bedouin woman does after she gets educated. Does she forget her duties as a mother? The difference between the Bedouins and the Egyptians is that when the Egyptian woman has a baby, she gives it to her mother to raise for her, and she takes it to day care. She doesn't do her duty to the child nor give it the required care. For example, she nurses only up to the fortieth day or at most for two months. And then she leaves it with her mother, her sister, or day care and goes out to work. But the Bedouin woman gives the child its due, even if she's educated and has an advanced degree. Not her mother, not anyone else—she herself does the work.

And she raises her child according to her customs. Let's say she's a Bedouin who marries an Egyptian or an educated Bedouin. She doesn't raise her child by the customs or traditions of the Egyptians. She raises her child with the customs and traditions of the Bedouin, except that she is slightly more informed. I mean, she tells her daughter, "This is shameful" and "That is right." Take an educated Bedouin girl like me, for example. If I were to marry an educated man and live the city life, I wouldn't let my daughter follow the ways of the Egyptians where a girl wears short dresses or goes out to clubs. No, of course that is wrong. We must be modest. It is wrong for us Bedouins, and we must respect our traditions. This is necessary. You wouldn't find an educated Bedouin woman allowing her daughter to do things that she could not do when she was with her family. Or maybe even if her parents permitted it, the girl herself would not do it. "No," she'd know, "that's wrong." Bedouin women are the ones who really know how to raise their daughters. They are better than Egyptians because the Egyptian woman won't hit her daughter. Very rarely do you find an Egyptian who can hit her daughter. But the Bedouin woman, if her daughter does something wrong, she must hit her. Even if she's not that young. She must hit her to teach her right and wrong. You don't learn right from wrong if you're not beaten. The Egyptians don't do it and their girls—well, you know . . .)

Poets have long reflected on the differences between Bedouins and their peasant neighbors. Only fragments are remembered, however, like the lines of a love story about a wealthy peasant and a beautiful Bedouin girl named Khawd. Drought had driven her family into his fields in search of pasture for their herds. He allowed them to stay and graze their animals when he saw Khawd. One day, though, his beloved announced that her family had decided to return to the desert; she asked him to migrate with them. In despair the young man answered:

O Khawd, I have no camels that I might travel your distances
I have nothing but buffalo and cows, who will find no pastures
    near you

Kamla's aunt Dhahab had once recited a short poem on a similar theme—it was her comment when I declined her polite suggestion that I marry her son so that I come could live with her. The song came, she said, from a story about a bull who fell in love with a camel and tried to follow her into the desert. She warned him that he would exhaust himself if he tried, since he had to eat and drink every day and she drank only every five days. He said that for her sake he'd drink only every other day, but she knew he couldn't keep up with her. She told him:

You'll kill yourself bellowing
O bull, if you try to follow . . .

Some women were tolerant of moral differences between themselves and Egyptians. I talked once about television with two poor women who had recently moved to the area from near the Libyan border. They said they found television entertaining to watch when they had no work to do. Their favorite shows, of course, were the Egyptian serialized dramas.

I was curious. "But the Egyptians on these programs are not like you, are they?"

One of them laughed. "The Egyptians are citified, not like the Bedouins, the poor things."

They explained that it didn't matter because they would never watch television with people they should respect and be modest in front of. Girls would never watch if their fathers were there; women would leave the room if their husbands had visitors.

"So you don't you feel embarrassed by what you see on television?"

"No, if you're by yourself it doesn't matter," replied the older of the two.

"What if you see people in love?"

The younger of the two women laughed. "They're free to do that. We don't worry about them. The Egyptians have no modesty. They have no religion. They just do everything. It's their way."

The older one agreed. "Yes, let them do what they want. We just laugh at them."

Kamla and Sabra had a younger sister who loved television. She thought her father was wrong not to let them have a TV set. Although she conceded that foreign films were immoral, she argued that Egyptian films were different. Haj Sagr had taken away the television set when he heard that the girls were watching films in which people hugged and kissed each other. "He didn't want us watching. He said it was shameful." But these films and stories, she persisted, always showed the correct path in the end, even though they had people doing such things in early scenes. Egyptian films show how the girl who went off with a man later realized that he had tricked and used her. The importance of proper moral behavior always became clear ultimately.

Kamla's sister wondered anyway what her father could be thinking when he worried about his daughters' exposure to these things. Realistically she asked, "Where do we ever go? Nowhere but this house or the rest of the camp, where it's all family. Where does he think these things could happen?"

Kamla's father did fear the influence of Egyptians on the Bedouin community. In his opinion, the most serious problem the Bedouins faced was that of intermarriage between Bedouins and Egyptians. In the past, he maintained, no Arab, even the simplest shepherd, would give his daughter in marriage to "a peasant," as they used to call all Egyptians, even if the man were a company president. Things were more difficult now. Whereas before the area had been almost completely Bedouin, now, in regions like theirs that were close to large towns, Egyptians made up fifty percent of the population.

The trouble with the Egyptian presence, he went on, was that the Egyptian girls looked so pretty. They always dressed up, combed out their hair, and wore short dresses. A group of Bedouin elders had met recently to discuss what to do about these women who "walk around naked." Their concern was that the young men would find them attractive and want to marry them. And their fathers, wanting to make them happy, might agree. If the young men married Egyptian girls, there would no longer be any difference between Bedouin and Egyptian in the next generation. Sagr had warned the elders of this danger at the meeting. He admitted, though, that the process would be hard to stop now that the boys see these girls in school. Although he was afraid that Bedouin girls might pick up attitudes and habits from Egyptians—like having boyfriends, which the Egyptian girls don't think twice about—his real fear was intermarriage. That would bring about the end of tribal bonds.

Europeans

Sagr sensed the gradual shift in the boundaries of the moral community. Egyptians and Awlad ʿAli are being brought together by roads, newspapers, radio, television, schools, agricultural cooperatives, the army, and Parliament. With foreigners—Europeans— however, the divide remains absolute. Even Kamla, who sometimes pleaded with me, exasperated with her rambunctious little brothers and sisters, to take her away with me ("Put me in your suitcase and get me out of here!") and who proudly told me about several young Bedouin women with M.A.'s in veterinary medicine who had been sent, tattoos and all, to London for further training— even she did not approve of the Godless Europeans. Unlike Egyptian Christians, she argued, Europeans do not recognize God. "Every Muslim, even the most ignorant and uneducated, knows that there is a God and that He created all things." Worse, Europeans do not pray. When I contradicted her to say that many prayed in church, she challenged me. "What? What kind of person prays with his shoes on? May God protect us!"

The Westerner's lack of faith in God provides powerful imagery for inhumanity. Kamla's uncle's wife once lamented her lost brother with a poem that exploited this view:

> The European, with all his lack of faith,
> wept when I told him of my condition . . .

To show the magnitude of their compassion for girls, women sang a wedding rhyme that also mentioned Europeans:

> God protect every girl
> even the Christian woman's daughter

Kamla has not seen the new tourists who visit the Western Desert, but she has heard about them. In 1986 a favorite commercial cassette was the song called "The Japanese Woman" by the young Bedouin star Si'daawy al-Git'aany. The singer, identifying himself by tribe, says he lost his heart to a foreigner. (Although he calls her Japanese, the details of his song suggest a melding of many nationalities.)

Spanning many verses, the tale begins with his first sight of the woman. She had come to Egypt to relax, he sings, and in the gardens of a summer resort hotel in Marsa Matruh she was swinging on a swing. Her father, sitting on a chair ("like a boss") was grotesque and frightening: a European Christian with a long beard eating platefuls of pork and drinking quantities of beer. "We are Bedouins who like the desert," the singer goes on, "and they are Europeans. Fate brought us together." In her company he forgot his cares, and although they were accustomed to different ways, she made him lose interest in Bedouin women, who only cared about tying up goats and waiting for the sheep to come home in the evening.

She wore a cross and made him sit on chairs. Oh, he knew their ways were different, but he went astray, unable to stop himself from falling in love with a Christian. As she sat under an umbrella they talked. He had been to school and knew her language. She asked him to come home with her, but he first wanted to show her his home and the desert snail shells. Then she telephoned the governor and got permission for him to travel with her. So there he found himself, walking behind her, carrying her suitcases to board an airplane. Like a bird it took off, and he was scared. Everything is by God's will—that a man from the desert should end up with a Japanese woman.

Contrasting her country with his, he finds that the sea is to the south instead of the north. Her country is famous for its buses and trucks, he sings, whereas our women know only how to spin and to churn butter in goatskin bags. The moral contrasts are harsher. There, women's hair is uncovered and men wear straw baskets on their heads instead of skull caps. Women go wherever they wish and everyone says hello to them.

Accompanying his lover to a nightclub, he found people dancing like birds as someone howled while playing the piano. People got drunk and started fighting and throwing things around. His story would make a good soap opera, he sings. Things were different once they got to her country and she lost interest in him. The song ends with a refrain about the treachery of women, an ending that always got a rise out of Kamla and her sisters. "He got what he deserved," they insisted. "Who told him to go chasing after the foreigner, carrying her suitcases?"

Piety

Kamla reflected, in her essay, on what aspects of Bedouin life she would like to see preserved. Her father would have been proud of the list of positive features she drew up.

We all know that everything in life has its good qualities and its bad. (Weren't you asking what was good about the Bedouins and what wasn't?) *The virtues of the Bedouins are:*
1. Their piety and their total adherence to the traditions of the Prophet, despite their lack of education. (This is the thing I hope will continue until Judgment Day. This is the best thing — that they are religious. Even though ninety percent of them aren't educated, they are pious. Long clothing, respect, and modesty. The woman is as pious as the man. No woman can talk with a man she doesn't know or have him visit her at home. And she doesn't show her face or talk with any older man. This is what I hope Bedouin women and girls will never abandon.)
2. Their total respectfulness. The old respect the young, and the young respect the old, whether they are strangers or kin.
3. Their generosity. (It's true. You won't find anything on this earth like the generosity of the Bedouins. Even someone they don't know — they must invite him to the house and bring him food. Maybe no one else has this quality. I hope the Bedouins will hold on to this.)

4. Hospitality and respect for the guest.

5. The ties of kinship that link various parts of the family and the cooperation of relatives in all situations. (The other thing I want them to hold onto is this mutual assistance—they help each other in all circumstances. For example, even someone from a family that is related distantly to another must help a person from that family. Even among the women. When a Bedouin woman sets up a loom, for instance, her neighbors come to help her. Others always come to help. I wish the whole world—never mind just families—the whole world would help each other and that Muslims would cooperate the way our religion tells us to. Ninety-nine percent of Bedouin women haven't been educated. But they are pious. They're ignorant and illiterate, but they dress the right way, they fear God, and they pray. Sometimes they don't even know how to pray properly, but they pray anyhow. They are totally respectable, and they follow the traditions of the Prophet. They say the Prophet used to do this, the Prophet used to do that. They learn it from their husbands or their educated sons.)

Interestingly, Kamla had little to say about any of the traditional virtues except the first, piety. Although she was vehement in asserting their importance, perhaps she could not afford to think through their implications. She was proud of her father's generosity and hospitality, for instance, but it was also a source of tension, since the burden of feeding his many guests fell on the overworked women of the household. And if she were to think about how the extensive bonds between kin are to be maintained, she would have to admit the virtues of marriages to paternal cousins, the kind of marriage she wanted desperately to avoid.

Piety was a different matter. Like many, Kamla was becoming defensive in the face of new pressure from those sympathetic to Islamic activists in Egypt. She was correct to point out how tied up with their faith her kin were. They reckoned the months by the Islamic lunar calendar, the years by the annual religious feasts, age by the number of years a person has fasted the month of Ramadan, and the hours of the day by the five times for prayer. All the older women and many of the younger ones prayed regularly. Doing without the accoutrements of city people, women simply prayed where they were, facing southeast and laying a small kerchief on the ground before them. The men like Kamla's father tended to know more. They would have learned as children to recite the Qur'an, and they continued to learn from the lectures at the mosque every Friday.

Their reactions to the sanctimonious Egyptians—and now to some Bedouins from the cities, who were becoming, as they put it, "followers of the model," meaning the life of the Prophet—have been mixed. The older women are not cowed. They argue, as Kamla did, that they have always worn modest clothing and covered their hair with a headcloth. They resent being told that some of the ways they have demonstrated their devoutness are wrong.

Kamla is more unsure. Sometimes she defends these Muslim Sisters and Brothers and sometimes she goes along with the old Bedouin women as they make fun of them. One evening, having recited some poetry and told some traditional tales for my benefit, Kamla's aunt Dhahab turned to her niece and asked, "Hey Kamla, have you given Lila any songs?"

Kamla was coy. "I'm not a song person. I'm just a simple person minding my own business. I'm with God. I'm pious and know my Lord."

Her sister hooted, perhaps thinking of Kamla's love of the radio and scandalous movie magazines. But Kamla went on, only half joking, "Auntie, I've become pious. I don't have anything to do with songs."

Her aunt mocked her, "What's this? You've become pious?" Everyone laughed as the old aunt continued, "God's blessings! God's blessings! So, you're joining the 'Beard Family'?"

There was a commotion, with everyone talking at once about the topic that was so often in the air these days: the Islamists. Kamla spoke on their behalf. "They say, 'We are religious people, . . . following God's path, the path to heaven.' "

Her aunt was hardly convinced. "I swear to God, they've never seen heaven. God is the only judge. God is present."

Sabra thought they should be more respectful. But she admitted, "May God protect them, they do some things that aren't necessary. Do you know what our aunt who lives out west says? She says they say that the sugar dolls are wrong, even the food we make to celebrate the Prophet's birthday. Rotten life! The special food for the birthday that the whole world celebrates—they say it is forbidden!"

Her aunt concurred. "Have you ever heard of such a thing!"

Some women were even more irreverent. Once when an old friend from the nearby town was visiting, the evening conversation turned to the topic of these new religious types. She complained that they had forbidden celebrations of saints' birthdays, including the candy and meat eaten at them. They had said it was wrong to call any holyman "Saint So-and-so." She said, "They have forbidden everything. Why, the next thing you know they'll forbid the clothes we wear and make us go around naked."

She then described to the group gathered around her how these people dressed. She told them about the wife of a Muslim Brother called Mr. Muhammad who had moved to her town. The woman was offering lessons on religion every Tuesday afternoon for any woman who wished to learn. She wore a veil that covered her head and her face, "except for her eyes"; she wore gloves, a dress down to the ground, and shoes. As the old woman put it, "She looks like a ghost."

Kamla showed off her knowledge of religion. "It is wrong for a woman to veil her face. What is required is that your head be covered; it is fine to expose your hands, your feet, and your face."

The old woman then commented on the men. "They all run around with those beards. Why, Doctor Ahmed's sticks out like this! It looks like pubic hair."

Kamla had to raise her voice to be heard over the wild laughter. "But Auntie, the beard is a tradition of the Prophet."

Kamla's cousin Salih had tried briefly to grow a beard, but the teasing had been merciless. No matter how many times Kamla told them it was the tradition of the Prophet, Gateefa and his other aunts accused him of looking like a Coptic priest. He finally shaved it off.

Kamla had confided to me that she would have liked to replace her kerchief with the new Islamic headcovering but she was afraid her family would object. A photograph of her with her school friends revealed that she was the only one among them not wearing the new modest dress. Yet Kamla criticized some of her classmates who wore this type of clothing but added flowers and multicolored headbands to their veils. She said their religion teacher had given them a real talking to and had confiscated their flowers and headbands saying, "If you want to take on the veil, do it seriously." Kamla said she would adopt this kind of headcovering "if God opens the way for me and I get to marry someone educated."

A New Order

The final part of Kamla's essay was to have been about what she hoped would change in her community. All she had written, though, was this:

As for the bad things, I will talk about them.

She read this final sentence and looked at me. "What are the wrongs I wish the Bedouins would finish with? I've already discussed these. First, their ideas about girls. They are totally meaningless and wrong. I wish they would give her the opportunity to get educated. They see her as a worthless being. You know this, Lila. . . . This is what I hope the Bedouins will leave behind. They should see that a girl is a person, a noble person created just as God created men. She has feelings, sensitivities, and desires.

"Another thing I wish is that they wouldn't let their customs and traditions rule them to such an extent that they believe that the customs of the city people are wrong and theirs right. Whenever they see that a person is educated, they say he's wrong, we're right. I wish they would respect the educated. I wish they would preserve their customs and traditions but be a bit more advanced. A girl who goes to school doesn't forget her customs and traditions, no matter how educated she becomes. Even if she goes to Europe or America, the Bedouin girl will preserve her customs and traditions. They should give her more freedom.

"Another thing I wish is that they would get more organized. I wish they would put a little order in their lives. Among Bedouins, order is completely lacking. In every area of their lives—in terms of food, in having too many children, in the way they raise the children—there's no order. And in the house—anything goes!"

I was curious about what Kamla meant by "order." She gave examples from close to home. "Say you've got two brothers living in one house. If they organized their lives, they'd put each one in his own house. And the business of marrying more than one wife—I wish they'd change their views on this. It is the biggest sin. The Prophet—it is not forbidden, but the Prophet said only if you can treat them fairly. But a man can't, it can't be done. Even if he has money, he can't. As a person, in his thoughts and his actions, he can't be fair. He'll like one more than another.

"The generation that's coming now, after my father's and mother's, they wouldn't think of it or do it. Why? So they won't have a house with thirty or forty people living in it. A household with two women in it will have thirty or forty people in it. Their lives will be lousy. They won't have good food, good clothes, or good childrearing. They won't be clean. A woman alone in her own house can handle her children. When there are two women, one will say, 'Why should I hit my children when that one doesn't hit hers?' They watch each other. When one does something, the other is looking. If one cleans and washes and the other doesn't, she says, 'Why should I do this when she doesn't?' If she is alone, a woman won't be able to say that. Who's going to do it for her? She'll do it herself and she'll know what's what. When she's alone she doesn't have to depend on anyone. And even her daughter will turn out well, like her mother. The other way they're always getting into fights over any little thing. Even without my saying this, you know it, Lila. This is what I wish would change.

"Bedouins think that as long as they have a house and can eat, drink, and be clothed, that's enough. That's life. And they marry and have kids and marry again. But a man should live a more ordered and relaxed life. Should a man come home at the end of his day tired from working and find it filthy and the kids and women fighting? He comes wanting to relax, and finds this? This is what makes someone say, 'No, there should be order.' "

For years I had heard Kamla's call for order. Living in a household of twenty or more, half of whom are under ten years old, can be chaotic. Fed up, Kamla would sometimes say, "This isn't a house, it's a breeding station!" She and Sabra often teased their mother, calling her Shalabiyya, the name of a character they had seen in a family planning advertisement on television. Shalabiyya was a woman with too many children: in her lap, on her shoulders, on her head. When she tried to draw water or milk the cow, they climbed all over her and trailed behind her. Gateefa would apologize, "We can't change the way we are."

When Kamla was young, she would come home from school announcing that she was going to marry an Egyptian doctor and have only one child. Other times she'd say she was going to have only two children, both daughters. She was going to live alone in a house with her husband, just them, no relatives. Bedouin men, she would say, make women work hard and don't pay attention to them. Even if the woman is ill, the man won't lift a finger to help, not even to pick up a crying baby. Egyptian men help their wives, respect them, and treat them well. When Kamla's younger sister, echoing their father, accused Egyptians of being stingy and not offering food to their guests, Kamla defended them to support her favorite theme. She argued that they just did things in an organized manner; they had special meal times, unlike the Bedouins who brought out food whenever anyone stopped by.

Perhaps because tensions between her father's wives had recently intensified, Kamla was impassioned in her final commentary. "Even without becoming educated, the Bedouins could organize their lives. It is enough to marry just one. Or if a man wants to marry more than one, he should put each wife in her own house.

They won't fight then. But if the two are together, you'll always find this one saying, 'That one did and said' and that one saying, 'This one said this and did that.' Even if they are friends, the people outside the household won't let them be. Someone will come and say, 'That one said this' and 'This one said that.' Women are famous for this kind of talk.

"Yes, Bedouin women are famous for their talk. The Prophet said, 'Women—if not for their tongues, women would go to heaven.' They asked him, 'Why should a woman go to heaven?' He said, 'Because she gives milk.' Praise be to God, milk flows from her. And beyond that, she works harder than a man. She's weaker—that's right, she's weak compared to the man, whom nothing bothers—but she has to work more. She has children and cares for them. They asked the Prophet, 'So what is it that keeps her from entering heaven?' He said, 'It is because of her tongue.' In a second she'll turn things around. She'll gossip about everyone. Women talk about people more than men do."

Kamla is critical of the older women in her community. She confessed, too, that she belonged to two worlds. With her sisters and cousins she talked about the things they knew, not letting on that she was different. But there were so many things she could talk to her school friends about that she could not talk about with the girls in her family—things like politics. Sometimes she seemed to accept her double life with equanimity. When I saw her spinning with her aunt one day, I asked, "Hey Kamla, so you know how to spin too?" She had laughed. "Yes, I can go either way. If it turns out I'm to be citified, I'll do that. And if it turns out I'll be a Bedouin, I'll know how."

When I suggested that she might be lonely if she moved into a house of her own, she was adamant: "No, I won't miss them at all." Yet this is someone who is fiercely proud of her father for being an important man who is also generous and pious. Despite occasional confrontations, she spends, like her sisters, nearly every evening sitting close to her mother and talking. Even her brood of little siblings only sometimes drives her really crazy. The youngest she can rarely resist grabbing to hug. Delighted by this two-year-old's every new accomplishment, she whispers new words in her ear and kisses her when she repeats them.

Most of the time, though, she says she wants to get out. I worry about Kamla's blithe confidence that life in the city will be so much better. I disagree with her assessment of Bedouin women's lives. I argue with Kamla that she deliberately ignores the richness of their relationships and the way they have always struggled back (and were expected to). Her own life is evidence. There was not a single woman in the camp who had not admired her for being a willful little girl. Even her father had been amused by her opinions and determination. As she had grown up, her strength of purpose had enabled her to withstand the social pressure against her going to school. The independence she displayed reminded me of her grandmother Migdim, with her stories of resistance to marriage and her struggles to have her way with her sons. It even reminded me of her mother, Gateefa, who had earned the respect of her husband.

Yet when her letter arrived I was happy for her—happy that it was her fate not to have to marry her cousin after all and glad that her father had been willing to take her wishes into consideration. Armed with romantic visions inspired by Egyptian radio melodramas, cloying love songs, and her tattered collection of hokey postcards showing blonde brides and grooms looking deeply into each other's eyes, she will go off to live with her Egyptianized, educated husband in a small and ordered household. She will never work outside the home. She will rarely even leave her apartment. She expects to clean house, cook meals, and serve her husband. If God brings children, she'll take care of them and raise them well.

Because she has none of his sister Aisha's feminine refinement, I was worried. What would her husband think when he first saw this sturdy young woman with her wide feet and callused hands? Because she is the daughter of a wealthy tribal leader, the fabric of her dresses would be expensive and she would bring many with her; but they would have been tailored by local seamstresses, whose renditions of city clothes are always awkward. And would she know how to dress for the wedding night, this girl who had to fight her mother's horrified accusations of immodesty when she wore a home-made bra? Would Engineer Ibrahim Saleem find charming her outspoken ways?

I wrote back to wish her all happiness and to apologize for not being able to attend the wedding. An older sister would sing at the henna party on the eve of the wedding, so I looked through my collection of Bedouin wedding songs to see if any seemed right. I ended my letter with three that I hoped would mean something to her. The first let her know how much I thought of her family:

Her father has a good name
and those who have come to marry will find happiness . . .

The second reminded her that I knew how much she wanted this:

Her morning is blessed
she got what she desired and was honored . . .

And the third expressed my best wishes for this young woman, vulnerable and beautiful as are all young brides heading off into the unknown:

Neighbors, come say farewell
a gazelle from our land is about to journey . . .

TRANSCRIPTIONS OF
ARABIC POEMS AND SONGS

Transcriptions of the Arabic poems seek to approximate the Awlad
ʿAli dialect except in distinguishing ḍ from ẓ to conform to the
system used by the *International Journal of Middle East Studies*. A
detailed explanation of the dialect and the transliteration system can
be found in my earlier study (Abu-Lughod 1986, xv–xix).

Chapter 1

1. Far away
    > bi ʿīd mā yjībak ʿilm
    > ḥaggā lū tahāyēt yā ʿalam . . .

2. Dear one
    > ʿazīz fil-manām girīb
    > w fi l-arḍ jūba yā ʿalam . . .

3. He took away
    > showwā twārfik yā ʿēn
    > il-yās fīk mō dāyir shway . . .

4. The heart
    > il-ʿagl hū illī mḥagūg
    > armā ḥjāyja rāḥan ḍilul . . .

5. You who guards
    > yā nāgir ʿal-anthā shāgī
    > yā nāgir ʿal-anthā shāgī
    > marra tzurr w marra tlāgi
    > marra tthūr tdugg sdādī

6. Praise be
   subḥān illī khallāk
   blā miʿīz yā ḍān ṣābra . . .

7. He's lifted
   ʿalēk shāl dhēl il-bēt
   idh-dhīb jāk yā rāʿi l-ghanam . . .

8. The sheep
   iḍ-ḍān wāradat wizrudat
   wil-kabsh hū illī māt min il-ʿaṭash . . .

9. In a late night
   zarrārat ʿagāb il-lēl
   shrib ḥalībhā rāʿi l-ghanam . . .

10. He struck
    shāl khēshtu mughṭāẓ
    khadhō mināyḥā rāʿi l-ghanam . . .

11. Little Kafy
    Kfēwa baʿd iṭ-ṭuhūr
    yirkab ḥṣān markābu dhahab . . .

12. A pity
    ḥāba yā ṣāḥib ha sh-shanna
    ḥāba yā ṣāḥib ha sh-shanna
    ḥāba yā ṣāḥib ha sh-shanna
    gālū shāyib min l-ashāyib
    māt w mā ʿuyūnī rāʿnnu
    ḥāba yā ṣāḥib ha sh-shanna

13. May they always
    ʿalēhum il-ʿizz ydūm
    ḍanā ḍanāy w āna bēnhum . . .

Chapter 2

1. My work is a strong steed
   nā ṣanaʿṭī mjammam
   yjī fis-sarāya yzāyid

lammā khālaṭ rumt il-kim
ykhallī ṭ-ṭawārif ginēyid
w l-ajwād tandā w tiʿzim
w ilhā fin-nakhāwa ʿawāyid
w il-andhāl min ligumt il-fam
minhā tʿān ish-shadāyid

2. Crows
   in-nās yafraḥo bil-ghrābēn w nā min ghrābēn khāyif
   yjībilnā zōl mishtāg mghawnin ʿalēna mrāyif

3. In my joy
   min farḥī lak
   fataḥtu lak
   w umm aḥmad miṭṭabāga

4. I'm not your prey
   lānī ṣayyidtak w lānak ṭērī
   w lā jʿibtak tarkab ʿalē srīrī
   yḥannin ʿalēk allāh w talgā ghērī

5. I forbid myself
   ḥarām ftāshik
   w ḥarām ʿalayya margadik w frāshik
   hātī j-jamal limmī ʿalēh dbāshik
   w dūrī wēn ṭubbī ṭīrī
   lānī ṣayyidtak w lānik ṭērak

6. Friends
   illī fir-rukhā ṣāḥīb
   fil ʿuzz ʿidā thārīthum . . .

7. Your worries
   tukhmīnik kthir yā ʿēn
   uṣḥē amrādh shēnāt tuligdī . . .

8. They watered
   iṣgō l-ʿēn bil-ḥawwāl
   mrār nīn ʿalēha rwī . . .

9. Despair of them
   khallāk yāshum yā ʿēn
   gharībin mā jāb wāldik . . .

10. Son, be like
    khallīk yā wlad kē halak
    shdād ʿazm w ʿuyūnhum gwā . . .
11. Even facing
    ḥattā fī ḥukūmat maṣr
    ʿuyūnhum gwā mā rayyabū . . .
12. All of his desires
    jamāʿ min shihāh gaḍā
    bḥaru rāg w glūʿa naṣab . . .

Chapter 3

1. Every day you give birth
   kul yōm tjīb miyya
   yā nā yā ʿaṭībt idh-dhirriyya
2. Hey old man
   Yā shēb yā ʿajūz
   yā bgērat gandūz
   yā sabʿa miʿza sūd
   yā ḥmayyir in-nahāg
   yā jrēwa il-wagwāg
   aʿṭīna min taʿashsha hal-lēla
   walla hamm, nākilkum
3. The one who's absent
   illī ghāyib nīn yjī
   w illī mistājaʿ nīn yishfī
   w iṣ-ṣghayyar nīn yakbar
4. I want a small herd
   nā wuddī fī giṭʿat lgīḥ
   w kōta tfīḥ
   w magʿid maʿā binit rājil mlīḥ
5. I want some milking camels
   nā wuddī fī giṭʿat shawāyil
   w markūb khāyil
   w magʿad maʿā binit shēkh il-gabāyil

6. I want to be up on a young mare
   nā wuddī fōg gabbāb gabba
   w l-ayyām dāla bidālu
   w nalḥag ṭlība taghghabbā
   w insī dēnna min hbālu

7. My dear, have you forgotten
   nsīt yā ʿazīz ghalāy
   yā ṭūl mā jāzēt bik . . .

Chapter 4

1. We're playing
   nalʿabū fī farḥan lilnā
   yinʿan būh illī kallimnā

2. Those who came to our wedding
   illī jāna fil-farḥ njūh
   illī mā jāna mā nibbūh

3. Those who come to congratulate
   illī bāraklak yā ghālī
   l-ʿugbā ʿindu nīn njīh

4. You who've come to keep me company
   yā lli annastu maṭraḥī
   khallī lēlitkun ṣabbāḥi

5. If you'd not been very dear
   lū mānak ghālī bil-ḥēl
   mā jīnāk ʿagāb il-lēl

6. My brothers
   khawātī w ʿiyāl ʿamāmī
   nazhā kēf yjū guddāmi

7. Go tell her aunt
   gūlū lil-ʿammā l-biʿīda
   tihḍar hal-lēla s-siʿīda

8. Uncle, those who've come
   illī bāraklak yā sīdī
   jamīla fōg ʿalē rāsī

9. A hundred blessings
   mīt mabrūk ʿalē ʿammitna
   illī dārat faraḥ w lammatna

10. You who've come here
    yā illī min gharba jītūna
    marḥabtēn w sharraftūna

11. The maternal and paternal aunts
    il-khālāt w il-ʿammāt
    frāḥā lghanwāk yā ʿalam . . .

12. He wore himself out
    gaḍā mnāb shāgī fīh
    brāwa ʿalē būk yā wlad . . .

13. If you dance
    kān ragaṣtī jāk ij-jūd
    fī farḥ wlēdik mardūd

14. Even if her topknot
    ḥattā nkān il-giṣṣa shēb
    fī farḥ ʿelēwa mā ʿēb

15. Even if she's gotten old
    ḥattā nkān ʿajūz kbīra
    taʿraf kēf tṣōb wtdīru

16. Out little boy
    barra wlad mā nakshī nāyib
    dars ʿajūz bḍāʿat shāyib

17. Gold dipped
    dhahab fī dhahab maṣbūb
    ʿazīz min l-ʿmāla l-awwilī . . .

18. Welcome, welcome
    marḥabtēn ahlān bij-jōda
    marḥabtēn ahlān bij-jōda
    marḥab yā mōl ij-jumma maḥrūda
    marḥab yā llī ʿēnik sōda
    marḥab yā llī kāḥil l-anẓār
    marḥab yā fāyiz ʿan jīlu

w tawwā yisʿidnī bil ḥēl
njībū ṣāfik bit-tiʿdīl
w nihkī guddām il-ḥuḍār
w nihkī guddām il-gāʿid
fīk (ghathīthin?) mā lhun ḥad
w intī lik sālif māḥ yṣāra . . .

19. Like a man
mithīl illī ṭāliʿ min bār
mithīl illī shārib sakrān
illī shārib min kul anwāʿ
yjī ysannid ʿas-sīsān
nmawwij rāyiḥ fī tayyār
nmawwij rāyiḥ fī daymūm

20. Praise be to God
subḥān illī khālig fīk
rgēb w ktūf w dhirʿēk
sghār w mangūshāt īdēk
w taḥt ʿugūdik raynā fīk
tawwa nihkī ʿanhin nawrīk
w nistādhan rāni shaʿār
tsamḥīnī dīrī maʿrūf
intī min ṣaḍrik ahū ōff
ykhuff illī ʿaglu sabbār
ykhuff illī gārī l-gurān
aʿūzu billāh min sh-shayṭān
anā ʿābid rabbī subḥān
w nṣallī w ʿārfīn ij-jīrān
lākin rakkabtī fīya jnān
il-mōlā khāliglik tidyān
mṣābī kē ḥabb ir-rummān
ydaffun man yirjib bardān

21. Take the sash
khudh il-maḥzam w ḥazzimnī
ʿalā ṭagra w nus ʿallimnī

249

22. Your mom's bloomers
    sirwāl ummik satānē
    hizzīhum willa aṭlāʿī

23. Hey beautiful
    yā ʿēnī mā shālla ʿalēha
    talʿab w t-khammis bīdēha

24. Our bride is fair
    ʿarūsitnā bēḍa w ḥamra
    w il-ḥāsid fī ʿēnu jamra

25. Into the eye
    il-ʿēn illī tiḥsid fin-nās
    nḥuṭṭu fīha misht nḥās

26. If you fear
    kuntī khāyfa mn l-ʿēn
    ḥuṭṭīlik khamsa w grēn

27. I don't want
    lubt il-ʿilwā nā ma nrīdu
    wuddī fī bājō jdīda

28. Mom, get me off this hill
    yamma fukkīni min l-ʿilwa
    lā ḥṭiba lā mayya ḥilwa

29. God damn
    yikhrib bēt wlad il-ʿamm
    rabbī mā ygarrib lā damm

30. O Lord, let them be many
    nʿanhā yā mōlāy tzīd
    il-farḥā bēn ʿiyyāl is-sīd

31. The bride belongs to us
    il-ʿarūsa ʿarūsitna
    w il-ʿarīs wlad ʿammitna

32. O Grandma, bless our joy
    yā ḥanna salmī saʿādna
    bnayyitna w ʿind wladna

33. Even on the scales
    ḥattā fil-wzān rdāʿ
    il-ʿēn kēfhā kēf il-ʿalam . . .

250

34. Silk on silk
    ḥarīr fī ḥarīr ykhīl
    khēr min talāmī ʿal-ghrub . . .

35. Some people travel
    in-nās ʿal-gharīb tjūl
    niḥnā min ʿaḍānā nākhadho . . .

36. A bird
    ṭēr fī smūm iryāḥ
    yḥūm mā minẓār ṣāyḍu . . .

37. The heart would be no hunter
    yabgā l-ʿagl mō ṣiyyāḍ
    in mā laʿab fī rīshhun . . .

38. Fair and her bangs
    bēḍa wij-jumma maṣfiyya
    binit tgūl ʿanāg ḥaṭṭiyya

39. Fair, unblemished
    bēḍa lā shāra lā māra
    kē l-gamar sāʿat māẓhāra

40. She takes after
    jat lil-khāla w il-ʿammāt
    dhahab bilūlī malḍūmāt

41. If you want love
    kān trīd ghalā ṣ-ṣabʿiyya
    ḥuṭṭ alfēn w shīl il-miyya

42. Her father doesn't care
    būha mō mkhaṣūs flūs
    yrīd l-himma win-nāmūs

43. The one you took
    illī khadhtī wlad siʿdāwī
    lā ṣāyiʿ lā btāʿ gahāwī

44. The boy you got
    ḥaṣṣaltī wlad mtsammī
    lā tibkī lā tgūlī yummī

45. Pastures
    rabīʿ fī manāzil halik
    bnī fīh yā ʿēn barūkī . . .

46. The dear one
    il-ʿen darijhā mabrūk
    armat abdhārhā fī wuṭunhā . . .

47. The dear one
    il-ʿēn darijhā mabrūk
    zraʿāt fī mʿālī wuṭnhā . . .

48. Apples from the gardens
    tuffāḥ fī janān ikhwān
    mā yāklāh ghēr in-nigī . . .

49. May God's mercies
    allāh ysāmḥik yā binit
    ʿalē ʿidād mōjāt il-bḥar . . .

50. God protect
    sallim būha illī rabbāha
    lin-nās iz-zēnīn aʿṭāha

51. If he doesn't bring a refrigerator
    in kān mā jāb it-tallājā
    mā ʿad ydhūg ʿindī l-ghadā

52. If he doesn't get a television
    kān mā jāb it-talfizyūn
    niḥlif mā nkaḥḥil l-iʿyūn

53. Anyone who tells me
    illī gāl il-ghālī maḥyūz
    nʿannu yrakkib kalākūz

54. Hey you
    yā bū ʿarbiyya lāmūnī
    ṭaffī n-nūr ʿamēt ʿuyūnī

55. The one who owns
    bū ʿarbiyya nagl kbīra
    lā yaskar lā yashrab bīra

56. Swing by
    mayyil mayyil bit-tayūta
    w iʿzignī ḥag il-baskūta

57. Put the bridal veil
    ḥuṭṭī l-kūsha fōg shaʿarhā

khallī ṣ-ṣawwār yṣawwirha

58. Hey woman, explain
    waṣṣī bintik yā wliyya
    rāh tirgid fij-jallābiyya

59. Him with the patterned red
    bū ṣmāda ḥamra mangūsha
    bizn illāh n'idd grūshu

60. Let's go, you and me
    yallā nā wiyyāk ḥabbabbī
    wil-maṣrūf yjībhā rabbī

61. You and I are the sweetest
    nā wiyyāk ḥalāwa ḥilwa
    yallā nal'abū 'al-'ilwā

62. My eyes will never forget
    'ēnī mā tansā ghālīha
    nīn gṭūr il-mōt yjīha

63. A girl
    bint tgūl gu'ūd fwākhir
    kē nagrabha tistākhar

64. Don't forget
    mā tinsē illī mitmawwiḥ
    kēf zarāg iz-zara' yrawwiḥ

65. No one has yet forgotten
    lissā mā nsāhum wālī
    mā zālō 'al-'ēn ghawālī

66. The tears of the eye
    dam' il-ēn 'alē fargāhun
    malla sab'a byār iḥdhāhun

67. Tonight's the night
    il-lēla lēlat ḥinnayāt
    w bukra 'inid 'azīz tbāt

68. The corners of the tent
    tḍāwan arkān il-bēt
    farḥān jāytā rīmat khala . . .

69. May she be good
    lᶜanhā tibgā binit ḥalāl
    tfājīna biᶜiyāl w māl

70. May she be a real Arab
    lᶜanhā tibgā binit ᶜarab
    tkhushsh ij-jimla mā tkharribsh

71. Make her dear mother happy
    Yā rab farriḥ maynitha
    ᶜar-rumma tinshir khirgithā

72. O Saint ᶜAwwaam
    yā sīdī il-ᶜawwām il-ᶜālī
    fīnā mā tshammit lā wālī

73. When the people
    sāᶜat ḥḍūr in-nās
    yā karīm tātī bil-faraj . . .

74. Behind us
    warāna ṭawāgī ḥumur
    ysālō ᶜalē mā nafᶜalu . . .

75. I'm confident
    ᶜazīz ᶜinid ḍumnī fī
    talgāh yā ᶜalam bāmantu . . .

76. Khwayyir doesn't tremble
    Khwayyir lā yrayyib lā ykhāf
    yjīb shārafhā ᶜar-rafrāf

77. Go tell your father
    yā Sulṭān gūl l-būk
    rāyat ish-sharaf fōg rūsna . . .

78. They lived like falcons
    ᶜāshan sgūriyyāt
    ṣayyāḍ il-khalā mā ṭālhun . . .

79. Bravo!
    brāwa ᶜalēha nūr
    illī ḥajāj būhā mā wṭī . . .

80. Look at her cloth
    unẓur khirgithā yā banāt
    tgūl mfaggis rummānāt

81. Little Selima, blessings
    yā Slēma mabrūk ᶜarīsik
    ḍawētī bwjūh tirīsik

82. Little Selima, bless you
    yā Slēma salmik dassāsa
    rawwaḥ khayyik kēf il-bāsha

83. Go tell her father
    gūlū lbūha tahanna
    damm il-bit nzil ᶜal-ḥinna

84. The cloak
    ij-jard illī ghaṭṭētik bīh
    nawwar wajhik nawwartīh

85. Like a crescent moon
    hilāl mā ᶜalēh zbūn
    sharaf il-ᶜēn yōbān yā ᶜalam . . .

Chapter 5

1. My warnings
   nṣūḥa minnī lish-shāyib
   illī ḥābis ḥurrīt ish-shab
   wnāsī ḥāja ismhā ḥub
   w ᶜaṭf w shōg w nār thib
   yā magwā nār il-ghāwī
   yā magwā nār il-ᶜajgin illī baᶜdhun mishtāgīn
   simaḥithā yagbō khāyfīn
   ygūl in-nāgir sāᶜa yjī
   ygūl in-nāgir sāᶜa yṭūg

2. O Khawd
   yā khōd mā ᶜindinā dhōd nīn narḥalō fī jibākum
   mā ᶜindī ghēr bgar w jamūs mā lhum mrātiᶜ iḥdhākum

3. You'll kill yourself
   yirdī ᶜalēk nᶜīr
   yā thōr tibīᶜak ilhun

4. The European
   naṣrāni glīl id-dīn
   shkētlu ʿalē ḥālī bkā
5. God protect
   rabna yusṭur kul bnayya
   ḥattā bit in-naṣrāniyya
6. Her father
   būhā msammā zēn
   w illī khālaṭō ṣāḥib saʿad . . .
7. Her morning
   il-ʿēn ṣubuḥḥā mabrūk
   ṭālat mnāhā washrafat . . .
8. Neighbors, come
   wadʿū yā jīrān
   ghazāl wuṭnā nāwya safar . . .

BIBLIOGRAPHY

Abou-Zeid, Ahmed M. 1966. "Honour and Shame Among the Bedouins of Egypt." In *Honour and Shame,* ed. J. G. Peristiany, 243–50. Chicago: University of Chicago Press.

Abu-Lughod, Lila. 1986. *Veiled Sentiments: Honor and Poetry in a Bedouin Society.* Berkeley and Los Angeles: University of California Press.

———. 1988a. "A Bedouin Community: Ethnography in a Different Voice." *Newsletter of the American Research Center in Egypt* 141:1–4.

———. 1988b. "Fieldwork of a Dutiful Daughter." In *Arab Women in the Field: Studying Your Own Society,* ed. Soraya Altorki and Camillia El-Solh, 139–61. Syracuse: Syracuse University Press.

———. 1989. "Zones of Theory in the Anthropology of the Arab World." *Annual Review of Anthropology* 18:276–306.

———. 1990a. "Can There Be a Feminist Ethnography?" *Women and Performance: A Journal of Feminist Theory* 5(1):7–27.

———. 1990b. "The Romance of Resistance: Tracing Transformations of Power Through Bedouin Women." *American Ethnologist* 17:41–55.

———. 1990c. "Shifting Politics in Bedouin Love Poetry." In *Language and the Politics of Emotion,* ed. Catherine Lutz and Lila Abu-Lughod, 24–45. New York: Cambridge University Press.

———. 1991. "Writing Against Culture." In *Recapturing Anthropology,* ed. Richard Fox, 137–62. Santa Fe, N.M.: School of American Research Press.

———. Forthcoming. "Islam and the Gendered Discourses of Death." *International Journal of Middle East Studies.*

Ahmed, Leila. 1987. "Women of Egypt." *Women's Review of Books* 5(2):7–8.

Altorki, Soraya, and Camillia El-Solh, eds. 1988. *Arab Women in the Field: Studying Your Own Society.* Syracuse: Syracuse University Press.

Appadurai, Arjun. 1988a. "Introduction: Place and Voice in Anthropological Theory." *Cultural Anthropology* 3:16–20.

———. 1988b. "Putting Hierarchy in Its Place." *Cultural Anthropology* 3:36–49.

Arens, William. 1979. *The Man-eating Myth: Anthropology and Anthropophagy*. New York: Oxford University Press.

Asad, Talal, ed. 1973. *Anthropology and the Colonial Encounter*. New York: Ithaca Press.

Asad, Talal. 1986. *The Idea of an Anthropology of Islam*. Occasional Papers Series, Center for Contemporary Arab Studies. Washington, D.C.: Georgetown University Press.

Atiya, Nayra. 1982. *Khul Khaal: Five Egyptian Women Tell Their Stories*. Syracuse: Syracuse University Press.

Bauman, Richard. 1986. *Story, Performance, and Event*. Cambridge: Cambridge University Press.

Beauvoir, Simone de. [1953] 1974. *Second Sex*. New York: Random.

Behar, Ruth. 1990. "Rage and Redemption: Reading the Life Story of a Mexican Marketing Woman." *Feminist Studies* 16:223–58.

Belenky, Mary, Blithe Clinchy, Nancy Goldberger, and Jill Tarule. 1986. *Women's Ways of Knowing*. New York: Basic Books.

Benjamin, Walter. 1968. "The Storyteller." In *Illuminations*, 83–110. New York: Schocken Books.

Boon, James. 1982. *Other Tribes, Other Scribes: Symbolic Anthropology in the Comparative Study of Cultures, Histories, Religions, and Texts*. Cambridge: Cambridge University Press.

Bourdieu, Pierre. 1977. *Outline of a Theory of Practice*. Trans. Richard Nice. Cambridge: Cambridge University Press.

Bowen, Elenore S. [1954] 1964. *Return to Laughter*. Garden City, N.Y.: Anchor Books.

Brettel, Caroline. 1982. *We Have Already Cried Many Tears: Portuguese Women and Migration*. Cambridge, Mass: Schenkman Publishing.

Briggs, Jean. 1970. *Never in Anger*. Cambridge, Mass.: Harvard University Press.

Brown, Karen McCarthy. 1991. *Mama Lola*. Berkeley and Los Angeles: University of California Press.

Bruner, Edward M. 1986. "Ethnography as Narrative." In *The Anthropology of Experience*, ed. Victor Turner and Edward Bruner, 139–55. Urbana: University of Illinois Press.

Burke, Edmund III, ed. In press. *Struggle and Survival in the Modern Middle East*. Berkeley and Los Angeles: University of California Press.

Butler, Judith. 1990. *Gender Trouble*. New York: Routledge.

Cesara, Manda. 1982. *Reflections of a Woman Anthropologist: No Hiding Place*. New York: Academic Press.

Chodorow, Nancy. 1978. *The Reproduction of Mothering*. Berkeley and Los Angeles: University of California Press.

Christ, Carol, and Judith Plaskow, eds. 1979. *Womanspirit Rising*. San Francisco: Harper & Row.

Cixous, Hélène. 1983. "The Laugh of the Medusa," trans. K. Cohen and P. Cohen. In *The SIGNS Reader*, ed. Elizabeth Abel and Emily Abel, 279–97. Chicago: University of Chicago Press.

Clifford, James. 1980. Review of *Orientalism*, by Edward Said. *History and Theory* 19:204–23.

———. 1983. "Power and Dialogue in Ethnography." In *Observers Observed: Essays on Ethnographic Fieldwork*, ed. George Stocking, Jr., 121–56. Madison: University of Wisconsin Press.

———. 1986a. "Introduction: Partial Truths." In *Writing Culture: The Poetics and Politics of Ethnography*, ed. James Clifford and George Marcus, 1–26. Berkeley and Los Angeles: University of California Press.

———. 1986b. "On Ethnographic Allegory." In *Writing Culture: The Poetics and Politics of Ethnography*, ed. James Clifford and George Marcus, 98–121. Berkeley and Los Angeles: University of California Press.

———. 1988a. "On Collecting Art and Culture." In *The Predicament of Culture*, 215–51. Cambridge, Mass.: Harvard University Press.

———. 1988b. "On Ethnographic Self-Fashioning." In *The Predicament of Culture*, 92–113. Cambridge, Mass.: Harvard University Press.

Clifford, James, and George Marcus, eds. 1986. *Writing Culture: The Poetics and Politics of Ethnography*. Berkeley and Los Angeles: University of California Press.

Collier, Jane, and Sylvia Yanagisako, eds. 1987. *Gender and Kinship*. Stanford: Stanford University Press.

Crapanzano, Vincent. 1980. *Tuhami: Portrait of a Moroccan*. Chicago: University of Chicago Press.

———. 1984. "Life Histories: A Review Essay." *American Anthropologist* 86:953–60.

Critchfield, Richard. 1978. *Shahhat: An Egyptian*. Syracuse: Syracuse University Press.

Davis, Natalie Zemon. 1988. *Fiction in the Archives: Pardon Tales and Their Tellers in Sixteenth-Century France*. Stanford: Stanford University Press.

di Leonardo, Micaela, ed. 1991. *Gender at the Crossroads of Knowledge*. Berkeley and Los Angeles: University of California Press.

Dumont, Jean Paul. 1978. *The Headman and I*. Austin: University of Texas Press.

Dwyer, Kevin. 1982. *Moroccan Dialogues*. Baltimore: Johns Hopkins University Press.

Echols, Alice. 1984. "The Taming of the Id: Feminist Sexual Politics 1968–

83." In *Pleasure and Danger,* ed. Carol Vance, 50–72. Boston: Routledge & Kegan Paul.

Eickelman, Dale. 1989. *The Middle East: An Anthropological Approach.* 2d ed. Englewood Cliffs, N.J.: Prentice-Hall.

Fabian, Johannes. 1983. *Time and the Other: How Anthropology Makes Its Object.* New York: Columbia University Press.

Fahim, Hussein, ed. 1982. *Indigenous Anthropology in Non-Western Countries.* Durham, N.C.: Carolina Academic Press.

Favret-Saada, Jeanne. 1980. *Deadly Words: Witchcraft in the Bocage.* Cambridge: Cambridge University Press.

Fernea, Elizabeth W. 1969. *Guests of the Sheik: An Ethnography of an Iraqi Village.* Garden City, N.Y.: Anchor Books.

Foucault, Michel. 1978. *Discipline and Punish.* New York: Pantheon Books.

———. 1980. *Power/Knowledge.* Ed. Colin Gordon. New York: Pantheon Books.

Fox, Richard. 1991. "Introduction: Working in the Present." In *Recapturing Anthropology,* ed. Richard Fox, 1–16. Santa Fe, N.M.: School of American Research Press.

Frank, Geyla. 1979. "Finding the Common Denominator: A Phenomenological Critique of Life History Method." *Ethos* 7:68–94.

Friedl, Erika. 1989. *Women of Deh Koh: Lives in an Iranian Village.* Washington, D.C.: Smithsonian Institution Press.

Friedrich, Paul. 1986. *The Princes of Naranja.* Austin: University of Texas Press.

Geertz, Clifford. 1973a. "The Impact of the Concept of Culture on the Concept of Man." In *The Interpretation of Cultures,* 33–54. New York: Basic Books.

———. 1973b. "Thick Description: Toward an Interpretive Theory of Culture." In *The Interpretation of Cultures,* 3–30. New York: Basic Books.

———. 1988. *Works and Lives.* Stanford: Stanford University Press.

Gilligan, Carol. 1982. *In a Different Voice.* Cambridge, Mass.: Harvard University Press.

Gilsenan, Michael. Forthcoming. *Lords of the Lebanese Marches.* London: I. B. Tauris.

Ginsburg, Faye, and Rayna Rapp. 1991. "The Politics of Reproduction." *Annual Review of Anthropology* 20:311–43.

Gordon, Deborah. 1988. "Writing Culture, Writing Feminism: The Poetics and Politics of Experimental Ethnography." *Inscriptions* 3/4:7–24.

Haraway, Donna. 1985. "A Manifesto for Cyborgs: Science, Technology, and Socialist Feminism in the 1980s." *Socialist Review* 80:65–107.

———. 1988. "Situated Knowledges: The Science Question in Feminism and the Privilege of Partial Perspective." *Feminist Studies* 14:575–99.

Harding, Sandra. 1987. "The Method Question." *Hypatia* 2:19–35.

Hartsock, Nancy. 1985. *Money, Sex, and Power: Toward a Feminist Historical Materialism.* Boston: Northeastern University Press.

Hatem, Mervat. 1988. "Feminist Analysis and the Subjective World of Women." *Association of Middle East Women's Studies News* 2(6):7–9.

Herzfeld, Michael. 1987. *Anthropology Through the Looking Glass: Critical Ethnography in the Margins of Europe.* Cambridge: Cambridge University Press.

The Holy Qur'an: English Translation of the Meanings and Commentary. 1410 A. H. Rev. and ed. Presidency of Islamic Researches, Ifta, Call, and Guidance. Al-Madinah al-Munawarah, Saudi Arabia: King Fahd Holy Qur'an Printing Complex.

Hymes, Dell, ed. 1969. *Reinventing Anthropology.* New York: Random House.

Irigaray, Luce. 1985a. *Speculum of the Other Woman.* Trans. Gillian C. Gill. Ithaca: Cornell University Press.

———. 1985b. *This Sex Which Is Not One.* Trans. Catherine Porter, with Carolyn Burks. Ithaca: Cornell University Press.

Jackson, Michael. 1986. *Barawa and the Ways Birds Fly in the Sky: An Ethnographic Novel.* Washington, D.C.: Smithsonian Institution Press.

———. 1989. *Paths Toward a Clearing: Radical Empiricism and Ethnographic Inquiry.* Bloomington: Indiana University Press.

Jameson, Fredric. 1984. "Postmodernism, or, the Cultural Logic of Late Capitalism." *New Left Review* 146:59–92.

John, Mary. 1989. "Postcolonial Feminists in the Western Intellectual Field: Anthropologists *and* Native Informants?" *Inscriptions* 5:49–73.

Kapferer, Bruce. 1988. "The Anthropologist as Hero: Three Exponents of Post-modernist Anthropology." *Critique of Anthropology* 8(2):77–104.

Keller, Evelyn Fox. 1985. *Reflections on Gender and Science.* New Haven: Yale University Press.

Kendall, Laurel. 1988. *The Life and Hard Times of a Korean Shaman.* Honolulu: University of Hawaii Press.

Kondo, Dorinne. 1986. "Dissolution and Reconstitution of Self: Implications for Anthropological Epistemology." *Cultural Anthropology* 1:74–88.

Kristeva, Julia. 1980. "Motherhood According to Giovanni Bellini." In *Desire in Language,* ed. Leon Roudiez, 237–70. New York: Columbia University Press.

———. 1981. "Women's Time," trans. Alice Jardine and Harry Blake. *Signs* 7:13–35.

Kuper, Adam. 1988. *The Invention of Primitive Society: Transformation of an Illusion*. Boston: Routledge & Kegan Paul.

Langness, L. L., and Geyla Frank. 1981. *Lives: An Anthropological Approach to Biography*. Novato, Calif.: Chandler & Sharp.

Lavie, Smadar. 1990. *The Poetics of Military Occupation: Mzeina Allegories of Bedouin Identity Under Israeli and Egyptian Rule*. Berkeley and Los Angeles: University of California Press.

Lazreg, Marnia. 1988. "Feminism and Difference: The Perils of Writing as a Woman on Women in Algeria." *Feminist Studies* 14:81–107.

Lutz, Catherine. 1988. *Unnatural Emotions*. Chicago: University of Chicago Press.

———. 1990. "Engendered Emotion: Gender, Power, and the Rhetoric of Emotional Control in American Discourse." In *Language and the Politics of Emotion,* ed. Catherine Lutz and Lila Abu-Lughod, 69–91. New York: Cambridge University Press.

———. Forthcoming. "Social Contexts of Postmodern Cultural Analysis." In *Modernity and Postmodernity,* ed. John Jones, Wolfgang Natter, and Theodore Schatzki. New York: Guilford Press.

MacKinnon, Catharine. 1982. "Feminism, Marxism, Method, and the State: An Agenda for Theory." *Signs* 7:515–44.

Mani, Lata. 1989. "Multiple Mediations: Feminist Scholarship in the Age of Multinational Reception." *Inscriptions* 5:1–23.

Marcus, George, and Dick Cushman. 1982. "Ethnographies as Texts." *Annual Review of Anthropology* 11:25–69.

Marcus, George, and Michael M. J. Fischer. 1986. *Anthropology as Cultural Critique*. Chicago: University of Chicago Press.

Mascia-Lees, Frances E., Patricia Sharpe, and Colleen Ballerino Cohen. 1989. "The Postmodernist Turn in Anthropology: Cautions from a Feminist Perspective." *Signs: Journal of Women in Culture and Society* 15:7–33.

Meis, Maria. 1983. "Towards a Methodology for Feminist Research." In *Theories of Women's Studies,* ed. Gloria Bowles and Renate Duelli Klein, 117–39. London: Routledge & Kegan Paul.

Mernissi, Fatima. 1988. *Doing Daily Battle: Interviews with Moroccan Women*. London: Women's Press.

Mills, Margaret. 1991. *Rhetorics and Poetics in Afghan Traditional Storytelling*. Philadelphia: University of Pennsylvania Press.

Mitchell, Juliet. 1974. *Psychoanalysis and Feminism*. New York: Pantheon Books.

Mitchell, Timothy. 1988. *Colonising Egypt*. Cambridge: Cambridge University Press.

———. 1990. "The Invention and Reinvention of the Egyptian Peasant." *International Journal of Middle East Studies* 22:129–50.

Mohanty, Chandra Talpade. 1984. "Under Western Eyes: Feminist Scholarship and Colonial Discourses." *Boundary 2* 12:333–58.

Mohsen, Safia. 1975. *Conflict and Law Among Awlad ʿAli of the Western Desert.* Cairo: National Center for Social and Criminological Research.

Moore, Henrietta. 1988. *Feminism and Anthropology.* Minneapolis: University of Minnesota Press.

Morgen, Sandra. 1989. *Gender and Anthropology: Critical Reviews for Research and Teaching.* Washington, D.C.: American Anthropological Association.

Mudimbe, V. Y. 1988. *The Invention of Africa: Gnosis, Philosophy, and the Order of Knowledge.* Bloomington: Indiana University Press.

Munson, Henry, Jr. 1984. *The House of Si Abd Allah.* New Haven: Yale University Press.

Narayan, Kirin. 1989. *Storytellers, Saints, and Scoundrels: Folk Narrative in Hindu Religious Teaching.* Philadelphia: University of Pennsylvania Press.

O'Brien, Mary. 1981. *The Politics of Reproduction.* Boston: Routledge & Kegan Paul.

Ong, Aihwa. 1988. "Colonialism and Modernity: Feminist Re-Presentations of Women in Non-Western Societies." *Inscriptions* 3/4:79–93.

Ortner, Sherry. 1974. "Is Female to Male as Nature Is to Culture?" In *Woman, Culture, and Society,* ed. Michelle Rosaldo and Louise Lamphere, 67–87. Stanford: Stanford University Press.

Pandolfo, Stefania. 1991. " 'The Angel of Death Replied': Absence and Longing in a Moroccan Space of Memory." Ph.D. diss., Princeton University.

Personal Narratives Group. 1989. *Interpreting Women's Lives: Feminist Theory and Personal Narratives.* Bloomington: Indiana University Press.

Rabinow, Paul. 1977. *Reflections on Fieldwork in Morocco.* Berkeley and Los Angeles: University of California Press.

Reinharz, Shulamit. 1983. "Experiential Analysis: A Contribution to Feminist Research." In *Theories of Women's Studies,* ed. Gloria Bowles and Renate Duelli Klein, 162–91. London: Routledge & Kegan Paul.

Rich, Adrienne. 1979. "Toward a Woman-centered University." In *On Lies, Secrets, and Silence,* 125–56. New York: Norton.

———. 1986. *Of Woman Born: Motherhood as Experience and Institution.* 10th ann. ed. New York: Norton.

Riesman, Paul. 1977. *Freedom in Fulani Social Life.* Chicago: University of Chicago Press.

———. 1982. "Fieldwork as Initiation and as Therapy." Paper presented at the 81st Annual Meeting of the American Anthropological Association, Washington, D.C.

Rosaldo, Michelle Z. 1974. "Woman, Culture, and Society: A Theoretical Overview." In *Woman, Culture, and Society,* ed. Michelle Rosaldo and Louise Lamphere, 17–42. Stanford: Stanford University Press.

Rosaldo, Renato. 1989. *Culture and Truth: The Remaking of Social Analysis.* Boston: Beacon Press.

Rose, Dan. 1987. *Black American Street Life: South Philadelphia, 1969–1971.* Philadelphia: University of Pennsylvania.

Rose, Hilary. 1983. "Hand, Brain, and Heart: A Feminist Epistemology for the Natural Sciences." *Signs* 9:73–90.

———. 1986. "Women's Work: Women's Knowledge." In *What Is Feminism?: A Re-Examination,* ed. Juliet Mitchell and Ann Oakley, 161–83. New York: Pantheon Books.

Ruddick, Sara. 1989. *Maternal Thinking: Toward a Politics of Peace.* Boston: Beacon Press.

Said, Edward. 1978. *Orientalism.* New York: Pantheon Books.

———. 1989. "Representing the Colonized: Anthropology's Interlocutors." *Critical Inquiry* 15:205–25.

Sanday, Peggy, and Ruth Goodenough, eds. 1990. *Beyond the Second Sex.* Philadelphia: University of Pennsylvania Press.

Sangren, Steven. 1988. "Rhetoric and the Authority of Ethnography." *Current Anthropology* 29:405–24.

Schleifer, Aliah. 1986. *Motherhood in Islam.* Cambridge: Islamic Academy.

Scott, David. 1989. "Locating the Anthropological Subject: Postcolonial Anthropologists in Other Places." *Inscriptions* 5:75–84.

Sharawi, Huda. 1986. *Harem Years.* Trans., ed., and intro. by Margot Badran. London: Virago Press.

Shostak, Marjorie. 1981. *Nisa: The Life and Words of a !Kung Woman.* Cambridge, Mass.: Harvard University Press.

Smith, Dorothy. 1987. *The Everyday World as Problematic.* Boston: Northeastern University Press.

Smith, Mary F. [1954] 1981. *Baba of Karo, a Woman of the Muslim Hausa.* New Haven: Yale University Press.

Spivak, Gayatri Chakravorty. 1987. *In Other Worlds.* New York: Methuen.

Stacey, Judith. 1988. "Can There Be a Feminist Ethnography?" *Women's Studies International Forum* 11:21–27.

Stahl, Sandra Dolby. 1989. *Literary Folkloristics and the Personal Narrative.* Bloomington: Indiana University Press.

Stanley, Liz, and Sue Wise. 1983. *Breaking Out: Feminist Consciousness and Feminist Research.* London: Routledge & Kegan Paul.

Stewart, John O. 1989. *Drinkers, Drummers, and Decent Folk: Ethnographic Narratives of Village Trinidad.* Albany: State University of New York Press.

Stewart, Kathleen. 1988. "Nostalgia—A Polemic." *Cultural Anthropology* 3:227–41.

———. 1991. "On the Politics of Cultural Theory: A Case for 'Contaminated' Cultural Critique." *Social Research* 58:395–412.

Stocking, George W., Jr. 1989. "The Ethnographic Sensibility of the 1920s and the Dualism of the Anthropological Tradition." In *Romantic Motives: Essays on Anthropological Sensibility,* History of Anthropology, vol. 6, ed. George W. Stocking, Jr., 208–76. Madison: University of Wisconsin Press.

Stoller, Paul. 1989. *The Taste of Ethnographic Things: The Senses in Anthropology.* Philadelphia: University of Pennsylvania Press.

Stoller, Paul, and Cheryl Olkes. 1987. *In Sorcery's Shadow.* Chicago: University of Chicago Press.

Strathern, Marilyn. 1987. "An Awkward Relationship: The Case of Feminism and Anthropology." *Signs* 12:276–92.

Tannen, Deborah. 1989. *Talking Voices: Repetition, Dialogue, and Imagery in Conversational Discourse.* Cambridge: Cambridge University Press.

Taussig, Michael. 1987. *Colonialism, Shamanism, and the Wild Man.* Chicago: University of Chicago Press.

Tedlock, Barbara. 1991. "From Participant Observation to the Observation of Participation: The Emergence of Narrative Ethnography." *Journal of Anthropological Research* 47:69–94.

Tedlock, Dennis. 1983. *The Spoken Word and the Work of Interpretation.* Philadelphia: University of Pennsylvania Press.

———. 1987. "Questions Concerning Dialogical Anthropology." *Journal of Anthropological Research* 43:325–37.

Trawick, Margaret. 1990. *Notes on Love in a Tamil Family.* Berkeley and Los Angeles: University of California Press.

Turner, Edith. 1987. *The Spirit and the Drum: A Memoir of Africa.* Tucson: University of Arizona Press.

Tyler, Stephen. 1986. "Post-modern Ethnography: From Document of the Occult to Occult Document." In *Writing Culture,* ed. James Clifford and George Marcus, 122–40. Berkeley and Los Angeles: University of California Press.

———. 1987. "On 'Writing-Up/Off' as 'Speaking-For.'" *Journal of Anthropological Research* 43(4):338–42.

Visweswaran, Kamala. 1988. "Defining Feminist Ethnography." *Inscriptions* 3/4:27–44.

Wagner, Roy. 1981. *The Invention of Culture*. Chicago: University of Chicago Press.

Watson, Lawrence, and Maria-Barbara Watson-Franke. 1985. *Interpreting Life Histories*. New Brunswick, N.J.: Rutgers University Press.

Weintraub, Karl Joachim. 1978. *The Value of the Individual: Self and Circumstance in Autobiography*. Chicago: University of Chicago Press.

Wolf, Eric. 1982. *Europe and the People Without History*. Berkeley and Los Angeles: University of California Press.

Wolf, Margery. 1968. *The House of Lim*. New York: Appleton-Century-Crofts.

Young, Robert. 1990. *White Mythologies: Writing History and the West*. London: Routledge.